Holt Literature & Language Arts

Second Course

UNIVERSAL ACCESS Interactive Reading

- **Word Analysis, Fluency, and Systematic Vocabulary Development**
- **Reading Comprehension**
- **Literary Response and Analysis**

HOLT, RINEHART AND WINSTON

A Harcourt Classroom Education Company

Austin · New York · Orlando · Atlanta · San Francisco · Boston · Dallas · Toronto · London

Credits

Editorial

Project Director: Kathleen Daniel
Editor: Amy Fleming
Managing Editor: Mike Topp
Manager of Editorial Services: Abigail Winograd
Senior Product Manager: Don Wulbrecht
Editorial Staff: Susan Kent Cakars, Steven Fechter,
    Rob Giannetto, Kerry Johnson, Brenda Sanabria, Dan Unger
Project Administration: Elizabeth LaManna
Editorial Support: Renée Benitez, Louise Fernandez, Soojung Christine Han,
    Bret Isaacs, Laurie Muir
Editorial Permissions: David Smith, Carrie Jones
Conceptual Framework and Writing: e2 Publishing Services, Inc.

Art, Design, and Production

Director: Athena Blackorby
Senior Design Director: Betty Mintz
Series Design: Proof Positive/Farrowlyne Associates, Inc.
Design and Electronic Files: Proof Positive/Farrowlyne Associates, Inc.
Photo Research: Proof Positive/Farrowlyne Associates, Inc.
Production Manager: Catherine Gessner

Printed in the United States of America
ISBN 0-03-065029-1

26 27 28 29 30 0877 17 16 15 14 13 12
4500369114

Contents

Interactive Readings for Independence

CHAPTER 7   ## Literary Criticism: The Person Behind the Text

Getting Ready

Graphic Organizers

for *Holt Literature and Language Arts*, Chapter 7

CHAPTER 8   Reading for Life   306

Getting Ready

Graphic Organizers

for *Holt Literature and Language Arts,* Chapter 8

Interactive Readings for Independence

Mastering the California Standards in Reading*

 Chapter 1   Structures: Patterns of Meaning
Standards Focus

Vocabulary Development 1.2   Understand the most important points in the history of English language, and use common word origins to determine the historical influences on English word meanings.

Reading Comprehension (Focus on Informational Materials) 2.2   Analyze text that uses proposition and support patterns.

Literary Response and Analysis 3.2   Evaluate the structural elements of the plot (for example, subplots, parallel episodes, climax), the plot's development, and the way in which conflicts are (or are not) addressed and resolved.

 Chapter 2   Characters: Doing the Right Thing
Standards Focus

Vocabulary Development 1.2   Understand the most important points in the history of English language, and use common word origins to determine the historical influences on English word meanings.

Reading Comprehension (Focus on Informational Materials) 2.3   Find similarities and differences between texts in the treatment, scope, or organization of ideas.

Literary Response and Analysis 3.3   Compare and contrast motivations and reaction of literary characters from different historical eras confronting similar situations or conflicts.

 Chapter 3   Being There: Setting
Standards Focus

Vocabulary Development 1.3   Use word meanings within the appropriate context, and show ability to verify those meanings by definition, restatement, example, comparison, or contrast.

Reading Comprehension (Focus on Informational Materials) 2.1 (Grade 6 Review)   Identify the structural features of popular media.

Literary Response and Analysis 3.4   Analyze the relevance of the setting (for example, place, time, customs) to the mood, tone, and meaning of the text.

 Chapter 4   We Still Believe
Standards Focus

Vocabulary Development 1.3   Use word meanings within the appropriate context, and show ability to verify those meanings by definitions, restatement, example, comparison, or contrast.

Literary Response and Analysis 3.5   Identify and analyze recurring themes (for example, good versus evil) across traditional and contemporary works.

---

* Unless otherwise noted, the standards listed are grade-level standards.

Chapter 5   Imagine That! Literary Devices
Standards Focus

Vocabulary Development 1.1   Analyze analogies, metaphors, and similes to infer the literal and figurative meanings of phrases.

Reading Comprehension (Focus on Informational Materials) 2.8 (Grade 6 Review)   Note instances of fallacious reasoning in text.

Literary Response and Analysis 3.6   Identify significant literary devices (for example, metaphor, symbolism, dialect, irony) that define a writer's style and use those elements to interpret the work.

Chapter 6   Sound and Sense: Forms of Poetry
Standards Focus

Reading Comprehension (Focus on Informational Materials) 2.4   Compare the original text to a summary to determine whether the summary accurately captures the main ideas, includes critical details, and conveys the underlying meaning.

Literary Response and Analysis 3.1   Determine and articulate the relationship between the purposes and characteristics of different forms of poetry (for example, ballad, lyric, couplet, epic, elegy, ode, sonnet).

Chapter 7   Literary Criticism: The Person Behind the Text
Standards Focus

Vocabulary Development 1.1   Analyze idioms to infer the literal and figurative meanings of phrases.

Vocabulary Development 1.3   Use word meanings within the appropriate context, and show ability to verify those meanings by definition, restatement, comparison, or contrast.

Reading Comprehension (Focus on Informational Materials) 2.7   Evaluate the unity, coherence, logic, internal consistency, and structural patterns of text.

Literary Response and Analysis 3.7   Analyze a work of literature, showing how it reflects the heritage, traditions, attitudes, and beliefs of its author (biographical approach).

Chapter 8   Reading for Life
Standards Focus

Reading Comprehension (Focus on Informational Materials) 2.1   Compare and contrast the features and elements of consumer materials to gain meaning from documents (for example, warranties, contracts, product information, instruction manuals).

Reading Comprehension (Focus on Informational Materials) 2.5   Understand and explain the use of a complex mechanical device by following technical directions.

Reading Comprehension (Focus on Informational Materials) 2.6   Use information from a variety of consumer, workplace, and public documents to explain a situation or decision and to solve a problem.

To the Student

A Book for You

....

A book is like a garden carried in the pocket.
—Chinese Proverb

....

Picture this: a book chock full of intriguing stories that you want to read and informational articles that are really interesting. Make it a book that actually tells you to write in it, circling, underlining, adding your own questions, jotting down responses. Fill it with graphic organizers that encourage you to think in a different way. Make it a size that's easy to carry around. That's *Interactive Reading*—a book created especially for you.

A Book Designed for Success

....

Reading is a creative activity. You have to visualize the characters, you have to hear what their voices sound like.
—Madeleine L'Engle

....

Interactive Reading is designed to accompany *Holt Literature and Language Arts.* Like *Holt Literature and Language Arts,* it's designed to help you interact with the literature and master the California language arts content standards.

Each chapter has three parts:
- Getting Ready
- Graphic Organizers for use with the selections in *Holt Literature and Language Arts*
- Interactive Readings for Independence

Getting Ready

Actors, athletes, dancers, and musicians all prepare before they perform. Getting Ready helps you prepare to read each chapter in *Holt Literature and Language Arts.*

To help you prepare, Getting Ready provides—
- an overview of what to expect in the chapter
- a strategy that will help you read the selections successfully and master the standards

- a Practice Read that is easy and fun to read
- questions and comments to help you interact with the Practice Read and apply the strategy
- a graphic organizer or chart for applying the strategy

Graphic Organizers for *Holt Literature and Language Arts*

Reading effectively involves interacting with the text. Graphic organizers give you a visual and fun way to organize, interpret, and understand the selections in *Holt Literature and Language Arts.*

To help you organize, interpret, and understand the selections, the graphic organizers provide—

- support for reading each literary and informational selection
- support for mastering the standards
- a creative way for you to think about and interact with the selections

Interactive Readings for Independence

Each chapter ends with new selections for you to read as you build toward independence. These selections provide new opportunities for you to apply your skills and strategies and interact with the text.

In this section, you will find—

- new literary and informational selections
- information for author study
- questions and comments to guide your reading and help you interact with the text
- projects that help you explore ideas and extend your knowledge

A Book for Your Thoughts and Ideas

....

Reading helps you think about things, it helps you imagine what it feels like to be somebody else . . . even somebody you don't like!
—Paula Fox

....

Reading is about you. It is about your own thoughts and feelings. It is about making connections between what you read and your own life and experience. The more you give of yourself to your reading, the more you will get out of it.

A Walk Through the Book

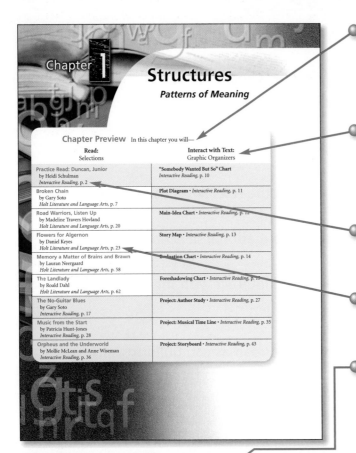

Chapter Preview
Knowing what to expect helps you be more successful. The Chapter Preview provides an overview of what's in each *Interactive Reading* chapter.

Read and Interact
In each chapter you will read both literary and informational texts and use graphic organizers as one way of interacting with the selections.

Highlighted Selections
The highlighted selections appear only in *Interactive Reading*.

Other Selections
The unhighlighted selections appear only in *Holt Literature and Language Arts.*

Strategy Launch
This page is designed to give you an advantage. Like strategies used in sports and business, reading strategies help you reach your goal—mastery of the standards.

Literary Focus
This feature introduces a literary focus for the chapter. The focus ties into a California reading standard.

A Strategy That Works
This feature introduces a reading strategy that will be used throughout the chapter. Each strategy helps you make sense of the text and understand the literary focus. It guides you in exploring and interpreting the text in a creative way while mastering the standard.

Pointers
See at a glance how to use the strategy. Pointers make each strategy easy to follow and use.

Reading Standards
Here are the California reading standards that are covered in this chapter. Each part of the chapter is designed to help you master these standards.

Practice Read

Here's a story that will probably be easy to identify with. It's about a teen who wants a dog. You've already gotten a head start, because now you know what the "somebody" (a teen) "wants" (a dog). Read on to find out the specifics.

Duncan, Junior

Heidi Schulman

SOMEBODY WANTED BUT SO

Pause at line 16. What's the "But" part of this plot, or the **conflict**?

_____
_____
_____
_____
_____
_____
_____
_____

VOCABULARY DEVELOPMENT

canine (kā′nīn′) *adj.:* of or like a dog.

Canine is from the Latin word *canis* for "dog."

I turned fourteen about two months ago, and that's when I decided it was time to get a dog. After all, my family and I live way out in the country, and the place is about as close to doggie heaven as anywhere on earth. For shade, we've got bushy pine trees that go up a hundred feet into the air. We've got a wide, muddy river to splash in, and in the spring and summer the meadows are filled with purple and yellow wildflowers and tall grasses so soft they'd tickle a pup's paws. It's quiet enough to hear a cat meow a quarter
10 of a mile away, and between the beavers and birds and old jackrabbits that like to come close to the back door and jiggle their whiskers, a dog can sniff all day and never get bored. It's perfect.

I explained my decision to my parents. They had other ideas for me, though, and none of them had anything to do with the word **"canine."**

"Jeremy," said my father. That's my name, by the way—Jeremy.

"Jeremy," dad said, "who's going to walk the dog in the
20 middle of winter when it's five below zero and the sky is pitch black and the wind is howling and sleet is blowing into your face?"

I had a feeling dad would say that. I was prepared.

"I won't have to walk him," I answered. I'll just let him out and he can walk himself. This is the country, Dad. There's land everywhere."

My comeback was brilliant, if I do say so myself. And it was completely based on fact. Our house sits in the middle of a huge meadow that stretches, gosh, I don't know how
30 far it really stretches, but trust me, this meadow is seriously huge. You can't even see any other houses from where we live. In fact, our closest neighbors are the birds that hang out in the pine trees.

My mother, of course, had her own strong opinion. You can always count on that with mom.

"Jeremy Gottlieb. Do you think I'm going to let an animal run around outside by himself, get filthy dirty, and then track mud and pine needles inside all over my clean carpet? I don't think so."
40 It was time for brilliant comeback number two. I'd really worked on this one.

"I'll make him dog boots, mom. Little rubber things with Velcro closings. That way he'll be clean when he comes in."

"Nice try," said my mom. "How about a fish instead?"

I couldn't blame my parents for being down on the dog idea. The last time we'd had a dog, we lived in New York City in a crowded two-bedroom **apartment** on the fifth floor of an old brick apartment building. If you tried
50 to compare the place we lived then to the place we live now,

EVALUATE

Underline Jeremy's replies to his parents' objections. How effectively does he reply to their reasons for not having a dog?

_____
_____
_____
_____
_____
_____
_____
_____
_____
_____
_____
_____
_____

VOCABULARY DEVELOPMENT

apartment (ə-pärt′mənt) *n.:* room or group of rooms to live in.

In England, apartments are called *flats,* because they are usually on one floor.

Practice Read
A Practice Read is an easy-to-read selection that gives you practice in applying the strategy and interacting with the text. Using the Practice Read helps you warm up before reading the selections in *Holt Literature and Language Arts.*

Before You Read
This feature tells you what the selection is about and gives you background information.

Side-Column Notes
Each selection is accompanied by notes in the side columns. They guide your interaction with the selection and show you how to apply the reading strategy. Many notes ask you to circle or underline in the text itself. Others provide lines on which you can write your responses to questions.

Types of Notes
The different types of notes throughout the selection help you—
- apply the reading strategy
- use reading skills to comprehend and interpret
- focus on a literary element
- build vocabulary
- develop word knowledge
- decode unfamiliar words

Vocabulary Development
Vocabulary words for you to learn and own are set in boldface in the selection, letting you see words in context. Vocabulary words are defined for you right there in the side column.

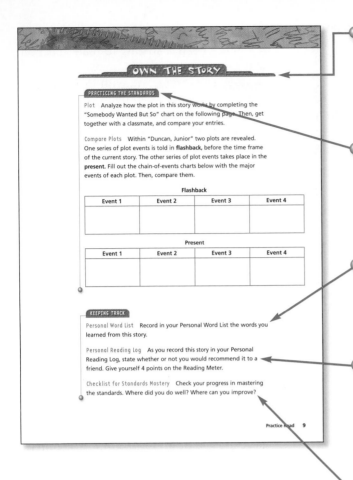

Own the Story, Text, or Poem
The meaning you take from a selection is based on the thought and reflection you put into it. Make each selection your own. Mark it up with your own comments and questions.

Practicing the Standards
You have a major goal in front of you: to master the California standards. This feature appears at the end of each selection to help you practice the skill in the standard.

Personal Word List
At the back of the book, you will find a Personal Word List for recording words you have learned and words you especially like.

Personal Reading Log
The more you read, the better you will read. Keep track of how much you read in your Personal Reading Log at the end of the book. By the year's end the Reading Meter will show the approximate number of words you have read in the book.

Checklist for Standards Mastery
With each selection you read and each standard you master, you come closer and closer to reaching your goal. Keep track of your progress with the Checklist for Standards Mastery at the end of the book.

Reading Strategy Graphic Organizer
At the end of every Practice Read is a graphic organizer that guides you in applying the reading strategy to the selection.

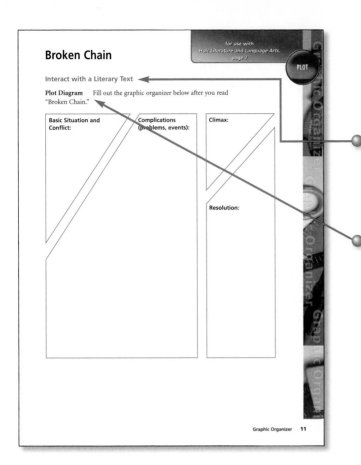

Holt Literature and Language Arts

Now that you have prepared and practiced, it's time to turn to the selections in *Holt Literature and Language Arts.*

Interact with a Literary Text

For every literary selection in *Holt Literature and Language Arts,* there is a graphic organizer to help you read the text with increased understanding.

Reading Standard

Each graphic organizer reinforces the literary focus and moves you closer toward mastering a California reading standard.

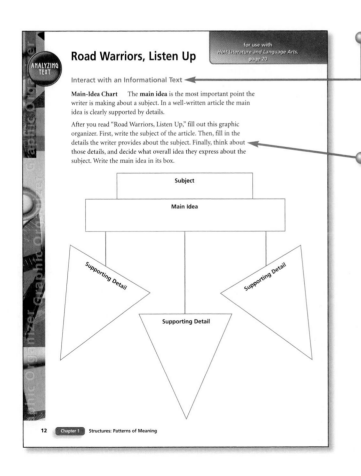

Interact with an Informational Text

For every informational selection in *Holt Literature and Language Arts,* there is a graphic organizer to help you read the text with increased understanding.

Reading Standard

Each graphic organizer reinforces the informational focus and moves you closer toward mastering a California reading standard.

Literature

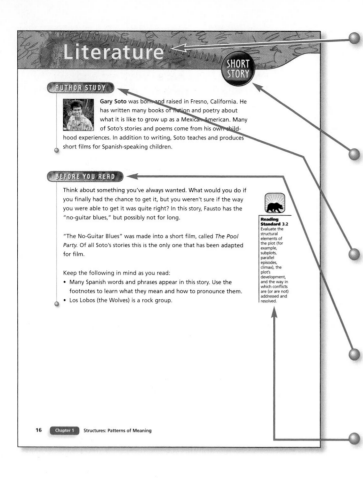

SHORT STORY

AUTHOR STUDY

Gary Soto was born and raised in Fresno, California. He has written many books of fiction and poetry about what it is like to grow up as a Mexican American. Many of Soto's stories and poems come from his own childhood experiences. In addition to writing, Soto teaches and produces short films for Spanish-speaking children.

BEFORE YOU READ

Think about something you've always wanted. What would you do if you finally had the chance to get it, but you weren't sure if the way you were able to get it was quite right? In this story, Fausto has the "no-guitar blues," but possibly not for long.

"The No-Guitar Blues" was made into a short film, called *The Pool Party.* Of all Soto's stories this is the only one that has been adapted for film.

Keep the following in mind as you read:
• Many Spanish words and phrases appear in this story. Use the footnotes to learn what they mean and how to pronounce them.
• Los Lobos (the Wolves) is a rock group.

Reading Standard 3.2
Evaluate the structural elements of the plot (for example, subplots, parallel episodes, climax), the plot's development, and the way in which conflicts are (or are not) addressed and resolved.

16   Chapter 1   Structures: Patterns of Meaning

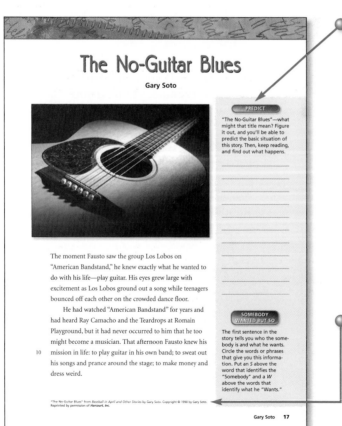

The No-Guitar Blues

Gary Soto

PREDICT

"The No-Guitar Blues"—what might that title mean? Figure it out, and you'll be able to predict the basic situation of this story. Then, keep reading, and find out what happens.

The moment Fausto saw the group Los Lobos on "American Bandstand," he knew exactly what he wanted to do with his life—play guitar. His eyes grew large with excitement as Los Lobos ground out a song while teenagers bounced off each other on the crowded dance floor.

He had watched "American Bandstand" for years and had heard Ray Camacho and the Teardrops at Romain Playground, but it had never occurred to him that he too might become a musician. That afternoon Fausto knew his mission in life: to play guitar in his own band; to sweat out his songs and prance around the stage; to make money and dress weird.

SOMEBODY WANTED BUT SO

The first sentence in the story tells you who the somebody is and what he wants. Circle the words or phrases that give you this information. Put an *S* above the word that identifies the "Somebody" and a *W* above the words that identify what he "Wants."

10

"The No-Guitar Blues" from *Baseball in April and Other Stories* by Gary Soto. Copyright © 1990 by Gary Soto. Reprinted by permission of *Harcourt, Inc.*

Gary Soto   **17**

Interactive Selections
After you read the selections in a chapter of *Holt Literature and Language Arts,* build toward independence by reading the selections at the end of each *Interactive Reading* chapter.

Types of Literature
Effective readers are skilled at reading many different types of text. Each text type is identified so that you can keep track of your mastery.

Author Study
Some interactive selections give you an opportunity to read more by an author you have studied in *Holt Literature and Language Arts.*

Before You Read
This feature tells you what the selection is about and gives you background information.

Reading Standard
The California reading standard you will concentrate on with each interactive selection is identified here in the side column.

Side-Column Notes
Each selection is accompanied by notes in the side columns. They guide your interaction with the selection and show you how to apply the reading strategy. Many notes ask you to circle or underline in the text itself. The different types of notes are designed to help you—

• apply the reading strategy
• use reading skills to comprehend and interpret
• focus on a literary element
• build vocabulary
• develop word knowledge
• decode unfamiliar words
• understand text structures
• build fluency

Footnotes
Difficult or unusual terms are defined in footnotes.

OWN THE STORY

PRACTICING THE STANDARDS

Plot   Analyze how the plot in this story works, based on the "Somebody Wanted But So" notes that are printed next to the story text. Identify elements of the plot such as **conflict, complications, climax,** and **resolution.** With a partner, discuss the resolution of Fausto's problem. Did you think it was a believable resolution?

_____

_____

_____

_____

_____

_____

_____

_____

_____

_____

_____

KEEPING TRACK

Personal Word List   List the vocabulary words for this story in order of difficulty in your Personal Word List. Don't forget to add the new Spanish words you learned, too!

Personal Reading Log   How much did you enjoy this short story, and why? Write your response to it in your Personal Reading Log, and award yourself 5 points on the Reading Meter.

Checklist for Standards Mastery   You are learning a lot as you read these stories! Use the Checklist for Standards Mastery to see how well you have done mastering the standards and where you can improve.

Own the Story, Text, or Poem

The meaning you take from a selection is based on the thought and reflection you put into it. Make each selection your own. Mark it up with your own comments and questions.

Practicing the Standards

This feature appears at the end of each selection to help you check your mastery.

Personal Word List

Record words you have learned and words you especially like in your Personal Word List at the end of the book.

Personal Reading Log

Keep track of how much you read in your Personal Reading Log at the end of the book. By the year's end the Reading Meter will show the approximate number of words you have read in this book.

Checklist for Standards Mastery

With each selection you read and each standard you master, you come closer and closer to reaching your goal. Keep track of your progress with the Checklist for Standards Mastery at the end of the book.

Project Graphic Organizer

Don't just stop after you read the selection. The project graphic organizer helps you go beyond the selection and extend your knowledge and understanding.

The No-Guitar Blues ■ *Interactive Reading,* page 17

PROJECT

Go Beyond a Literary Text

Author Study   Use your library and the Internet to find out more about Gary Soto. Find five books by Gary Soto, and fill out the book list below.

Works of Gary Soto

Title	Date	Genre (novel, short story, poetry, nonfiction)	Brief Description

Chapter 1

Structures
Patterns of Meaning

Chapter Preview In this chapter you will—

Strategy Launch: "Somebody Wanted But So"

LITERARY FOCUS: PLOT

Plot is the chain of related events that tells us what happens in a story. When a plot is well mapped out, it hooks us and we say we can't put the story down. The "hook" of the plot, the part that grabs us and keeps us reading, is usually a **conflict,** or problem faced by a character. When the outcome of the conflict is decided one way or another, the plot reaches a **climax,** the most exciting moment in the story. We want to learn how the conflict is **resolved**—in other words, how the story turns out.

A STRATEGY THAT WORKS: "SOMEBODY WANTED BUT SO"

"Somebody Wanted But So" is a very effective strategy you can use to keep track of the plot. To use this strategy, keep the following ideas in mind as you read: "Somebody" is the main character; "Wanted" is what the character wants; "But" means that complications develop that make it harder for the character to get what he or she wants; and "So" is how things work out at the end.

POINTERS FOR USING "SOMEBODY WANTED BUT SO"

⟫➤ *Somebody:* The plot begins with the main character facing a conflict. Start by identifying your "Somebody."

⟫➤ *Wanted:* Ask yourself, "What does this character want?"

⟫➤ *But:* Then, ask yourself, "What's keeping the character from getting what he or she wants?" This is the conflict.

⟫➤ *So:* Finally, ask yourself, "So what happens when the main character tries to solve the problem?" This is the resolution.

Put the four parts together in a sentence, and you've got a summary of the plot.

Reading Standard 1.2
Understand the most important points in the history of the English language, and use common word origins to determine the historical influences on English word meanings.

Reading Standard 2.2
Analyze text that uses proposition and support patterns.

Reading Standard 3.2
Evaluate the structural elements of the plot (for example, subplots, parallel episodes, climax), the plot's development, and the way in which conflicts are (or are not) addressed and resolved.

Here's a story that will probably be easy to identify with. It's about a teen who wants a dog. You've already gotten a head start, because now you know what the "somebody" (a teen) "wants" (a dog). Read on to find out the specifics.

Duncan, Junior

Heidi Schulman

**SOMEBODY
WANTED BUT SO**

Pause at line 16. What's the "But" part of this plot, or the **conflict**?

Even though the Place where he lived was perfect for a dog his parents didn't want to get one.

**VOCABULARY
DEVELOPMENT**

canine (kā′nīn′) *adj.*: of or like a dog.

Canine is from the Latin word *canis* for "dog."

I turned fourteen about two months ago, and that's when I decided it was time to get a dog. After all, my family and I live way out in the country, and the place is about as close to doggie heaven as anywhere on earth. For shade, we've got bushy pine trees that go up a hundred feet into the air. We've got a wide, muddy river to splash in, and in the spring and summer the meadows are filled with purple and yellow wildflowers and tall grasses so soft they'd tickle a pup's paws. It's quiet enough to hear a cat meow a quarter

10 of a mile away, and between the beavers and birds and old jackrabbits that like to come close to the back door and jiggle their whiskers, a dog can sniff all day and never get bored. It's perfect.

I explained my decision to my parents. They had other ideas for me, though, and none of them had anything to do with the word **"canine."**

"Jeremy," said my father. That's my name, by the way—Jeremy.

"Jeremy," dad said, "who's going to walk the dog in the
20 middle of winter when it's five below zero and the sky is
pitch black and the wind is howling and sleet is blowing
into your face?"

I had a feeling dad would say that. I was prepared.

"I won't have to walk him," I answered. I'll just let him
out and he can walk himself. This is the country, Dad.
There's land everywhere."

My comeback was brilliant, if I do say so myself. And it
was completely based on fact. Our house sits in the middle
of a huge meadow that stretches, gosh, I don't know how
30 far it really stretches, but trust me, this meadow is seriously
huge. You can't even see any other houses from where we
live. In fact, our closest neighbors are the birds that hang
out in the pine trees.

My mother, of course, had her own strong opinion.
You can always count on that with mom.

"Jeremy Gottlieb. Do you think I'm going to let an
animal run around outside by himself, get filthy dirty, and
then track mud and pine needles inside all over my clean
carpet? I don't think so."

40 It was time for brilliant comeback number two. I'd
really worked on this one.

"I'll make him dog boots, mom. Little rubber things
with Velcro closings. That way he'll be clean when he
comes in."

"Nice try," said my mom. "How about a fish instead?"

I couldn't blame my parents for being down on the
dog idea. The last time we'd had a dog, we lived in New
York City in a crowded two-bedroom **apartment** on the
fifth floor of an old brick apartment building. If you tried
50 to compare the place we lived then to the place we live now,

EVALUATE

Underline Jeremy's replies to
his parents' objections. How
effectively does he reply to
their reasons for not having
a dog?

His replies on
the objections
were good reasons
and were
well thought.
It could convince
his parents to
buy a dog.

VOCABULARY
DEVELOPMENT

apartment (ə·pärt′mənt) n.:
room or group of rooms to
live in.

In England, apartments are
called *flats,* because they are
usually on one floor.

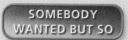

SOMEBODY WANTED BUT SO

Pause at line 58. What do you know about "Somebody" so far?

Jeremy use to have a dog when he lived in a city and now he is living in a long meadow.

VOCABULARY DEVELOPMENT

exercise (ek′sər·sīz′) *n.*: activity for the purpose of training or developing the body or mind.

humidity (hyoo·mid′ə·tē) *n.*: moistness; dampness.

When you come to a long word, you can often find a shorter word inside it that you already know. Circle the smaller word inside *humidity*.

the only thing you could say was they were exact opposites. Here, we have nature, nature, and more nature. There, we had cement, cement, and more cement. Our street was just one six-story brick apartment building after another. There were no trees and there was no grass. The only things that grew were scrawny little weeds trying to bust out from the cracks in the sidewalks.

It wasn't exactly a good place for a pet who needs **exercise.** But my aunt was moving and couldn't take her
60   10-year-old dog Duncan with her. I remember the night I convinced my parents to take him. I begged. I promised to walk the dog every day. I did everything but have a tantrum, because I knew for sure that would backfire on me.

It was about 95 degrees that night. The **humidity** was high and we were all sweating like pigs. I think the reason my parents finally gave in and took the dog was that the heat had gone to their brains and they just wanted to go to sleep.
70   So Duncan came to live with us. He was a black poodle who'd never had a haircut and looked like a stringy mop that had come to life. He had a limp, and because of it, he'd trip sometimes and run into the couch or a table. But it never seemed to bother him.

Duncan and I became close pals. But I hardly ever walked him.

I can still remember the way my mother looked at me on freezing mornings as she put her woolly brown winter coat on over her pajamas to take Duncan for his walk. I got
80   out of it by pretending to be asleep. I was never really sure why my parents let me get away with it, but I think it was probably because they came to love Duncan, too.

Duncan lived a long life, by the way. We had my mom to thank for that. She refused to believe the vet when he said Duncan had a slipped disc and should be put down because he'd never be able to walk right. She just marched the dog out of the vet's office, borrowed a baby's playpen from neighbors, and made Duncan stay in there with a heating pad wrapped around his bad leg. Duncan got

90 better, and lived to be fifteen. But me, I never got better about taking him out.

So, to be honest, my parents had a pretty good reason for saying no to me when I said I wanted another dog. I didn't exactly have a great track record. But that didn't mean I was going to take "no" for an answer. I knew my parents loved dogs, and I've got a strong will just like my mom. So I just kept bringing it up, and bringing it up until, well, you get the picture.

When they finally gave in, I named the dog Duncan

100 Junior.

Every dog has his own personality. Which is my way of saying Duncan Junior turned out to be a lot different from Duncan Senior. He was a big guy, very muscular and strong. He had a short shiny coat and was all white, except for two black ears. DJ, which is what I called him for short, had more energy than a tornado, and his favorite thing in the whole entire world was running. We got him in the spring, and he and I would spend every afternoon and weekend running near the river. He'd run along the muddy

110 river bank, leaping over the limbs of willow trees that had blown down in the spring winds. There was my big white dog, practically up to his little black ears in muddy water, following the current, trying to pick up every stick and tree branch that floated by, brown eyes shining, the happiest

INFER

What does the story about Duncan have to do with Jeremy's asking for a dog in the country?

The story about Duncan gave Jeremy memories of how nice it was having a dog.

WORD KNOWLEDGE

In line 106, Jeremy compares Duncan Junior to a tornado, which is a violent whirling column of air, with wind speeds up to three hundred miles per hour.

Tornado came into English from the Spanish word *tornar,* meaning "turn." Spanish, in turn, borrowed from a Latin word meaning "thunder."

The snowstorm was a problem for Jeremy because he needed to walk the dog and there was a snowstorm and it was cold. Jeremy would rather stay in bed but he had to walk DJ.

animal you'd ever seen. When he finally came back to shore, he dropped a stick at my feet, like he was bringing me a gold medal from a swimming event at the Dog Olympics.

By the time winter came, my puppy weighed a hundred pounds and took up an awful lot of room on my
120 bed. He kept me pretty warm, though, and that's probably why I didn't notice how cold it was that October morning when I woke up to see we'd had our first snow. It was a big one. When I looked outside my bedroom window, everything was white. Not the pretty kind of white, but the kind of white that's still coming down, the kind that stops you from telling the difference between the ground and the sky and the trees and the cars. Total white-out.

The clock-radio came on and the announcer told us it was twenty-five degrees and we were in for the worst winter
130 ever on record.

DJ was smart, of course, but not smart enough to understand it was too cold to go out. So when he whined, even though I knew exactly what he wanted, I pulled the covers up over my head. It was a Sunday morning and the reason I remember exactly what happened is that I wrote it down.

(1) DJ whined.

(2) I ignored him, and pulled the pillows over my head.

140 (3) DJ pawed at my face.

(4) I turned over, face down.

(5) DJ barked.

(6) My mother yelled from the other room, "Jeremy, take your dog out."

(7) I pretended to be asleep.

(8) My father yelled out "Right now!"

(9) I kept pretending. After all, it worked in New York
City.

150　(10) My mother groaned and said to my father, "Here
we go again, Sam."

(11) My father said, "Helen" (that's my mom) "don't
do it."

(12) My mom said, "I'm doing it just this once, and
never again."

(13) I thought: "Yes!"

What happened next wasn't very pretty.

I heard my mom's slippers on the floor and heard the
back door open.

"Let's go, DJ," she said. Then her voice got louder. "DJ,
160　let's go now!"

DJ whined. I heard my mother shuffle back into bed.
DJ came back into my room and whined again.

My mother called out, "Jeremy, we know you're just
pretending to be asleep. But you'd better get up. Your dog
won't go outside with me."

You can only listen to a dog whine up to a certain
point, and that point is exactly four minutes and 11
seconds. When DJ reached that mark, I faced the awful
truth. My dog wouldn't go out of the house with anyone
170　but me. Not only that, but he wouldn't even walk if I was
at the back door waiting for him. I had to walk with him.

"You're carrying loyalty too far," I said to DJ the next
morning. It was 6 A.M., and I was outside walking my dog.
I was wearing at least three sweaters, and my teeth were
chattering because the temperature was so low the snow
had turned to ice.

But DJ just smiled and ran along, waiting for me at
every turn. You practically couldn't see him in the snow.

SOMEBODY
WANTED BUT SO

Pause at line 172. The plot
develops to a climax. What
does Jeremy do?

Jeremy gets out
of bed and walks
DJ after DJ
refuses to go
on a walk
with his mom.
The only person
DJ would go on
a walk with is
Jeremy.

responsibility
(ri·spän′sə·bil′ə·tē) *n.:* duty
or obligation.

FLUENCY

Read the boxed paragraph
aloud with natural expression. If you have trouble with
*getting-up-before-the-crack-
of-dawn-and-walking-him,*
pretend there are no
hyphens in it. Read each
word separately. You'll probably find that the words are
pretty easy. Now, use the
hyphens to help you read the
whole phrase smoothly, as if
it were one long word.

INTERPRET

How is the story's **resolution**
successful for Jeremy? How
is it unsuccessful?

The resolution was
successful for Jeremy
because he got a
new dog. It was
unsuccessful because
he had to walk it
in the cold winters.

180   His white body blended in to everything else, and the only
reasons you could spot him at all were those little black ears
and hot doggy breath and that smile he smiled when I'd
finally catch up with him.

So that's how my life has turned out so far. I've got a
dog, and the dog walks me. Sometimes I hear my mother
whispering to my father how good it is that this dog has
taught me **responsibility.** Maybe she's right. I'm not sure I
even know what she means. But what I do know is that
walking with DJ, I've seen some very cool things I wouldn't
have seen without him. Like the day he started squealing,
190   took my coat jacket in his mouth, and dragged me to a tree
to show me two tiny kittens, meowing and hungry. Do the
kittens live with us now? What do you think? Or the day DJ
suddenly stopped dead in his tracks, let his favorite
chewed-up stick fall out of his mouth, and motioned for
me to look up to the sky. High above us, floating on the
wind current, was a golden eagle—with wings so broad he
moved like he owned the sky. DJ and I just stood there
watching him until he floated out of our view and we
headed home.

200   Of course, it's not all perfect. There's still the getting-
up-before-the-crack-of-dawn-and-walking-him part of this
story, and I don't like it any better than I used to. I keep
having this dream that one day, my parents are going to
take over the job again. I don't know how I'm going to get
them to do it, but believe me, I'm working on it.

OWN THE STORY

Plot   Analyze how the plot in this story works by completing the "Somebody Wanted But So" chart on the following page. Then, get together with a classmate, and compare your entries.

Compare Plots   Within "Duncan, Junior" two plots are revealed. One series of plot events is told in **flashback,** before the time frame of the current story. The other series of plot events takes place in the **present.** Fill out the chain-of-events charts below with the major events of each plot. Then, compare them.

Flashback

Event 1	Event 2	Event 3	Event 4
Jeremy got a dog	He hardly ever walked him	The dog stayed in a baby play pin	The dog lived until 15

Present

Event 1	Event 2	Event 3	Event 4
Jeremy kept asking for a dog until he got one	they went to the river every afternoon	the dog would only go on a walk with Jeremy	Jeremy walked the dog and stopped pretending to be asleep.

KEEPING TRACK

Personal Word List   Record in your Personal Word List the words you learned from this story.

Personal Reading Log   As you record this story in your Personal Reading Log, state whether or not you would recommend it to a friend. Give yourself 4 points on the Reading Meter.

Checklist for Standards Mastery   Check your progress in mastering the standards. Where did you do well? Where can you improve?

Duncan, Junior ▪ *Interactive Reading,* page 2

Interact with a Literary Text

"Somebody Wanted But So" Chart   Work alone or with a partner.
Fill out the columns of the "Somebody Wanted But So" chart for
"Duncan, Junior." If you wish, use two SWBS statements connected
by *Then.* Or write a single statement covering the whole story, if
you can.

Somebody	Wanted	But	So
Jeremy			
Then Jeremy			

Broken Chain

Interact with a Literary Text

Plot Diagram   Fill out the graphic organizer below after you read
"Broken Chain."

Basic Situation and Conflict:

Alfonso didn't like the way he looked.

Complications (problems, events):

· Alfonso didn't like how his teeth were.

· He met a cute girl that went to his school.

· Ernie was jelous Alfonso might have found himself a girlfriend.

· Alfonso pushes on his teeth occasionally.

· Sandra rode on the bike with Alfonso to go on the date.

Climax:

Sandra put her hand over Alfonsos.

Resolution:

Sandra agrees to go on a date with Alfonso and they go on a bike.

Road Warriors, Listen Up

for use with
Holt Literature and Language Arts,
page 20

Interact with an Informational Text

Main-Idea Chart   The **main idea** is the most important point the writer is making about a subject. In a well-written article the main idea is clearly supported by details.

After you read "Road Warriors, Listen Up," fill out this graphic organizer. First, write the subject of the article. Then, fill in the details the writer provides about the subject. Finally, think about those details, and decide what overall idea they express about the subject. Write the main idea in its box.

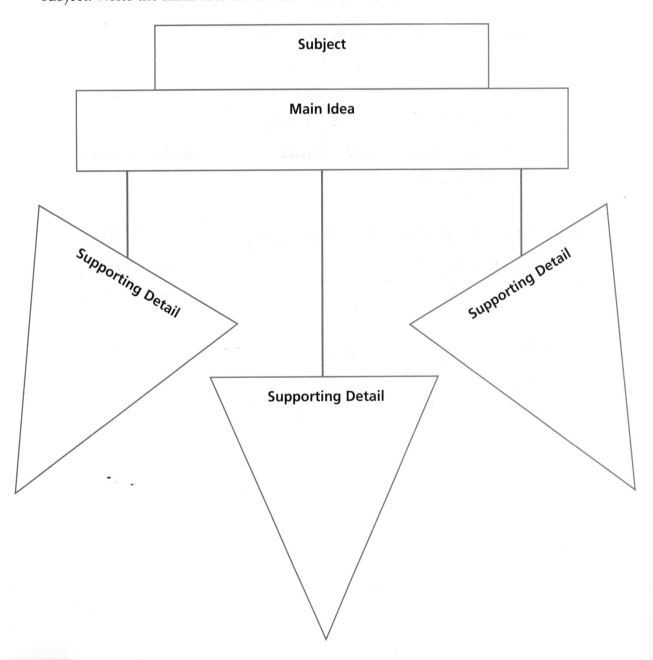

Flowers for Algernon

Interact with a Literary Text

Story Map   Long stories and novels are likely to have more plot complications than short stories. "Flowers for Algernon" certainly has a more complicated plot than the other stories you are reading in Chapter 1. Fill out the story map below as you read "Flowers for Algernon" to be sure you understand the plot events.

Main Characters	Descriptions
Charlie Gordon	Brain proccesses slower than others
Miss Kinnan	Teaches people like Charlie Gordon
Algernon	Mouse that is very smart
Dr. Strauss	Used Charlie for an experiment

Conflict

Charlie Gordon wanted to be smart and normal like everyone else but he is retarted.

What Happens?

Complication 1: Charlie was offered a once in a lifetime offer to become the smarted person on Earth but die in 2 years.

Complication 2: He took the opperation and became smart but people saw him as a freak

Complication 3: Charlie began to forget everything a little before 2 years has passed.

Complication 4: He dies after 2 years

Climax

He became smart and was finally able to beat Algernon in a race.

Resolution

Charlie took the opperation and became the smartest person on Earth.

Memory a Matter of Brains and Brawn

Interact with an Informational Text

Evaluation Chart   In an effective informational or persuasive text, the main idea is stated as a proposition at the beginning. The proposition is then supported by reasons. The first sentence of "Memory a Matter of Brains and Brawn" is the proposition: "The brain is like a muscle: Use it or lose it."

Below are the reasons that the writer of the article gives for believing that proposition. For each reason, decide whether it is a fact, a statistic, an example, an anecdote, a definition, or an expert opinion. Then, evaluate how effective you think each reason is. Rate the reasons on a scale of 1–4, with 4 the highest rating. If you think a reason could be made stronger, say how you would change it.

Reason	Type of Reason	Effectiveness	How I Would Change It
Mental exercise seems crucial to retaining brainpower.	expert opinion	2	
Bad memory linked to lifestyle risks that people can change	fact	3	
Alzheimer's patients can be helped by mental exercise.	fact	3	
"Read, read, read. . . . Anything that stimulates the brain to think."	Example	2	
The brain continually rewires and adapts itself, even growing some new neurons.	fact	4	
Alzheimer's linked to less education and poor reading habits	anecdote	3	

The Landlady

Interact with a Literary Text

Foreshadowing Chart When you read a suspenseful story, you make predictions about what might happen next. Clever authors usually include clues—details that foreshadow a later event—to help readers make predictions.

Fill out the foreshadowing chart as you read "The Landlady."

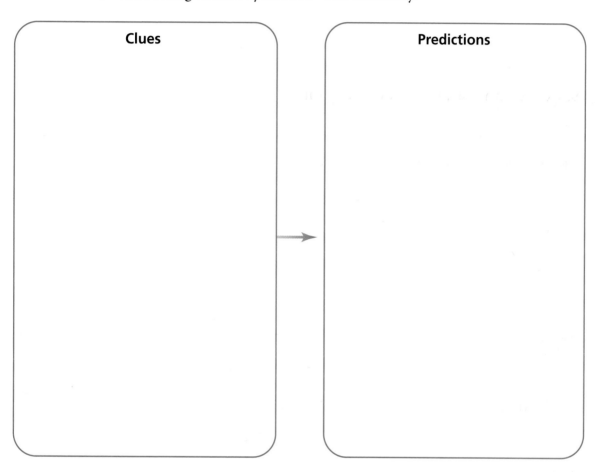

Clues	Predictions

Main Event Foreshadowed

Literature

AUTHOR STUDY

Gary Soto was born and raised in Fresno, California. He has written many books of fiction and poetry about what it is like to grow up as a Mexican American. Many of Soto's stories and poems come from his own childhood experiences. In addition to writing, Soto teaches and produces short films for Spanish-speaking children.

BEFORE YOU READ

Think about something you've always wanted. What would you do if you finally had the chance to get it, but you weren't sure if the way you were able to get it was quite right? In this story, Fausto has the "no-guitar blues," but possibly not for long.

"The No-Guitar Blues" was made into a short film, called *The Pool Party.* Of all Soto's stories this is the only one that has been adapted for film.

Keep the following in mind as you read:
- Many Spanish words and phrases appear in this story. Use the footnotes to learn what they mean and how to pronounce them.
- Los Lobos (the Wolves) is a rock group.

Reading Standard 3.2
Evaluate the structural elements of the plot (for example, subplots, parallel episodes, climax), the plot's development, and the way in which conflicts are (or are not) addressed and resolved.

The No-Guitar Blues

Gary Soto

PREDICT

"The No-Guitar Blues"—what might that title mean? Figure it out, and you'll be able to predict the basic situation of this story. Then, keep reading, and find out what happens.

The moment Fausto saw the group Los Lobos on "American Bandstand," he knew exactly what he wanted to do with his life—play guitar. His eyes grew large with excitement as Los Lobos ground out a song while teenagers bounced off each other on the crowded dance floor.

He had watched "American Bandstand" for years and had heard Ray Camacho and the Teardrops at Romain Playground, but it had never occurred to him that he too might become a musician. That afternoon Fausto knew his mission in life: to play guitar in his own band; to sweat out his songs and prance around the stage; to make money and dress weird.

10

SOMEBODY WANTED BUT SO

The first sentence in the story tells you who the somebody is and what he wants. Circle the words or phrases that give you this information. Put an *S* above the word that identifies the "Somebody" and a *W* above the words that identify what he "Wants."

"The No-Guitar Blues" from *Baseball in April and Other Stories* by Gary Soto. Copyright © 1990 by Gary Soto. Reprinted by permission of *Harcourt, Inc.*

_____

_____

_____

_____

_____

_____

_____

_____

_____

_____

SOMEBODY WANTED BUT SO

Re-read lines 32–45 to find a **complication** in the story's **plot.** In what way don't things turn out as Fausto had hoped?

_____

_____

_____

_____

_____

_____

_____

_____

_____

Fausto turned off the television set and walked out-side, wondering how he could get enough money to buy a guitar. He couldn't ask his parents because they would just say, "Money doesn't grow on trees" or "What do you think we are, bankers?" And besides, they hated rock music. They were into the *conjunto*[1] music of Lydia Mendoza, Flaco Jimenez, and Little Joe and La Familia. And, as Fausto

20 recalled, the last album they bought was *The Chipmunks Sing Christmas Favorites.*

But what the heck, he'd give it a try. He returned inside and watched his mother make tortillas. He leaned against the kitchen counter, trying to work up the nerve to ask her for a guitar. Finally, he couldn't hold back any longer.

"Mom," he said, "I want a guitar for Christmas."

She looked up from rolling tortillas. "Honey, a guitar costs a lot of money."

"How 'bout for my birthday next year," he tried again.

30 "I can't promise," she said, turning back to her tortillas, "but we'll see."

Fausto walked back outside with a buttered tortilla. He knew his mother was right. His father was a warehouseman at Berven Rugs, where he made good money but not enough to buy everything his children wanted. Fausto decided to mow lawns to earn money, and was pushing the mower down the street before he realized it was winter and no one would hire him. He returned the mower and picked up a rake. He hopped onto his sister's bike (his had two flat

40 tires) and rode north to the nicer section of Fresno in search of work. He went door-to-door, but after three hours he managed to get only one job, and not to rake

---

1. *conjunto* (kän·khōōn′tō): style of music popular near the U.S.-Mexico border.

leaves. He was asked to hurry down to the store to buy a loaf of bread, for which he received a grimy, dirt-caked quarter.

He also got an orange, which he ate sitting at the curb. While he was eating, a dog walked up and sniffed his leg. Fausto pushed him away and threw an orange peel skyward. The dog caught it and ate it in one gulp. The dog

50   looked at Fausto and wagged his tail for more. Fausto tossed him a slice of orange, and the dog snapped it up and licked his lips.

"How come you like oranges, dog?"

The dog blinked a pair of sad eyes and whined.

"What's the matter? Cat got your tongue?" Fausto laughed at his joke and offered the dog another slice.

At that moment a dim light came on inside Fausto's head. He saw that it was sort of a fancy dog, a terrier or something, with dog tags and a shiny collar. And it looked

60   well fed and healthy. In his neighborhood, the dogs were never licensed, and if they got sick they were placed near the water heater until they got well.

This dog looked like he belonged to rich people. Fausto cleaned his juice-sticky hands on his pants and got to his feet. The light in his head grew brighter. It just might work. He called the dog, patted its muscular back, and bent down to check the license.

"Great," he said. "There's an address."

The dog's name was Roger, which struck Fausto as

70   weird because he'd never heard of a dog with a human name. Dogs should have names like Bomber, Freckles, Queenie, Killer, and Zero.

PREDICT

Pause at line 52. What will the dog have to do with Fausto's getting what he wants?

_____

_____

_____

_____

_____

_____

_____

_____

_____

_____

_____

_____

_____

_____

_____

_____

_____

_____

_____

_____

_____

_____

SOMEBODY WANTED BUT SO

What is Fausto's new plan?

_____

_____

_____

_____

_____

_____

_____

_____

_____

_____

_____

VISUALIZE

Pause at line 105. Imagine that you are Fausto. How do you feel about the place where the dog lives?

_____

_____

_____

_____

_____

_____

_____

_____

Fausto planned to take the dog home and collect a reward. He would say he had found Roger near the freeway. That would scare the daylights out of the owners, who would be so happy that they would probably give him a reward. He felt bad about lying, but the dog *was* loose. And it might even really be lost, because the address was six blocks away.

80   Fausto stashed the rake and his sister's bike behind a bush, and, tossing an orange peel every time Roger became distracted, walked the dog to his house. He hesitated on the porch until Roger began to scratch the door with a muddy paw. Fausto had come this far, so he figured he might as well go through with it. He knocked softly. When no one answered, he rang the doorbell. A man in a silky bathrobe and slippers opened the door and seemed confused by the sight of his dog and the boy.

"Sir," Fausto said, gripping Roger by the collar. "I

90   found your dog by the freeway. His dog license says he lives here." Fausto looked down at the dog, then up to the man. "He does, doesn't he?"

The man stared at Fausto a long time before saying in a pleasant voice, "That's right." He pulled his robe tighter around him because of the cold and asked Fausto to come in. "So he was by the freeway?"

"Uh-huh."

"You bad, snoopy dog," said the man, wagging his finger. "You probably knocked over some trash cans, too,

100   didn't you?"

Fausto didn't say anything. He looked around, amazed by this house with its shiny furniture and a television as large as the front window at home. Warm bread smells filled the air and music full of soft tinkling floated in from another room.

"Helen," the man called to the kitchen. "We have a visitor." His wife came into the living room wiping her hands on a dish towel and smiling. "And who have we here?" she asked in one of the softest voices Fausto had ever heard.

110 "This young man said he found Roger near the freeway."

Fausto repeated his story to her while staring at a **perpetual** clock with a bell-shaped glass, the kind his aunt got when she celebrated her twenty-fifth anniversary. The lady frowned and said, wagging a finger at Roger, "Oh, you're a bad boy."

"It was very nice of you to bring Roger home," the man said. "Where do you live?"

"By that vacant lot on Olive," he said. "You know, by 120 Brownie's Flower Place."

The wife looked at her husband, then Fausto. Her eyes twinkled triangles of light as she said, "Well, young man, you're probably hungry. How about a turnover?"

"What do I have to turn over?" Fausto asked, thinking she was talking about yard work or something like turning trays of dried raisins.

"No, no, dear, it's a pastry." She took him by the elbow and guided him to a kitchen that sparkled with copper pans and bright yellow wallpaper. She guided him to the 130 kitchen table and gave him a tall glass of milk and something that looked like an empanada.[2] Steamy waves of heat escaped when he tore it in two. He ate with both eyes on the man and woman who stood arm-in-arm smiling at him. They were strange, he thought. But nice.

---

2. **empanada** (em'pə·nä'də) *n.:* filled, baked pastry popular in Latin America. Empanadas may contain meat, vegetables, or fruit.

Gary Soto   21

Look up *deceitful* (line 144) in a dictionary. What is the word's origin? What does *deceitful* mean? What are some related forms of the word?

_____

_____

_____

_____

_____

_____

_____

_____

_____

PREDICT

Pause at line 158. What do you think Fausto will do with the money?

_____

_____

_____

_____

_____

_____

"That was good," he said after he finished the turnover. "Did you make it, ma'am?"

"Yes, I did. Would you like another?"

"No, thank you. I have to go home now."

As Fausto walked to the door, the man opened his
140 wallet and took out a bill. "This is for you," he said. "Roger is special to us, almost like a son."

Fausto looked at the bill and knew he was in trouble. Not with these nice folks or with his parents but with himself. How could he have been so deceitful? The dog wasn't lost. It was just having a fun Saturday walking around.

"I can't take that."

"You have to. You deserve it, believe me," the man said.

"No, I don't."

"Now don't be silly," said the lady. She took the bill
150 from her husband and stuffed it into Fausto's shirt pocket. "You're a lovely child. Your parents are lucky to have you. Be good. And come see us again, please."

Fausto went out, and the lady closed the door. Fausto clutched the bill through his shirt pocket. He felt like ringing the doorbell and begging them to please take the money back, but he knew they would refuse. He hurried away, and at the end of the block, pulled the bill from his shirt pocket: It was a crisp twenty-dollar bill.

"Oh, man, I shouldn't have lied," he said under his
160 breath as he started up the street like a zombie. He wanted to run to church for Saturday confession,[3] but it was past four-thirty, when confession stopped.

He returned to the bush where he had hidden the rake and his sister's bike and rode home slowly, not daring to

---

3. In the Roman Catholic religion, a person seeks God's forgiveness by telling his or her sins to a priest. This is called **confession**.

touch the money in his pocket. At home, in the privacy of his room, he examined the twenty-dollar bill. He had never had so much money. It was probably enough to buy a secondhand guitar. But he felt bad, like the time he stole a dollar from the secret fold inside his older brother's wallet.

170   Fausto went outside and sat on the fence. "Yeah," he said. "I can probably get a guitar for twenty. Maybe at a yard sale—things are cheaper."

His mother called him to dinner.

The next day he dressed for church without anyone telling him. He was going to go to eight o'clock mass.

"I'm going to church, Mom," he said. His mother was in the kitchen cooking *papas*[4] and *chorizo con huevos*.[5] A pile of tortillas lay warm under a dish towel.

"Oh, I'm so proud of you, Son." She beamed, turning
180   over the crackling *papas*.

His older brother, Lawrence, who was at the table reading the funnies, mimicked, "Oh, I'm so proud of you, my son," under his breath.

At Saint Theresa's he sat near the front. When Father Jerry began by saying that we are all sinners, Fausto thought he looked right at him. Could he know? Fausto **fidgeted** with guilt. No, he thought. I only did it yesterday.

Fausto knelt, prayed, and sang . But he couldn't forget the man and the lady, whose names he didn't even know,
190   and the empanada they had given him. It had a strange name but tasted really good. He wondered how they got rich. And how that dome clock worked. He had asked his mother once how his aunt's clock worked. She said it just worked, the way the refrigerator works. It just did.

---

4. *papas* (pä'päs) *n.:* potatoes.
5. *chorizo con huevos* (chō·rē'zō kôn wā'vōs): sausage with eggs.

VOCABULARY
DEVELOPMENT

fidgeted (fij'it·id) *v.:* moved in a restless, a nervous, or an uneasy way.

VOCABULARY
DEVELOPMENT

reluctantly (ri·luk′tənt·lē)
adv.: unwillingly.

If you felt you just had to
give away twenty dollars,
would you be eager to give
the money away? If you
understand how Fausto feels
in this situation, you'll understand the word *reluctantly.*

_____

_____

_____

_____

_____

_____

_____

VOCABULARY
DEVELOPMENT

charity (char′i·tē) *n.:*
voluntary giving of money
or help to those in need.

· · · · · · Notes · · · · · ·

_____

_____

_____

_____

_____

_____

_____

Fausto caught his mind wandering and tried to
concentrate on his sins. He said a Hail Mary and sang, and
when the wicker basket came his way, he stuck a hand
reluctantly in his pocket and pulled out the twenty-dollar
bill. He ironed it between his palms, and dropped it into
200 the basket. The grown-ups stared. Here was a kid dropping
twenty dollars in the basket while they gave just three or
four dollars.

There would be a second collection for Saint Vincent
de Paul,[6] the lector announced. The wicker baskets again
floated in the pews, and this time the adults around him,
given a second chance to show their **charity,** dug deep into
their wallets and purses and dropped in fives and tens. This
time Fausto tossed in the grimy quarter.

Fausto felt better after church. He went home and
210 played football in the front yard with his brother and some
neighbor kids. He felt cleared of wrongdoing and was so
happy that he played one of his best games of football ever.
On one play, he tore his good pants, which he knew he
shouldn't have been wearing. For a second, while he
examined the hole, he wished he hadn't given the twenty
dollars away.

Man, I coulda bought me some Levi's, he thought. He
pictured his twenty dollars being spent to buy church
candles. He pictured a priest buying an armful of flowers
220 with *his* money.

Fausto had to forget about getting a guitar. He spent
the next day playing soccer in his good pants, which were
now his old pants. But that night during dinner, his mother
said she remembered seeing an old bass *guitarron* the last
time she cleaned out her father's garage.

---

6. **St. Vincent de Paul** (1580?–1660?) was a French priest who helped the
   poor. Today, St. Vincent de Paul Societies carry on that mission.

"It's a little dusty," his mom said, serving his favorite enchiladas. "But I think it works. Grandpa says it works."

Fausto's ears perked up. That was the same kind the guy in Los Lobos played. Instead of asking for the guitar, he waited for his mother to offer it to him. And she did, while gathering the dishes from the table.

"No, Mom, I'll do it," he said, hugging her. "I'll do the dishes forever if you want."

It was the happiest day of his life. No, it was the second-happiest day of his life. The happiest was when his grandfather Lupe placed the *guitarron,* which was nearly as huge as a washtub, in his arms. Fausto ran a thumb down the strings, which vibrated in his throat and chest. It sounded beautiful, deep, and eerie. A pumpkin smile widened on his face.

"OK, *hijo,*[7] now you put your fingers like this," said his grandfather, smelling of tobacco and aftershave. He took Fausto's fingers and placed them on the strings. Fausto strummed a chord on the *guitarron,* and the bass **resounded** in their chests.

The *guitarron* was more complicated than Fausto imagined. But he was confident that after a few more lessons he could start a band that would someday play on "American Bandstand" for the dancing crowds.

230

240

SOMEBODY WANTED BUT SO

Just when he thinks he has to give up his dream, Fausto finds a solution to his problem. State it as a sentence beginning with "So."

_____

_____

_____

_____

_____

_____

_____

_____

_____

_____

VOCABULARY DEVELOPMENT

resounded (ri·zound'id) *v.:* echoed or filled with sound.

EVALUATE

If you had been Fausto, what would you have done with the money?

_____

_____

_____

_____

---

7. *hijo* (ē'hô) *n.:* Spanish for "son."

OWN THE STORY

Plot   Analyze how the plot in this story works, based on the "Somebody Wanted But So" notes that are printed next to the story text. Identify elements of the plot such as **conflict, complications, climax,** and **resolution.** With a partner, discuss the resolution of Fausto's problem. Did you think it was a believable resolution?

_____

_____

_____

_____

_____

_____

_____

_____

_____

_____

_____

_____

_____

KEEPING TRACK

Personal Word List   List the vocabulary words for this story in order of difficulty in your Personal Word List. Don't forget to add the new Spanish words you learned, too!

Personal Reading Log   How much did you enjoy this short story, and why? Write your response to it in your Personal Reading Log, and award yourself 5 points on the Reading Meter.

Checklist for Standards Mastery   You are learning a lot as you read these stories! Use the Checklist for Standards Mastery to see how well you have done mastering the standards and where you can improve.

The No-Guitar Blues

PROJECT

Go Beyond a Literary Text

Author Study Use your library and the Internet to find out more about Gary Soto. Find five books by Gary Soto, and fill out the book list below.

Works of Gary Soto

Title	Date	Genre (novel, short story, poetry, nonfiction)	Brief Description

Information

BEFORE YOU READ

Imagine that you're growing up in ancient Greece. What kind of music would you be listening to, and how would you be listening to it? There would be nothing electronic, but some other aspects of music listening might be familiar. For example, you might attend a crowded concert where weirdly dressed, highly paid superstars sing the latest hits!

Reading Standard 2.2 Analyze text that uses proposition and support patterns.

from Archaeology's dig, June/July 2000

Music from the Start

Patricia Hunt-Jones

TEXT STRUCTURE

In this informational article the writer presents a **proposition,** an important idea or opinion, and supports the proposition with reasons. The proposition is the main idea. Circle the proposition in the first paragraph of this article.

VOCABULARY DEVELOPMENT

archaeologists (är′kē·äl′ə·jists) *n.:* scientists who study ancient people and their culture.

TEXT STRUCTURE

Propositions are supported with statistics and other facts, examples, anecdotes, and expert opinions. Underline a detail that supports the proposition.

And I've often wondered how did it all start?
Who found out that nothing can capture a heart,
Like a melody can? Well, whoever it was, I'm a fan.

—from the song "Thank You for the Music"
by the 1970s rock-and-roll group ABBA

When you're hanging out in your room listening to the sounds of 'N Sync, Britney Spears, or Fresh Prince, did you ever wonder when people started making music? Well, hold onto your headphones because, believe it or not, people

10 have been playing musical instruments for more than 10,000 years. In fact, **archaeologists** recently discovered flutes in China that are around 9,000 years BMTV (Before Music Television), making them among the oldest playable multinote musical instruments ever found.

But the story of how people developed music is about more than the discovery of old instruments. Through

Assyrian musicians in a parade, about 7th century B.C.

representation
(rep′rē·zen·tā′shən) *n.:* image
or likeness of.

Like many long words, *representation* is built upon a base
word plus a prefix and suffix.
What is the prefix? What is
the suffix? What is the base
word? Divide the word to
show the three parts.

_____

_____

_____

_____

_____

_____

_____

sculpture, paintings, writing on tablets and tombs, and
even Bible stories, archaeologists have learned how
people of ancient cultures created and improved the
20   music they loved.

Ancient Music Makers

The earliest **representation** of people playing musical
instruments appeared on Sumerian writing tablets in
Mesopotamia (now modern Iraq) around 3000 B.C.
Sumerian music was first played on drums and bird-bone
flutes (both of which archaeologists have found in the
area). The Sumerians later developed stringed instruments
such as lutes, harps, and lyres. As the centuries passed,
Sumerian kings paid musicians to write and play music for
30   festivals and religious holidays.

The English word *lyric* comes
from the Greek word *lyra,*
"stringed instrument"
(line 28).

In English a *lyric* is a poem
that does not tell a story
but instead expresses the
speaker's thoughts or feelings. *Lyrics* are the words to
a song.

transformed (trans·fôrmd′)
v.: changed the form or
appearance of.

The prefix *trans-* is from
a Latin word meaning
"over, on the other side
of, through, or across."
What is a *transformer*? a
transfusion? *transportation*?

_____

_____

_____

_____

_____

_____

_____

_____

_____

_____

_____

· · · · · · **Notes** · · · · · ·

_____

_____

_____

_____

_____

Appreciation for the sound of Sumerian stringed instruments carried over to ancient Egypt. During the next 1,000 years, Egyptian musicians **transformed** the harp, originally a three-string instrument, into a 20-string instrument.

An Egyptian harpist in a mural painting from about 1100 B.C.

The History of Music BMTV (Before Music Television)	
9000 B.C.	The Chinese invent a flute out of hollow bird bones. It is among the first multinote, playable musical instruments.
3000 B.C.	The first stringed instruments, such as harps, lutes, and lyres, are developed in Sumer, a city in Mesopotamia.

(continued)

40

The History of Music BMTV (continued)	
2134–1600 B.C.	Portable harps are invented in Egypt. Priests and dancers play them at festivals and religious ceremonies.
1550–1080 B.C.	Many new kinds of instruments are created in Egypt including pipes, trumpets, drums, and tambourines. These folks knew how to party.
8th Century B.C.	The famous Greek poet Homer describes many instruments and songs in his famous poems, the *Iliad* and the *Odyssey*.
600 B.C.	As described in the Bible, a golden statue of the Assyrian king Nebuchadnezzar is dedicated as a full orchestra plays.
427–322 B.C.	In their writings, the famous Greek philosophers Plato and Aristotle say music is important in the education of Greek citizens.
50 B.C.	The water organ is invented by the Romans using old cows' stomachs to hold the water.
A.D. 284	The Roman emperor Carinus throws a huge party with an orchestra of 200 flutes, 100 harps, and 100 trumpets.
A.D. 1000–1500	The Aztecs in Mexico play percussion instruments and horns, primarily during religious ceremonies.

50

60

70

TEXT STRUCTURE

How many years does this time line span?

· · · · · · Notes · · · · · ·

INTERPRET

Is it just a coincidence that English has the word *music* and ancient Greek had the word *mousike*? Explain.

_____

_____

_____

_____

_____

_____

WORD KNOWLEDGE

Underline the definition of the word *musicology* (line 100).

The suffix *-logy* is from a Greek word meaning "word" or "study of" or "theory of." What is *biology*? *psychology*? *theology*?

_____

_____

_____

_____

_____

_____

What does *octave* mean (line 104)? How do you know?

_____

_____

_____

While we have a lot of information about Egyptian music, musicians, and instruments, we have no idea how their music sounded. We do know that the ancient Egyptians so enjoyed music that their cow-goddess, Hathor, ruled over love, joy, and—you guessed it—music. Paintings and reliefs in royal tombs show Egyptians—from the wives

80 of pharaohs to the lowliest slaves—playing music as far back as 2600 B.C. In Egypt, music was mostly played during religious ceremonies, great festivals, and large parades. Even divorcing Egyptian couples would fight over who owned the rights to instruments, written music, and musicians (who were slaves).

Besides stringed instruments, Egyptian musicians also played pipes and trumpets. In fact, two trumpets, one of bronze and gold, the other silver, were found in the tomb of the boy king, Tutankhamen. They are now in the Cairo

90 Museum, as is the mummified body of Harmosis, ancient Egypt's greatest musician.

The Greek Beat

The ancient Greeks weren't the first culture to develop *mousike* (their word for music) and instruments, but they made the biggest contribution to the art of Western music as we know it today. The instruments found in Greece were similar to those in Sumer and Egypt. How do we know this? Herodotus, a 5th-century B.C. Greek historian, writes about Greeks traveling to Sumer and Egypt to study and

100 borrow their instrument-making skills and musicology (the science of writing and creating music). Pythagoras, the 6th-century mathematician, also went to Sumer to study the science of music. He would eventually develop the octave, the group of eight notes—do, re, mi, etc.—that became the foundation for modern Western music.

Scene from a Greek vase, about 5th century B.C.

VOCABULARY DEVELOPMENT

harmonious (här·mō′nē·əs) *adj.:* having musical tones combined to give a pleasing effect.

This writer provides many definitions in context. Underline the context definitions of *melody* and *harmony* (lines 111–112). Underline the **analogy,** or comparison, she uses to help you understand what a head harness is (line 114).

WORD KNOWLEDGE

Lever (line 119) can be pronounced with the first e long or short. Both pronunciations are correct.

VOCABULARY DEVELOPMENT

accompaniment (ə·kum′pə·nə·mənt) *n.:* music performed together with the main part.

Use a dictionary to find words that have the same root as *accompaniment.*

_____

_____

_____

_____

_____

_____

Which instruments made the Greeks get up and boogie? Ancient writings tell of how audiences loved the *aulos,* which was a double-pipe flute. The two pipes were played at the same time, and archaeologists believe this
110 created a **harmonious** sound. We don't know which pipe carried the melody (main music line) and which carried the harmony (complementary music line), or even how they sounded together. We do know that the flute players had to wear a head harness (much like a retainer) to hold the pipes to their lips.

The ancient Greeks also developed the *phorminx,* a seven-string lyre, and the cithara, which was a popular instrument used in local concerts. They also created one of the first organs. The organ player would move a lever
120 which would drive air into a pipe using water pressure to create a sound.

In Greece, music was so popular that it was played as **accompaniment** to everyday chores and during battle training for soldiers. During concerts, audiences shoved and pushed each other for the best seats. Musicians

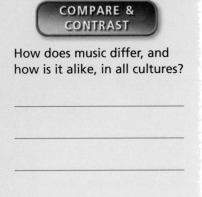

COMPARE & CONTRAST

How does music differ, and how is it alike, in all cultures?

_____

_____

_____

_____

performed and composed original music, wore fancy costumes, made tons of money, and were worshiped by adoring fans. The Greeks might also be the first Western culture that put words to music. They would recite their

130 historical or romantic poetry while instruments played in the background. And we have the Greeks to thank for many of our modern music words, such as *chorus, choir, orchestra,* and *harmony.*

OWN THE TEXT

PRACTICING THE STANDARDS

Analyzing Text   Imagine you were giving a lecture and you wanted to summarize information from the article "Music from the Start." The point of the lecture is to identify the main propositions of the article and the details that support the propositions. Prepare index cards that you would use to help you give your lecture. On each card, write one proposition, followed by a bulleted list of the statistics, facts, examples, or anecdotes that support the proposition. Exchange cards with a partner, and review each other's work.

KEEPING TRACK

Personal Word List   Write the new words from this selection in your Personal Word List. To check your understanding, use each word in a sentence about something other than music.

Personal Reading Log   What reading problems did you encounter in this selection? How did you deal with them? Give yourself 2 points on the Reading Meter.

Checklist for Standards Mastery   Mastery of the standards is a long-term process. Track your progress using the Checklist for Standards Mastery.

Music from the Start *Interactive Reading,* page 28

Go Beyond an Informational Text

Musical Time Line   In "Music from the Start," you learned about the origins of music and musical instruments. Go beyond what you've learned, and make a musical time line of rock-and-roll music. Do research in the library and on the Internet. You may also want to interview a music teacher in your school to learn of other resources.

Once your research is done, convert what you've learned into time line form, using the blanks below.

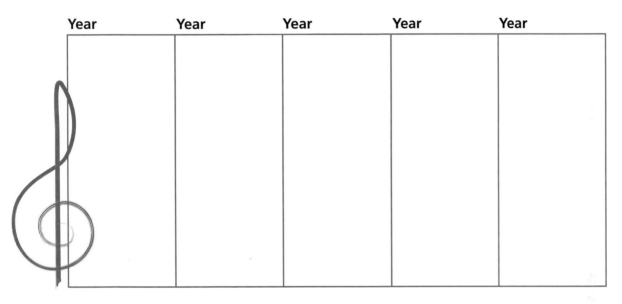

Year	Year	Year	Year	Year

Year	Year	Year	Year	Year

Literature

 MYTH

BEFORE YOU READ

Who do you think is the greatest musician alive today? Imagine that person playing music so beautiful that it even tames animals. Imagine this musician going down into the world of the dead and making the dead weep. Sound strange? Ancient peoples told such a story about the greatest musician in the world.

Reading Standard 3.2 Evaluate the structural elements of the plot, the plot's development, and the way in which conflicts are (or are not) addressed and resolved.

ORPHEUS AND THE UNDERWORLD

a Greek myth retold by Mollie McLean and Anne Wiseman

IDENTIFY

Pause at line 6. Circle the two different names given for the place being described.

VOCABULARY DEVELOPMENT

wicked (wik′id) *adj.:* morally bad or wrong.

Wicked comes from the Old English *wicce,* meaning "witch."

WORD KNOWLEDGE

Mercury (line 12) is the name of a Roman god (his Greek name is Hermes).

Mercury is also the name of a planet and of a chemical element.

The Underworld

Many times the Greeks told of a dark kingdom called Hades (hā′dēz′). They said people went to this place when they died. No one was sure where Hades was. Some said it was at the edge of the world. Others said it was under the very ground upon which men walked. That is why some people called it the Underworld.

The kingdom of Hades had two parts—one beautiful, one ugly. The beautiful part was filled with sunlight and happiness. Here lived those who had been good on earth.

10 The other part was dark and sad. Those who had been **wicked** lived here.

When a man died, Mercury came to take him to the Underworld. He led him down a dark road until they came to a great river. This river was called the Styx (stiks). Here Charon (ker′ən), an old boatman, was waiting. If the dead man had a penny in his mouth, Charon would take him across the river in his boat. He would not take him if the dead man's friends had forgotten the money.

20 Once across the river, they came to a dark **palace.** Here lived Pluto, king of the Underworld, and his beautiful wife, Proserpina. Outside the gate sat Cerberus (sʉr′bər·əs), a fierce three-headed dog with a hissing snake for a tail. He would let everyone pass into the palace. He would let no one out.

Inside the palace, it was cold and dark. The king and queen sat quietly on black chairs. Their pale faces were sad. They were so still that they looked as if they were made of stone.

Into this room, Mercury would lead the man who had 30 died. Pluto would ask Mercury if the man with him had led a good life. If the messenger-god said yes, the king sent the man to the beautiful part of Hades. If Mercury said no, Pluto gave the man some terrible labor.

Pluto had given terrible labors to many wicked men. One man had to roll a giant rock up a hill. Just as he came to the top, a magic power pushed the rock away from him. Down it would go, and the man would have to try once more. He would push the rock to the top again and again. Each time it would roll back.

40 Tantalus had been a cruel man on earth. In Hades, he had to stand in water which came up to his shoulders. But when he tried to take a drink, the water would run away. He was always thirsty. Over his head grew apples and oranges. But when he put his hand out for them, they would fly away. He was always hungry.

Pluto had also given hard labors to cruel women. Three sisters who had been wicked and mean had to carry water from a well in a sieve.

IDENTIFY

If somebody wanted to get across the River Styx to the Underworld, what would he or she need?

_____

_____

_____

VOCABULARY DEVELOPMENT

palace (pal′əs) *n.:* residence of a king, an emperor, a bishop, and so on.

Palace comes from the Latin *palatium,* after *Palatium,* one of the Seven Hills of Rome, where Augustus lived.

WORD KNOWLEDGE

Look up *tantalize* in a dictionary. Explain how its meaning is related to the mythic Tantalus (line 40).

_____

_____

_____

_____

_____

_____

_____

50 The people of the world were afraid of Hades. They
did not want to go to this dark place until their time had
come. Once in a long time a mighty hero had to go to the
Underworld. The next story tells of one of these heroes.

Orpheus Goes to the Underworld

In all of Greece there was no better singer than Orpheus
(ôr′fē·əs). When he sang and played his **lyre,** people would
stop their work and hurry to his side. Animals of the forest
would come near. Fierce monsters would sit quietly at his
feet. Even tall trees would bend their heads to hear his
song.

Orpheus went from place to place singing his songs of
love and battle. One day he saw a beautiful girl in the
crowd. He fell in love with her at once. He stopped playing
10 and walked over to her.

"What is your name?" he asked.

"I am called Eurydice (yo͞o·rid′i·sē′)," she said quietly.

"I shall sing my next song for you," said Orpheus.

He picked up his lyre and sang a beautiful song. When
Eurydice heard the song, she fell in love with the singer.

For many days, Orpheus stayed in this place. No longer
did he wish to go about the world singing. He wanted only
to please Eurydice. Every day he sang her a new song of
love.

20 Then one fine day, Orpheus and Eurydice were married. All their friends came to wish them happiness. There
was a great feast. There was dancing and singing. Everyone
was very happy until an old man stepped out of the crowd

and said, "Stop the dancing! Stop the singing! There is something I must say!"

"What is it, old man?" asked Orpheus.

"I have seen a bad sign in the sky. There is sadness ahead for you and your wife," he answered.

30 "How can there be sadness for us?" laughed Orpheus. "We love each other too much to be unhappy."

"We shall see. We shall see," said the old man as he walked quietly away.

After the old man had gone, a dark **shadow** fell on the feast. Soon everyone went home.

The next day, Orpheus and Eurydice took a walk beside the river. As they came near a field, Eurydice saw some beautiful red flowers. She ran to pick them. All at once, she fell. Orpheus raced to her side. Just as he came near, he saw a snake moving away in the grass.

40 "My foot! My foot!" cried Eurydice. "Something has hurt my foot!"

Orpheus picked her up in his powerful arms. He ran as fast as he could. He wanted to get to the river to wash her foot. As soon as he put her down on the ground, he knew she was dead.

For a long time after this, Orpheus went about the world singing and playing his lyre. No more did he sing of love and battle. His songs now told of the great sadness he felt in his heart. Each song asked how he might get

50 Eurydice back. He sang to the people of the world. He sang to the gods on Mount Olympus. No one could help him.

At last, Orpheus knew he must go to Hades. He went at once to the black cave which led to the Underworld. Down, down the dark road he went, singing his song of sadness all the way. Soon he was at the River Styx. Here

VOCABULARY DEVELOPMENT

shadow (shad′ō) *n.:* feeling of gloom or depression.

Shadow can also refer to the shade cast when light rays are blocked by an object.

SOMEBODY WANTED BUT SO

Pause at line 45. What is the "But" part of the plot—the problem that arises for "Somebody"?

_____

_____

_____

_____

_____

SOMEBODY WANTED BUT SO

So, what does "Somebody" do about getting what he wants?

_____

_____

_____

_____

_____

_____

VOCABULARY DEVELOPMENT

fierce (firs) *adj.:* of a violently cruel nature; savage; wild.

SOMEBODY WANTED BUT SO

Re-read lines 59–68. Circle the part that tells what Orpheus wants and his reason for wanting it.

Pause at line 78. What is the "But" that Pluto makes as a condition for Orpheus to get what he wants?

_____

_____

_____

_____

_____

_____

_____

_____

PREDICT

Pause at line 78. What do you think is going to happen?

_____

_____

_____

_____

_____

_____

stood the **fierce** old boatman. He had heard Orpheus coming. He, too, had felt the magic power of the hero's song. He took him across the river without a word.

On into the kingdom of Hades walked Orpheus. At the
60   sound of his singing, Tantalus forgot how hungry and thirsty he was. The man pushing the rock stopped his hard labor. The three sisters put their sieves on the ground and listened to the beautiful music. Orpheus walked on. He passed the cruel three-headed dog and went into the palace of Pluto. Here he saw the king and queen. He fell on his knees before them. Looking up, he said, "I have come to ask you to give me back my beautiful Eurydice. I cannot live without her."

The king and queen had heard the young hero's song.
70   Their hearts had been moved by its sadness. Pluto said, "No one has ever left Hades before. We will let Eurydice go because of your beautiful singing."

"You are very kind, Pluto," said Orpheus. "Where shall I look for her?"

"Do not look for her," said the king. "Go back the way you have come. She will follow you. Do not look back at her until you can see the light of the sun. If you once turn, she will be lost forever. Now, go! Remember my words!"

Orpheus started the long trip back. Out of the palace
80   he went. He passed the three-headed dog. He went over the river. Soon he was on the dark road which led up to the world. As he walked, he listened for footsteps behind him. He heard nothing. He began to wonder if Pluto had played some terrible trick on him. He walked on. Still he could hear nothing. Orpheus could stand it no longer. Just as he reached the end of the road, he turned around.

"Eurydice!" he called.

There before him, he saw a gray shadow. It was his beautiful wife.

90   "Orpheus!" she cried. "You should not have turned so soon! We were almost free! Goodbye! Goodbye!"

    With a sad smile, she went back to the Underworld. Orpheus followed her, but this time no one would listen to his song. He knew she was lost forever.

    After a time, Orpheus went back to the world. Never again did he sing a song of love!

Orpheus and his lyre in a scene from a Greek vase, about 6th century B.C.

SOMEBODY
WANTED BUT SO

Complete a "Somebody Wanted But So" statement to summarize the plot.

_____

_____

_____

_____

_____

_____

_____

_____

_____

_____

_____

_____

_____

_____

_____

_____

_____

_____

_____

_____

_____

_____

OWN THE STORY

Plot Imagine you were to "pitch," or try to sell, your idea for a movie version of the Orpheus myth. You have five minutes to sell your idea to the movie company. Plan your presentation by writing a summary of the story, giving emphasis to plot complications and the story's climax. Then, rehearse your presentation with a partner present to provide feedback.

_____

_____

_____

_____

_____

_____

_____

_____

_____

_____

KEEPING TRACK

Personal Word List In your Personal Word List, write the new words you learned from reading this myth. Don't forget to add the names of gods and mythic beings and places and to tell who or what they are.

Personal Reading Log Give some advice to a writer who might want to retell the myth of Orpheus for today. Be specific about difficulties and strengths in the version you read. Give yourself 3 points on the Reading Meter for this selection.

Checklist for Standards Mastery Once you've grasped the plot of the story, enter your progress on the Checklist for Standards Mastery.

Orpheus and the Underworld

Interactive Reading, page 36

PROJECT

Go Beyond a Literary Text

Storyboard   When a story is turned into a movie or television drama, the director often uses a storyboard to map out the plot. The storyboard consists of separate frames, like those in a comic book. Each frame illustrates a different scene. Reading the storyboard, you can see the plot developing from beginning to end. Often a storyboard is made on thick paper or cardboard and hung on an easel, bulletin board, or wall.

Draw two frames of a storyboard for "Orpheus and the Underworld." They do not have to represent two scenes that are right next to each other in the myth. On the lines below each drawing, write a description of that scene.

1. _____

_____

_____

2. _____

_____

_____

Chapter 2

Characters
Doing the Right Thing

Chapter Preview   In this chapter you will—

Strategy Launch:
"Compare and Contrast"

LITERARY FOCUS: CHARACTER AND MOTIVATION

Good writers make their characters seem like real people. They do this through **characterization.** Characterization includes showing what the character looks like, what the character says, and how the character acts. Characterization also might include information about how other people feel about the character and what the character thinks. Well-drawn characters have believable **motivations:** They do things for reasons that are convincing.

One interesting way to analyze characters' motivations and actions is to compare characters from different time periods. Ask yourself: "Would these characters have acted differently in another setting or another time frame?"

A STRATEGY THAT WORKS: "COMPARE AND CONTRAST"

You compare and contrast things all the time in real life. You may, for example, note similarities between two new bands, or you may note differences in the quality of food at competing restaurants.

When you read, you also use your skills of comparing and contrasting. Here's how.

POINTERS FOR USING "COMPARE AND CONTRAST"

⟫➡ Read both selections, and take notes on a comparison grid like the one that follows the Practice Reads.

⟫➡ Identify the key actions taken by each character. Then, look for motives for each character's actions.

⟫➡ Evaluate the characters' historical setting or the writer's historical period. Does the time frame affect the attitudes, motivations, and dreams of the characters in any way?

Reading Standard 1.2
Understand the most important points in the history of the English language, and use common word origins to determine the historical influences on English word meanings.

Reading Standard 2.3
Find similarities and differences between texts in the treatment, scope, or organization of ideas.

Reading Standard 3.3
Compare and contrast motivations and reactions of literary characters from different historical eras confronting similar situations or conflicts.

Following this account of John Adams is an editorial from a student newspaper. You will compare and contrast the editorial with this account of John Adams.

Here are some facts you should know before you read "John Adams: The Forgotten Man."

- John Adams was born in 1735 in Braintree, Massachusetts. He died in Braintree on July 4, 1826.
- Adams was regarded by his contemporaries as one of the most important statesmen of the revolutionary era.
- His reputation faded in the nineteenth century, but a modern edition of the correspondence between Adams and his wife, Abigail, has helped bring both Adamses back into the spotlight.

John Adams: The Forgotten Man

Mara Rockliff

VOCABULARY DEVELOPMENT

nominated (näm′ə·nāt′əd) *v.:* named; here, specifically, named as a candidate for something.

Nominate is from the Latin word for "name." What is a *nominee*?

_____

_____

_____

He **nominated** George Washington to head the Continental Army, and he persuaded Thomas Jefferson to draft the Declaration of Independence. He was our country's first vice president and second president. Few men contributed more to the formation of the United States, but Adams's face does not appear on any U.S. coin or bill. What was it about earnest, hardworking John Adams that people wanted to forget?

The problem was his personality. John Adams was
10 so totally honest he sometimes seemed rude. He held

passionate beliefs, and he flew into such tempers that Benjamin Franklin said he was "absolutely out of his senses." He was stubborn and conceited—and fiercely independent. He was driven only by his conscience and his sense of public duty.

Adams was not a people person. More than anything, he loved to read. "You'll never be alone with a poet in your pocket," he wrote his fourteen-year-old son.

20 As a boy in Massachusetts, though, John Adams never studied if he could avoid it. He liked to be outdoors, hunting and fishing, wrestling, swimming, and skating. He was a daydreamer, a prankster, a school-skipper. He hated Latin grammar, and he begged his father to let him work at something else instead. "Well," his father said, "my meadow yonder needs a ditch." After two days of digging ditches, John was happy to return to his Latin.

Doing the Right Thing

Adams went on to Harvard, where he found learning more exciting. Then he turned to a career in the law. This was
30 the mid-1700s. As a young Boston lawyer, Adams found himself in the thick of events that would lead to the Revolutionary War. He protested the British stamp tax and, like most Americans, objected to the regiments of British soldiers sent to America to enforce it.

In 1770, when panicked British Redcoats fired into an angry, rock-hurling mob in Boston, his fellow **patriots** seized the chance to whip up anti-British feeling. John's cousin Samuel Adams called the incident the "Boston Massacre." Silversmith Paul Revere engraved a picture
40 showing British soldiers killing peaceful citizens.

IDENTIFY

Underline the sentence in the first paragraph of the article that asks a question. Underline the sentence in the second paragraph that answers that question.

· · · · · · Notes · · · · · ·

_____

_____

_____

_____

_____

_____

_____

_____

VOCABULARY DEVELOPMENT

patriots (pā′trē·əts) *n.:* those who love and support their own country.

Patriot is from the Greek word *pater,* meaning "father." How does the idea of father enter into the words *patron* and *patrimony*?

_____

_____

_____

IDENTIFY

Underline the line in this section that explains the heading "Doing the Right Thing" (line 27).

INTERPRET

What does Abigail Adams mean in lines 60–61 when she says that her husband should be more generous to the ladies "than your ancestors"?

_____

_____

_____

_____

_____

_____

Restate Abigail Adams's reasoning in lines 61–64 in your own words.

_____

_____

_____

_____

_____

_____

_____

And John Adams? He did what his principles told him was right. He lent his legal talents to the conflict—on the soldiers' side. He believed that everyone deserved a fair trial, and he knew the British soldiers would never get one without a good lawyer. Adams managed to convince a Boston jury that the British soldiers shot in self-defense. Radical newspapers called Adams a traitor. But in his own eyes, defending those soldiers did not make him less of a patriot.

A Love Story—and a Shared Sense of Public Duty

50

For ten years Adams lived in Paris and London, working for his country. He hardly ever saw his family. Abigail, his wife, called herself a widow. She ran the farm, managed his business affairs, and raised their four children on her own. She wrote often to her husband—sometimes three times a day. Abigail also had strong principles and a strong sense of public duty. During the debates about the Declaration of Independence, Abigail urged her husband to "remember

60   the ladies, and be more generous and favorable to them than your ancestors." If the colonists would not obey the unjust laws the British passed, she pointed out, why should women obey unjust laws that men passed without giving them a voice? Abigail said that she gave up the comfort of her husband's presence for all those years as a sacrifice for her country.

"The Most Insignificant Office"

When Adams came home in 1789, he found his reputation had improved in his absence—perhaps because he hadn't

70   been around to pick fights with people. When Washington,

the hero of the war, became the nation's first president, Adams was elected vice president.

Adams hated the vice presidency. He called it "the most insignificant office that ever the invention of man contrived or his imagination conceived."

By the beginning of their second term, Adams had lost some of his popularity and most of his teeth. President Washington, still universally admired but also toothless, wore ivory dentures set in wood and attached by a metal
80 spring. To prevent his mouth from popping open, he had to keep his jaw clenched all the time, which may have added to his image as a dignified and silent man. Adams refused to get false teeth. He would let nothing interfere with his talking, even if the missing teeth made him hard to understand.

Washington declined a third term. Who would take his place? In '89 and '92, the vote for Washington had been **unanimous.** So in a way, 1796 was the first real election— which meant the bugs weren't quite worked out.
90 The Federalists backed Adams for president and Thomas Pinckney for vice president. The Democratic-Republicans backed Jefferson for president and Aaron Burr for vice president. But all the candidates got lumped together in one vote. The man with the most votes would be president; the man with the second most votes would be vice president.

And whose job was it to count the votes? Why, the current vice president and presiding officer of the Senate.

Whatever flaws Adams had, no one who knew him
100 ever doubted his honesty. He made his careful count and solemnly announced the result: the new president of the United States was . . . "John Adams." And the vice

INTERPRET

What does this detail about the teeth reveal about John Adams's character (lines 76–85)?

_____

_____

_____

_____

_____

_____

VOCABULARY DEVELOPMENT

unanimous (yoo·nan'ə·məs) *adj.*: based on complete agreement.

Unanimous is built on the Latin words *unus,* meaning "one," and *animus,* meaning "mind." What other words can you think of that are based on these Latin words?

_____

_____

IDENTIFY

How did the voting system in 1796 differ from the system we use today (lines 93–96)?

_____

_____

_____

_____

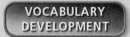

tyrant (tī′rənt) *n.:* absolute ruler, especially one who is cruel.

Tyrant is from the Greek word *tyrannos.* Which dinosaur gets its name from the word *tyrant*?

_____

_____

_____

COMPARE & CONTRAST

How does the writer compare and contrast Adams and Jefferson? Underline the points of comparison.

_____

_____

_____

INFER

Why is it fitting that both Jefferson and Adams died on July 4?

_____

_____

_____

_____

_____

_____

_____

president was his opponent and head of the rival party, Thomas Jefferson.

Enemy Attacks

Adams hated party politics, but he could not escape them. Because he supported a strong central government, his rivals, who wanted to keep power with the states, said he was a **tyrant.**

110   It was a bizarre twist: Jefferson, the Virginia aristocrat, with his 5,000-acre estate at Monticello, his white-columned mansion, and his two hundred slaves, now stood for democracy and equality. And Adams, a plain Yankee farmer who split his own firewood and cut his own hay, said *set* for *sit* and *ain't* for *isn't,* and refused on moral grounds ever to own a slave, was seen as an elitist. (The irony wasn't lost on Adams. In later years, he called his modest Massachusetts farm Montezillo—"small mountain"—a joke on Jefferson's "big mountain," Monticello.)

120 ## Old Patriots, Old Rivals, Old Friends

Adams lost his battle for reelection in 1800. He turned the "splendid misery" (as Abigail called the White House) over to his old rival, Jefferson, which must have seemed a fair revenge. Adams stayed away from the inauguration, and the two men didn't speak for years. After Jefferson retired, though, they renewed their friendship, and a steady stream of letters moved between Montezillo and Monticello for the rest of their lives.

        Adams died on July 4, 1826, the fiftieth birthday of the
130   nation he helped found. His last words were "Thomas Jefferson survives." He didn't know his friend and rival had died that morning.

Do the Right Thing: A Simple Plan

Rosemont High Register editorial staff

OCTOBER 2001

Here is a real-life drama. It happened right here at
Rosemont High last month.

The girls' basketball team sat around the room looking
glum. "You would think in the year 2001 things would be
fair," muttered one player. "Yeah, right," replied another.

At Rosemont High, not everyone was happy. Because
of budget cuts, the girls' basketball team would suffer. One
coach was let go, the season was shortened, and the school

10   bus would be unavailable for travel to games.

The boys' basketball team was not affected by cuts.

The girls' team got the news right after their first
practice of the season. The next day they met to talk over
the news.

"What I want to know is how come the boys' team isn't
affected by all this?" The speaker was Raisa.

"Are you kidding? The boys are gods!" That was
Thelma.

A small voice joined in the conversation. "What can we

20   _do_ about the situation? Is it too late to protest?"

The team looked in some surprise at Ana. She was the
shortest, shyest person on the team. No one knew her well
because she had recently moved to town.

Ana went on in her quiet voice. "I mean, _I_ know it's
unfair, and _you_ know it's unfair, and I bet even the school

IDENTIFY

What unfair situation does
the girls' basketball team
face? Underline the results
of the budget cut.

WORD KNOWLEDGE

Administrators (ad·min′ə·strā′tərz) are people who manage a business, a government, or an institution. *Administrator* is built on the Latin *ministrare,* meaning "serve."

IDENTIFY

Pause at line 32. What actions might the team take in protest? Underline their suggestions.

IDENTIFY

What peaceful solution do the girls use to resolve their problem?

_____

_____

_____

_____

_____

_____

_____

_____

_____

_____

_____

_____

administrators know deep down inside it's unfair. So there's got to be a way to convince them to undo the cuts."

Silence met Ana's comment.

Then there was a flurry of excitement as suggestions
30 started flying around the room. "Let's steal the boys' uniforms—just kidding!" "Let's hold a hunger strike!" "I know, we'll chain ourselves to the basketball equipment!"

Ana spoke up again, this time more confidently. "I was thinking we could start a petition, getting signatures of kids who support us and our team. Then we could show up at the Board of Education meeting next Tuesday to present our case. They've got to see that they're being unfair."

"That's a good idea," said Raisa. "Let's try to get the signatures of parents and teachers, too, to show we've got
40 adult support. Let's get to work on this petition so we can get it copied and signed."

The team threw themselves into the project, and their petition was signed by more than six hundred people. Needless to say, the Board of Ed restored the funding to the team. Everyone is happy again at Rosemont High. And little Ana, the quiet voice of reason, is a big hero to the basketball team.

OWN THE SELECTIONS

Compare Literary Characters   John Adams and the Rosemont High girls' basketball team come from different times and places, and the importance of their actions varies greatly. Still, you can compare and contrast their actions and motivations. After you re-read the selections, fill in the comparison grid on the next page. Review your completed chart, and discuss with a partner the similarities and differences you found between the characters in the two selections.

Character Grid   Fill out a character grid like the one that follows to show what you learned about the character of John Adams. Then, compare John Adams and his wife with people in public life today. What similarities and differences do you find? Do the different historical periods explain some of the differences in the characters?

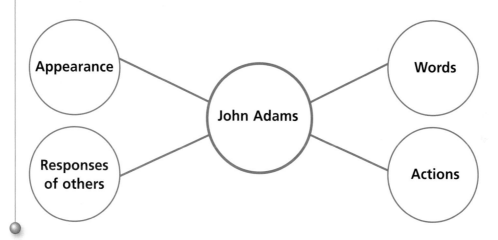

KEEPING TRACK

Personal Word List   Record the vocabulary words in your Personal Word List. Then, choose one word to use in conversation this week.

Personal Reading Log   Record these selections in your Personal Reading Log. Give yourself 4 points on the Reading Meter.

Checklist for Standards Mastery   Read through the Checklist for Standards Mastery. Check off the standards you have covered so far.

John Adams: The Forgotten Man;
Do the Right Thing ▪ *Interactive Reading,* page 46

Interact with Literary Texts

Comparison Grid   Use this comparison grid to analyze the similarities and differences between John Adams and the Rosemont High girls. Then, review the information you gather, and fill in the comment box.

Characters	Actions	Motivations	Historical Influences
John Adams			
Girls' Basketball Team			

Comments

_____

_____

_____

_____

from Harriet Tubman: Conductor on the Underground Railroad

for use with
Holt Literature and Language Arts,
page 87

CHARACTER

Interact with a Literary Text

What If? Chart   Fill out the following chart after you read the excerpt from *Harriet Tubman: Conductor on the Underground Railroad.* Jot down Tubman's actions, the motives for those actions, and her beliefs. Then, when you've finished the chart, think about what Tubman might have been if she had lived in a different time period.

Character: Harriet Tubman

Actions
Motives
Tubman's Beliefs
What If?   If Tubman lived in _____ she might have been . . .   _____   _____

COMPARE & CONTRAST

The Fugitive Slave Acts of 1793 and 1850

for use with
Holt Literature and Language Arts,
page 101

Interact with an Informational Text

Venn Diagram   A Venn diagram shows visually how two things are similar and different. The diagram is simply two intersecting ovals or circles. When the two things have a trait in common, write that trait in the area where the two circles intersect. If a trait belongs to only one of the two things, write it in the part of the circle that does not intersect with the other circle.

Compare and contrast the Fugitive Slave Acts of 1793 and 1850 by filling out the Venn diagram below.

Fugitive Slave Acts

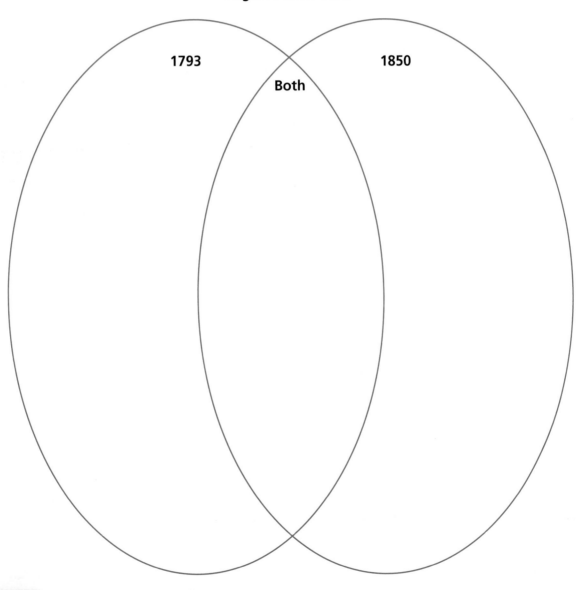

1793   Both   1850

Graphic Organizer   Graphic Organizer   Graphic Organizer

Barbara Frietchie

Interact with a Literary Text

Character-Traits Cluster   A character-traits cluster allows you to
create a profile of a character. Using details from the poem, fill out
the character-traits cluster below. At the end of the cluster, write
your profile of Barbara Frietchie.

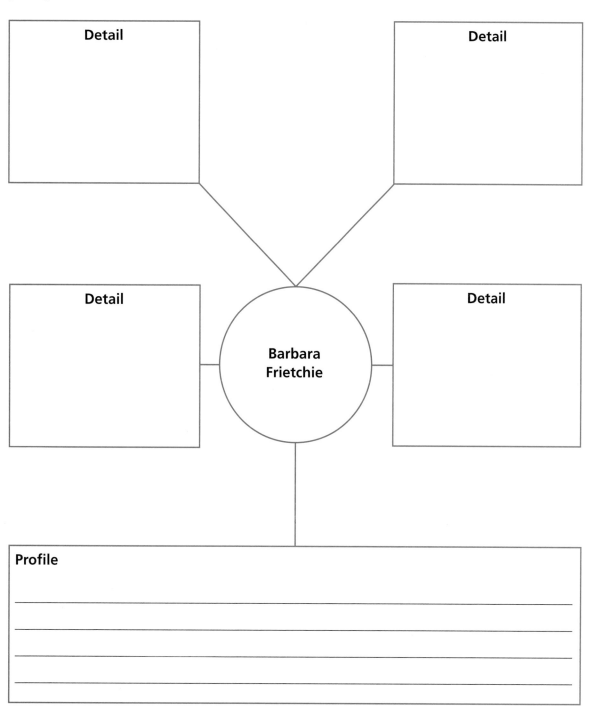

Detail

Detail

Detail

Barbara
Frietchie

Detail

Profile

_____

_____

_____

_____

Too Soon a Woman

CHARACTER

Interact with a Literary Text

Motivations Web   Characters have reasons, or motivations, for acting as they do. To learn more about why Mary, the main character in "Too Soon a Woman," acts as she does, fill in this motivations web. Then, review Mary's actions and motivations to come up with a conclusion about her character.

Character: Mary

| Action/Motivation | _____ |

↓

| Action/Motivation | _____ |

↓

| Action/Motivation | _____ |

Conclusion About Mary's Character:

_____

_____

_____

_____

_____

_____

_____

_____

_____

Union Pacific Railroad Poster; Home, Sweet Soddie

Interact with Informational Texts

Comparison Chart   Compare and contrast the Union Pacific Railroad advertisement and the article "Home, Sweet Soddie" by filling out the chart below.

	Advertisement	Article
Writers		
Purpose		
Audience		
"Slant" or bias		
Biased details		

Mrs. Flowers

CHARACTER

Interact with a Literary Text

Problem-Resolution Chart In this part of her autobiography, the writer tells a little story about a big event in her young life. Trace the actions that Mrs. Flowers takes to solve Marguerite's problem— to get Marguerite to talk again. At the end, describe the effects of Mrs. Flowers's actions.

Problem: Marguerite has stopped talking.

Event 1: _____
_____
_____
_____

Event 2: _____
_____
_____
_____

Event 3: _____
_____
_____
_____

Event 4: _____
_____
_____
_____

Event 5: _____
_____
_____
_____

Resolution: _____
_____
_____

Mrs. Flowers's Recipes

Interact with an Informational Text

Process Chart   A process chart shows the steps that are involved in a process leading to a product. The steps are shown in the order they are taken. Represent Mrs. Flowers's recipe for sugar cookies in the form of a process chart. You decide how to divide the process into steps.

Process: _____

Step:
Step:
Step:
Step:
Step:
Step:
Step:
Step:
Step:
Step:
Step:
Product:

Literature

AUTHOR STUDY

The excerpt "Mrs. Flowers" from Maya Angelou's *I Know Why the Caged Bird Sings* creates a vivid picture of the young Marguerite and the woman who helped change her life. In Angelou's "New Directions" you will meet Mrs. Annie Johnson, Angelou's grandmother, who decided "to step off the road and cut me a new path."

Maya Angelou was born in St. Louis, Missouri, in 1928, and raised in Stamps, Arkansas, where she lived with her grandmother. After leaving Stamps, Angelou won a scholarship to the California Labor School, where she took evening classes in dance and drama. In 1954 and 1955, she toured Europe and Africa in a State Department–sponsored production of the opera *Porgy and Bess.* In addition to her many short stories, magazine articles, and poems, Angelou has written and produced a ten-part television series on Africanisms in American life. In 1992, she wrote and read a poem for the inauguration of President Bill Clinton.

BEFORE YOU READ

You are about to read about two characters living in different times and places. Despite their differences, both characters face hardships with courage and strength.

Here are some details about these selections:

- "New Directions" is an essay about Mrs. Annie Johnson, Maya Angelou's grandmother, who lived in Arkansas in the early twentieth century.
- "Field Work" is a true narrative that focuses on the field workers in the Salinas Valley in California in the later part of the twentieth century.
- Both texts are about people who are not afraid of hard work.

Reading Standard 3.3
Compare and contrast motivations and reactions of literary characters from different historical eras confronting similar situations or conflicts.

New Directions

Maya Angelou

In 1903 the late Mrs. Annie Johnson of Arkansas found herself with two toddling sons, very little money, a slight ability to read and add simple numbers. To this picture add a disastrous marriage and the burdensome fact that Mrs. Johnson was a Negro.

When she told her husband, Mr. William Johnson, of her dissatisfaction with their marriage, he conceded that he too found it to be less than he expected, and had been secretly hoping to leave and study religion. He added that

10 he thought God was calling him not only to preach but to do so in Enid, Oklahoma. He did not tell her that he knew a minister in Enid with whom he could study and who had a friendly, unmarried daughter. They parted amicably, Annie keeping the one-room house and William taking most of the cash to carry himself to Oklahoma.

Annie, over six feet tall, big-boned, decided that she would not go to work as a **domestic** and leave her "precious babes" to anyone else's care. There was no possibility of being hired at the town's cotton gin or lumber mill, but

20 maybe there was a way to make the two factories work for her. In her words, "I looked up the road I was going and back the way I come, and since I wasn't satisfied, I decided to step off the road and cut me a new path." She told herself that she wasn't a fancy cook but that she could "mix groceries well enough to scare hungry away and keep from starving a man."

IDENTIFY

What do you learn about the time and place Mrs. Johnson lived in?

_____

_____

_____

_____

WORD KNOWLEDGE

The word *amicably* (line 13) means "in a friendly way" and comes from the Latin word *amicus,* which means "friend."

The Spanish word *amigo* comes from the same Latin word.

VOCABULARY DEVELOPMENT

domestic (də·mes'tik) *n.:* servant for the home, such as a maid or cook.

In this context, *domestic* is a noun meaning "household servant." It comes from the Latin *domus,* meaning "house" or "home." More often *domestic* is used as an adjective, meaning "having to do with a home."

_____

_____

_____

_____

_____

WORD KNOWLEDGE

A *cotton gin* (line 40) was the building where the seeds were removed from the newly picked cotton. A gin was the device that removed the seeds.

WORD KNOWLEDGE

Savories (line 41) are tasty bits of food. The word is more commonly used in Canada and England.

Savor (sā′vər) is a verb meaning "enjoy with great delight."

INTERPRET

Pause at line 51. What do Mrs. Johnson's actions reveal about her personality?

_____

_____

_____

_____

_____

She made her plans meticulously[1] and in secret. One early evening to see if she was ready, she placed stones in two five-gallon pails and carried them three miles to the cotton gin. She rested a little, and then, discarding some rocks, she walked in the darkness to the sawmill five miles farther along the dirt road. On her way back to her little house and her babies, she dumped the remaining rocks along the path.

That same night she worked into the early hours boiling chicken and frying ham. She made dough and filled the rolled-out pastry with meat. At last she went to sleep.

The next morning she left her house carrying the meat pies, lard, an iron brazier,[2] and coals for a fire. Just before lunch she appeared in an empty lot behind the cotton gin. As the dinner noon bell rang, she dropped the savories into boiling fat and the aroma rose and floated over to the workers who spilled out of the gin, covered with white lint, looking like specters. Most workers had brought their lunches of pinto beans and biscuits or crackers, onions and cans of sardines, but they were tempted by the hot meat pies which Annie ladled out of the fat. She wrapped them in newspapers, which soaked up the grease, and offered them for sale at a nickel each. Although business was slow, those first days Annie was determined. She balanced her appearances between the two hours of activity.

So, on Monday if she offered hot, fresh pies at the cotton gin and sold the remaining cooled-down pies at the lumber mill for three cents, then on Tuesday she went first

---

1. **meticulously** (mə·tik′yo͞o·ləs·lē) *adv.:* extremely carefully; with great attention to detail.
2. **brazier** (brā′zhər) *n.:* metal container that holds burning coals or charcoal, used to warm a room or grill food.

to the lumber mill presenting fresh, just-cooked pies as the lumbermen covered in sawdust emerged from the mill.

> For the next few years, on balmy spring days, blistering summer noons, and cold, wet, and wintry middays, Annie never disappointed her customers, who could count on seeing the tall, brown-skin woman bent over her brazier, carefully turning the meat pies. When she felt certain that the workers had become dependent on her, she built a stall between the two hives of industry and let the men run to her for their lunchtime **provisions.**
>
> She had indeed stepped from the road which seemed to have been chosen for her and cut herself a brand-new path. In years that stall became a store where customers could buy cheese, meal, syrup, cookies, candy, writing tablets, pickles, canned goods, fresh fruit, soft drinks, coal, oil, and leather soles for worn-out shoes.
>
> Each of us has the right and the responsibility to assess the roads which lie ahead, and those over which we have traveled, and if the future road looms **ominous** or unpromising, and the roads back uninviting, then we need to gather our resolve and, carrying only the necessary baggage, step off that road into another direction. If the new choice is also unpalatable,[3] without embarrassment, we must be ready to change that as well.

60

70

3. **unpalatable** (un·pal′it·ə·bəl) *adj.:* unpleasant. *Unpalatable* often means "tasting bad."

PERSONAL NARRATIVE

Field Work

Rose Del Castillo Guilbault

INTERPRET

What does the narrator mean when she says, "The fields were the stage where life's truths were played out . . ." (lines 10–11)?

_____

_____

_____

_____

_____

_____

_____

VOCABULARY DEVELOPMENT

despondent (di·spän'dənt) *adj.:* sad; dejected.

• • • • • • **Notes** • • • • • •

_____

_____

_____

_____

El fiel' was what my parents and their friends called it— their Anglicism[1] for the field. The first jobs I ever had were working el fiel'. I grew up in the Salinas Valley, where if you're young and Mexican, the only available summer jobs are agricultural work.

Although there is absolutely nothing romantic about working the fields, it did offer a fertile environment for learning important life lessons about work, family values, and what it means to grow up Mexican in the United

10 States. The fields were the stage where life's truths were played out—the struggles, hardships, humiliations; the humor, friendships, and compassions. For many young Mexicans, field work is practically a rite of passage.[2]

I can remember with uncanny clarity the first time I worked in the fields. It was the summer of my eleventh year, and I was feeling **despondent** and bored. I wanted to go on vacation, as many of my classmates did, but my parents couldn't afford it.

My mother was sympathetic; she was yearning to see

20 her family in Mexico. She came up with the idea that we

---

1. **Anglicism** (aŋ'glə·siz'əm): here, word adapted from English for use in Spanish.
2. **rite of passage:** event marking an important change in a person's life, such as the movement from childhood to adulthood.

could earn the $50 we needed for Greyhound bus tickets to Mexicali[3] if we both worked the garlic harvest that was about to begin on the farm where we lived.

The first hurdle to earning the money was persuading my traditional Mexican father to let us do it. He had made it clear to my mother that he did not want her to work. To him, a working wife implied his inability to support his family.

30 To this day, I have no idea how she convinced him that it was all right. Maybe it was because the job was very short-term—five days—or maybe it was because we hadn't been to Mexico in more than a year. My father knew an annual visit to see relatives was my mother's lifeline. In any case, my father agreed to lobby his boss the next day to let us join the garlic-picking crew.

The boss was skeptical about employing us. Not because he was concerned about hiring a woman and a child; he worried more about our inexperience and **stamina.** After all, this was a man's job and he had a 40 deadline. What if we slowed things down and he had to keep a worker for an extra day?

"Since when is picking garlic such an art?" my mother retorted when my father told her that night about the boss's reservations. But then he added that the boss had decided to take a chance on us.

We started immediately—at 6 A.M. the next day. The August morning was cold and gray, still shrouded in damp fog. We wore layers of clothes—a T-shirt, a sweat shirt, a windbreaker—to protect us from the early-morning chill 50 and later discard when the afternoon sun got too hot. We

---

3. **Mexicali** (meks′i·kä′lē): city in northwestern Mexico, near the California border.

IDENTIFY

What do the narrator and her mother decide to do? Why do they decide to do it?

_____

_____

_____

_____

_____

IDENTIFY

Why does the narrator's father decide to get work for his wife and daughter? Underline his reasons.

VOCABULARY DEVELOPMENT

stamina (stam′ə·nə) n.: endurance; resistance to fatigue, illness, hardship, and so on.

· · · · · · Notes · · · · · ·

_____

_____

_____

_____

_____

_____

_____

_____

_____

_____

_____

_____

_____

_____

_____

_____

_____

_____

_____

_____

INFER

Pause at line 75. What inferences do you make about the narrator based on the ways she tries to keep the bag around her waist?

_____

_____

_____

_____

_____

_____

wrapped scarves around our heads and topped them with knit caps. This was our field work uniform, and it is the same uniform you'll see men and women wearing today as you drive by California's valley fields.

A foreman showed us the proper way to pick garlic. "You hook your sack to this special belt. This frees your hands so you can pick the garlic and toss it into your sack."

We watched carefully as he hooked the bag to his waist and sauntered down the row, stooping slightly, while his 60 hands whirled like a harvester machine, making garlic bulbs fly from the ground into the sack.

"Easy!" he said, straightening his back.

And I learned it was easy—until the sack started getting full. Then it not only wouldn't stay on the belt hook, it became nearly impossible for a skinny eleven-year-old to budge.

I spent the morning engineering ways to keep the bag around my waist. I tried belting it and looping it on different parts of my body with my scarf. But it was hopeless; 70 at a certain level of fullness, the thing just couldn't be moved. So I resorted to a more laborious yet effective method. I'd drag the sack with both my hands, then run back and forth, picking handfuls of garlic and depositing them in the stationary bag. I must have looked as silly as a Keystone Kop.[4]

I heard laughter echoing from the distant fields. I looked around, wondering what the joke was about, and slowly realized they were laughing at me! My stomach did a somersault when I heard the impatient crunch of the fore-80 man's boots behind me. Was I going to be told to go home?

---

4. **Keystone Kop:** character in slapstick comedy films who does things in a clumsy, bumbling way.

"No, no, you don't do it right." He gestured wildly in front of me.

"But I can't do it the same way you do. The sack's too heavy," I explained.

Suddenly men's voices called out: "Déjala, hombre! Leave her alone, man. Let the kid do it her way."

The foreman shrugged, rolled his eyes upward, and walked away, muttering under his breath. My mother walked toward me, smiling. It was lunchtime.

90   After lunch, the afternoon sun slowed me down. Perspiration trickled down my back, making me itchy and sticky. It was discouraging to see everyone passing me, working row after row. Afternoon dragged on as heavy as the half-filled garlic sack I lugged.

By the end of the day, my shoulders felt as if someone had stuck a hot iron between them.

The following days became a blur of aching muscles and garlic bulbs. The rows seemed to stretch like rubber bands, expanding with each passing day. My mother's smile

100 and words of encouragement—a salve the first few days— no longer soothed me.

Even at home I felt overpowered by the **insidious** garlic. It permeated my skin and clothes. No matter how much I scrubbed, the garlic seemed to ooze from my pores, the odor suffocating me in my sleep.

On what was to be the last morning, I simply couldn't get out of bed. My body was so sore that the slightest move sent waves of pain through my muscles. My legs were wobbly from all the bending, and my shoulders felt as if

110 they had been cleaved apart. My whole body was one throbbing ache. The field had defeated me.

WORD KNOWLEDGE

What might "Déjala, hombre!" (line 85) mean? Circle the context clues you find.

_____

_____

_____

_____

_____

WORD KNOWLEDGE

Underline the three comparisons used in lines 95–101. Which are **similes**? Which is a **metaphor**?

_____

_____

_____

_____

_____

_____

_____

VOCABULARY DEVELOPMENT

insidious (in·sid′ē·əs) *adj.:* steadily treacherous; spreading slowly but with dangerous effects (like an insidious rumor or an insidious disease).

EVALUATE

Underline the mother's statement in line 114. How do you feel about what she says?

_____

_____

_____

_____

_____

_____

_____

INFER

Why does the narrator go back to the fields? Circle the words that show the mixed emotions she feels toward her father.

_____

_____

_____

_____

_____

_____

_____

_____

_____

_____

_____

"I just can't do it," I sobbed to my mother, the tears tasting like garlic.

"Anything worth having is worth working for," she said gently.

"I don't care about the vacation. I'm too tired. It's not worth it," I cried.

"There are only a few rows left. Are you sure you can't finish?" my mother persisted.

120 But to me the few rows might as well have been hundreds. I felt bad about giving up after working so hard, but it just didn't seem fair to pay such a high price to go on vacation. After all, my friends didn't have to.

My mother was very quiet all day. I'd forgotten it was to have been her vacation, too. My father was surprised to see us sitting neatly dressed when he came home. He listened quietly to my mother's explanation, and after a thoughtful pause said, "Well, if we all pitch in, we can still finish up the rows tonight, right on schedule."

130 As I looked at my father's dust-rimmed, bloodshot eyes, his dusty hair and mud-stained overalls, I was over-whelmed with a strange mixture of pity and gratitude. I knew by the slope of his shoulders he was very tired from his own grueling field work. And finishing up our leftover work was nothing short of an act of love.

I was torn. The thought of doing battle with the field again filled me with dread. But I said nothing, swallowing my reluctance until it formed a lump in my throat.

That summer evening, the three of us worked side by side, teasing, talking, laughing, as we completed the task.
140 It was dark, and we had grown silent by the time the last of the garlic sacks were lined up. The rosy glow from the

setting sun made me feel as warm as the relief of knowing the work was finally over and done.

I worked every summer thereafter, some in the fields (never again picking garlic!) and later in the vegetable-packing sheds, always alongside my mother. Working together created an unusual bond between us. And through this relationship, and relationships with other Mexican families thrust into this agricultural society, I got an education as solid and rich as the earth we worked.

150

IDENTIFY

Underline the passages that tell what the narrator gains by working in the fields.

• • • • • • Notes • • • • • •

Picking the crops.

OWN THE SELECTiONS

Characters   Compare and contrast Mrs. Johnson and the narrator of "Field Work" to see how their actions and motivations were similar and different. Take into consideration the time period in which each character lived. Use the comparison chart on the following page to map out your response. Then, fill in the bottom section with a comment on how these characters are alike and different.

KEEPING TRACK

Personal Word List   Record the new words from these selections in your Personal Word List. Choose two words that tell you about people, and use them in sentences.

Personal Reading Log   Enter these selections in your Personal Reading Log. Give yourself 5 points on the Reading Meter.

Checklist for Standards Mastery   Check to see how much you have learned. Use the Checklist for Standards Mastery to record your progress.

New Directions; Field Work

Interactive Reading, page 63

COMPARE & CONTRAST

Interact with a Literary Text

Comparison Chart   When you compare characters, you learn a great deal about them. To gather information for your comparison, you must go back to the text and read it very carefully for details you might have missed in your first reading.

Remember that *compare* can mean looking for similarities *and* differences. *Contrast* means looking for differences only.

Complete this chart with details about Mrs. Johnson from "New Directions" and the narrator of "Field Work." Then, comment on how the times and places in which they lived affected their actions.

Characters	Actions	Motivations	Historical Influences
Mrs. Johnson			
Narrator of "Field Work"			

Comments:

_____

_____

_____

_____

BEFORE YOU READ

Did reading about Mrs. Johnson's meat pies make your mouth water? Evan Morris has found a connection between food and our language. According to him, food is the source of hundreds of common English idioms. All right, chow down!

Reading Standard 2.3 Find similarities and differences between texts in the treatment, scope, or organization of ideas.

from The Word Detective

You Took the Words Right Out of My Mouth...

Evan Morris

WORD KNOWLEDGE

The title of this news column is a common English idiom. What does it mean?

_____

_____

VOCABULARY DEVELOPMENT

prosperity (präs·per'ə·tē) *n.:* good fortune, success.

The word *prosperity* is built from the Latin stem *spes,* which means "hope." What connection do you see between *prosperity* and *hope*?

_____

_____

Anyone who doubts that food occupies a place of honor in the human imagination need only open a dictionary of slang or common English idioms. Hundreds of our most commonly heard expressions are drawn from the chow line, and more are added every year. Here are a few choice tidbits (*tidbit* means "small tasty morsel," from the English dialect word *tid,* "tender," plus *bit*).

a chicken in every pot: "Economic **prosperity.**" A very old metaphor, revived to take center stage as a campaign

10 slogan in the 1928 U.S. presidential election (immediately preceding the Great Depression).

easy as pie: "Very easy or simple," since the early twentieth century. Of **debatable** logic, since making a good pie is anything but easy. May be a mangling of *nice as pie,* "very nice," which makes much more sense.

eat humble pie: "To apologize and be forced to acknowledge one's errors," since about 1830. This phrase is actually a pun on *umble pie,* a lowly servants' dish made from the *umbles* ("innards," ultimately from the Latin *lumbus,* "loin") of deer, as opposed to the venison their masters ate.

20

milktoast: "An ineffectual or feeble man." Milktoast (toast soaked in milk, sometimes with added butter and sugar) has been fed to toothless infants for centuries and used as a metaphor for wimpiness just as long. Often spelled *milquetoast* in the United States, after Caspar Milquetoast, a popular old-time comic-strip character.

proof of the pudding is in the eating: "You can't judge a thing until you put it to its intended use," *proof* in this case meaning "test" or "trial." An old and oft-quoted proverb

30 dating back at least to the seventeenth century.

rhubarb: "An uproar or ruckus." Thought to have come from the practice of having extras in theatrical crowd scenes say "rhubarb" over and over, **simulating** the sound of an angry mob.

VOCABULARY DEVELOPMENT

inconsequential
(in·kän'si·kwen'shəl) *adj.:*
unimportant; trivial.

Deep within the word *inconsequential* is the Latin root, *sequi,* "follow."

partisans (pärt'ə·zənz) *n.:* persons who are unreasonably devoted to something.

DECODING TIP

Circle the prefix you see in the word *substandard* (line 55). This prefix means "below." What do you think *substandard* means?

_____
_____
_____
_____

WORD KNOWLEDGE

Can you think of any other common English expressions that derive from food? (Remember Evan Morris claims there are hundreds.)

_____
_____
_____
_____
_____
_____

small beer: "**Inconsequential** or trivial." In the sixteenth century, "weak or inferior beer" soon applied to anything not worth worrying about.

sour grapes: Now often taken to mean simply "the bitterness of a sore loser," *sour grapes* originally meant "to
40 disparage as unworthy that which you cannot attain." The phrase comes from Aesop's fable about the fox who, unable to reach the grapes he desired, announced that he didn't want them anyway because he knew
50 that they were sour.

tripe: "Nonsense, intellectual rubbish." Tripe is a dish made from the stomach of a cow or sheep, and although it has its **partisans,** tripe has been a synonym for "worthless" since the seventeenth century. Now usually applied to substandard writing or art.

the world is your oyster: "You have endless opportunities." From Shakespeare's *The Merry Wives of Windsor,* wherein a character announces "Why then the world's mine oyster, which I with sword will open" to extract the pearls of
60 wealth within.

OWN THE TEXT

Structure   Informational articles can be organized in many ways. The method of organization depends on the topic of the article. Here are four commonly used methods of organization:

1. The information can be organized according to **chronology—** the time order in which events occur.

2. The information can be organized by **cause and effect.** Such an article would relate a series of causes and their effects.

3. The information can be organized in **lists.** The lists can be alphabetically arranged or arranged in the order of importance.

4. The information can be organized in a **compare-contrast pattern.** In this organization the writer tells how two things or people or events are alike and different.

Write two sentences in which you describe the structural organization of "You Took the Words Right Out of My Mouth . . ." Would it be possible to organize this information in any other way?

_____

_____

_____

KEEPING TRACK

Personal Word List   Record new words in your Personal Word List. Jot down other food expressions in your Personal Reading Log.

Personal Reading Log   The author of "You Took the Words Right Out of My Mouth . . ." has a newspaper column and Web site where he answers questions about language. As you record this selection in your Personal Reading Log, jot down any questions about language you have for Evan Morris. Award yourself 1 point on the Reading Meter.

Checklist for Standards Mastery   Use the Checklist for Standards Mastery to track what you have learned.

You Took the Words Right Out of My Mouth . . . ▪ *Interactive Reading, page 74*

Go Beyond an Informational Text

Glossary Templates   "You Took the Words Right Out of My Mouth . . ." is a **glossary** of idioms related to food. A glossary is a list of terms (and their definitions) limited to a specific subject or field. This particular glossary includes the following features:

• a brief introduction
• a series of entries
• explanations of where the idioms come from
• examples of how the idioms are used

Choose a field or subject that interests you. It could be a sport, a hobby, a subject you like to study, and so on. Write a glossary of specialized terms used in that field. Include at least six terms, with a full entry for each. Use the templates that follow.

entry: _____	entry: _____
explanation: _____ _____	explanation: _____ _____
example: _____ _____	example: _____ _____

entry: _____	entry: _____
explanation: _____ _____	explanation: _____ _____
example: _____ _____	example: _____ _____

entry: _____	entry: _____
explanation: _____ _____	explanation: _____ _____
example: _____ _____	example: _____ _____

Literature

MYTH

BEFORE YOU READ

All cultures have stories telling how things came to be. The ancient Greeks and Romans told **myths** about how the world was created and how features of our earth came into being. Americans settling the West told **tall tales** about how land features were formed and how different inventions came about.

In the next two stories, you will meet two figures: Prometheus, who gives a great gift to humankind, and Paul Bunyan, who personifies the can-do spirit of the American West.

Reading Standard 3.3
Compare and contrast motivations and reactions of literary characters from different historical eras confronting similar situations or conflicts.

Prometheus Steals Fire from Heaven

a Greek myth, retold by Anne Terry White

There was a time when there were no gods. Heaven and Earth alone existed. They were the first parents, and from their union sprang the gigantic Titans. For ages the Titans ruled the world. But at last the gods, who were the children of the Titans, rebelled and overthrew them. Then it was that Zeus became supreme ruler of the universe and his wife and sister, Hera, became queen of heaven.

Now as yet there were no men on earth, and none of the animals seemed worthy to rule the rest. So the gods

10 decided to make still another kind of creature. One of the Titans, Prometheus[1]—whose name means "**forethought**"—was chosen for the task.

---

1. Prometheus (prō·mē′thē·əs).

IDENTIFY

Myths usually tell about the deeds of gods and heroes. Circle the names of gods and goddesses in the first paragraph. What famous ship was named after the Titans?

_____

VOCABULARY DEVELOPMENT

forethought (fôr′thôt′) *n.:* planning beforehand.

Fore comes from the Old English *foran,* meaning "before."

IDENTIFY

According to the myth, why do we stand upright?

_____

_____

_____

_____

_____

IDENTIFY

What gift does Prometheus give humans that will make up for their not having fur, feathers, scales, or a shell?

_____

_____

VOCABULARY DEVELOPMENT

cunning (kun′iŋ) *n.:* skill in deception; slyness.

quick-witted (kwik′wit′id) *adj.:* nimble of mind; alert.

IDENTIFY

Why does Zeus want to curb the power of humans?

_____

_____

_____

_____

_____

Down from heaven the Titan sped. He took clay and mixed it with water, kneaded it, and shaped it in the likeness of the gods. He made his creature stand upright, for he wanted man to look up at the stars and not down on the earth, like the animals. Then Prometheus thought:

"What gifts shall I give this work of my hands to make him superior to the rest of creation?"

20   Unfortunately, his brother Epimetheus[2]—which means "afterthought"—had already given all the great gifts to the animals. Strength and courage, **cunning** and speed—he had distributed them all. Wings, claws, horns, scales, shelly covering—nothing was left for man.

Then **quick-witted** Prometheus thought of fire. Oh, great and wonderful gift! "With fire," the Titan thought, "man can make weapons and subdue the beasts, forge tools, plow the earth, and master the arts. What matter that my creature has neither fur nor feathers, scales nor shell?

30   Fire will warm his dwelling, and he need fear neither rain nor snow nor the wild north wind."

Back to heaven Prometheus sped, lit his torch at the chariot of the sun, brought down fire to man, and went away rejoicing.

But up on high Olympus, great Zeus frowned as he sat with the gods feasting on nectar and ambrosia. For Zeus was ever jealous of his power.

"This creature that looks to heaven is truly more than a match for the beasts," he thought. "Indeed, he is almost a

40   match for the gods. But I will curb his ill-got power!"

Straightway Zeus made woman, lovely as a goddess. All the immortals bestowed gifts upon her to make her yet more captivating. And they called her Pandora—"Gift-of-

_____

2. Epimetheus (ep′ə·mē′thē·əs).

all." When she was finished, Zeus himself bore the dazzling creature to the Titans.

"Beware!" Prometheus cautioned his brothers. "I fear the gifts of wily Zeus. He bears me ill will because of the fire I stole from heaven and brought down to mankind."

But Epimetheus was enchanted with Pandora and took
50 her to his heart and home.

Now in that home Epimetheus had a jar in which he kept certain gifts he had not distributed among the animals when he had made them. He took great pains to tell Pandora she must leave this jar alone. "On no account must you open it," he warned her.

But, above all things else, the gods had endowed Pandora with curiosity. No sooner was she alone than she sped to the forbidden jar.

"Surely it will do no harm if I just peek in and see
60 what is there," thought she.

She slipped off the cover. And there flew out a host of evil plagues and all manner of disease, envy, spite, revenge—and scattered themselves far and wide. Pandora clapped on the lid. But it was too late. The jar was all but empty. Only hope had remained—hope which never leaves mankind.

There was no danger now that man would rival the gods—he had enemies far worse than wild beasts to contend with. But still Zeus could not forgive Prometheus.
70 "The thief who stole heaven's fire shall be punished as his love of man deserves!" Zeus declared. "He shall be chained to the highest rock of Mount Caucasus—where man can never climb. Scorched by the sun, he shall lie and groan. And I shall cause a vulture to prey upon his liver, which shall grow again as fast as it is devoured."

INTERPRET

Choose one word to describe Prometheus, one to describe Epimetheus, and one to describe Pandora.

_____

_____

_____

_____

_____

_____

_____

_____

INFER

Pause at line 66. How can hope make these plagues less devastating?

_____

_____

_____

_____

_____

IDENTIFY

Underline the horrible punishment Zeus gives to Prometheus.

Prometheus has inspired many artists and writers. In what ways is he heroic?

_____

_____

_____

_____

_____

_____

_____

_____

_____

_____

_____

_____

_____

_____

_____

_____

_____

_____

He summoned Hephaestus.[3] And high on the mountain where eagles make their home, heaven's lame smith—all unwilling—riveted the Titan to the rock. There Prometheus hung in his chains. But he neither groaned nor

80 besought pity, neither regretted what he had done nor bent his knee before the tyrant. The rock, the vulture, and the chain—all that the proud can feel of pain—he endured, and showed his agony to none.

Prometheus statue in Rockefeller Center, New York City.

---

3. Hephaestus (hē·fes′təs): god of fire and the forge.

*Paul Bunyan runs a lumber camp in the
North Woods. Before this episode in Paul's adventures
started, Paul had been tinkering with the Mississippi River.
Ole (ō′lē) in this story is one of Paul's workers.
Babe is Paul's fabulous blue ox.*

Paul's Popcorn

Walter Blair

Having got the water meandering around to make the soil
moist, Paul figured he'd test the land out with popcorn. So
he picked up a good healthy looking kernel, walked out to a
likely looking place that had been **irrigated** lately, and dug
a hole about a foot deep with his middle finger. He couldn't
use his forefinger or thumb, naturally, because he was
holding the corn between them.

Well, Paul had no more than started back to camp to
get Ole to act as a witness, than there was a sort of sputter-
10 ing up of brown dirt, and a cornstalk came skyhooting
through. In no time at all, the corn was up to Paul's knee.
And by the time he got back with Ole, the cornstalk had
grown so much that the top was buried in a cloud.

"Ole!" says Paul. "Climb up to the top of that baby and
chop the top off so she won't grow any more!"

Ole started shinning up the stalk at a great rate. But
the thing kept shooting up, and in a minute or so Ole, too,
was out of sight in that cloud. It was a handsome cloud
with cottony bumps and scallopy edges, but Ole said after-
20 wards that being inside of it wasn't different from being
inside any old cloud. "Nothing but fog inside it," he said.

IDENTIFY

Tall tales are filled with
exaggeration. In fact, the
details are as oversized as
the American West must
have seemed to the settlers.
As you read, circle the
exaggerated details.

**VOCABULARY
DEVELOPMENT**

irrigated (ir′ə·gāt′id) *v.*:
supplied (land) with water
by means of ditches or canals
or sprinklers.

**WORD
KNOWLEDGE**

The adjective *scallopy* (line
19) describes something that
has curved edges like a
scallop shell.

FLUENCY

Read the comic conversation
in the box aloud. Use different, appropriate voices for
the two characters and for
the narration.

_____

_____

_____

_____

_____

_____

_____

_____

_____

**VOCABULARY
DEVELOPMENT**

considerable
(kən·sid′ər·ə·bəl) *adj.:*
much or large.

PREDICT

Pause at line 54. What is Paul
Bunyan going to do with a
herd of frozen cattle? What
would you do with them if
you were Paul Bunyan?

_____

_____

_____

_____

_____

_____

_____

"When you chop the top off, throw her down," Paul
yelled.

Ole's voice came booming down. "The top's above me,"
he said. "I can't get *to* the thing." Ole's big voice had something like the effect of thunder, and the cloud rained away
from around him. But this new moisture made the stalk
grow even faster.

"This won't do!" Paul yelled. "Come down, and we'll
30 handle her some other way!"

"Can't come down, either," Ole yelled in a minute.
"Every time I go down one yard, this thing shoots up three,
and I'm losing ground. I'm getting hungry, too."

Paul yelled for Babe, right then. And while he was
waiting for Babe to come along, he used his shotgun to
shoot up a few crullers which he hoped—for the time
being, at any rate—would keep Ole from starving to death.

When Babe came along, Paul hurried with the beast
over to Jim Hill's railroad, the Great Northern, which (by
40 good luck) wasn't far away. Paul loaded Babe up with a pile
of steel rails, then hurried back to the cornstalk with them.

"I'll see if I can't choke off the moisture in this cornstalk," Paul said. And with that he started tying those rails
together and then knotting them around the cornstalk.

It worked, too.

Soon the ears of corn away up near the top stopped
getting moisture and started to dry out. Then the hot sun
hit them hard, and shortly the corn began to pop, making
considerable noise, too.

50 After a while, this popped corn came drifting down
like so many snowballs. Babe, who'd lived through so much
fierce weather, didn't do any more than shiver a little. But a
big herd of cattle grazing nearby decided they were in a
world-beating blizzard and promptly froze to death.

Meanwhile, growing in spite of those knotted steel rails the way it had, the cornstalk had been bitten into by the things, and had cut itself off of itself. Now it started to tumble, slow but sure. Ole rode it down to the ground, just like a logger standing on a log in white water; then at the

60 right time he jumped off lightly and headed back for Paul, following along the cornstalk.

When Ole got there, the owner of the cattle herd, who'd hurried over, was talking up right sassy to Paul. "Look what you did to my cattle, just when they were fat for market!" he yelled. "You'll have to pay for them."

"Course I will," Paul said. And he settled for the cattle, right on the spot, for Paul was always fair and square, regardless of cost.

"Hello, Ole," says Paul. "Glad to see you back. Just
70 bought me a herd of frozen cattle."

"Goodness gracious!" Ole said. "And with our camp so far from where the cattle are, if we ship them they're likely to spoil."

"That won't do," Paul said. "We'll have to figure a way to use the critters. Teddy Roosevelt wouldn't like it if we wasted all those natural **resources.** Let me think."

After thinking a while, Paul snapped his fingers. "I've got it!" he said. "If the popcorn froze them, the popcorn can keep them frozen."

80 With that, he strolled over to the railroad and called on the head man, Jim Hill. Jim rented him a raft of boxcars. Then, with the help of Babe, Paul stuffed those boxcars with animals *and* popcorn. And that way, the meat kept fine until it had been delivered at Paul's camp.

So, without knowing it at the time, Paul had gone and invented refrigerator cars.

OWN THE STORIES

PRACTICING THE STANDARDS

Compare and Contrast Write two brief paragraphs contrasting the stories of Paul Bunyan and Prometheus. *Contrast* means to find differences. The graphic on the next page will help you gather your details. Write about Prometheus in the first paragraph. Write about Paul Bunyan in the second.

_____

_____

_____

_____

_____

_____

_____

_____

_____

_____

_____

_____

_____

_____

_____

KEEPING TRACK

Personal Word List Record the words you learned from these tales in your Personal Word List.

Personal Reading Log Enter these two stories in your Personal Reading Log. Indicate which one you preferred and why. Then, award yourself 6 points on the Reading Meter.

Checklist for Standards Mastery Think about what you've learned about character, and use the Checklist for Standards Mastery to record your progress.

Prometheus Steals Fire from Heaven; Paul's Popcorn ■ *Interactive Reading,* page 79

Interact with Literary Texts

Contrast Chart   Use this grid to gather details that show how the stories of Prometheus and Paul Bunyan are different.

	Prometheus	Paul Bunyan
Country of origin		
Historical period		
Character traits		
Actions/quests		
Motives		
Enemies		
Resolution to quest		
Tone of story		

Chapter 3

Being There
Setting

Strategy Launch:
"Sketch to Stretch"

LITERARY FOCUS: SETTING

Think about the last good movie you saw in a movie theater. When the movie was over, you walked outside and may have had to blink a few times so your eyes could adjust to the sun. You may have felt that you had taken a long trip somewhere and were suddenly back home. Watching a good movie picks you up and drops you into a setting. Reading a good story can do the same thing, but you have to do more than just sit, watch, and eat popcorn. You have to experience the setting in your imagination.

Setting is the time and place in which a story occurs. The setting of a story affects character and plot just as *your* setting affects the things you do and the kind of person you are.

A STRATEGY THAT WORKS: "SKETCH TO STRETCH"

The "Sketch to Stretch" strategy is a good way to express your feelings about a story, especially a story with a strong setting. In "Sketch to Stretch," you draw a picture of something (an object, an animal, a person) that expresses your general feeling about the story and its message.

POINTERS FOR USING "SKETCH TO STRETCH"

))⟫ After you read the story, ask yourself, "What is this story saying to me?" or "How does this story make me feel?"

))⟫ Capture your response in a sketch or drawing. You can draw symbols and objects that aren't in the story, if they help capture the story's essence for you.

))⟫ Remember: The point is not to illustrate the story. For example, let's say the story is about a couple who fall in love on a ship that later sinks into freezing-cold water. The sketch might be a simple heart shape that is broken by a wedge of ice. It's not an illustration of the ship. It is a symbol that suggests the meaning behind the story.

Reading Standard 1.3 Use word meanings within the appropriate context, and show ability to verify those meanings by definition, restatement, example, comparison, or contrast.

Reading Standard 2.1 (Grade 6 Review) Identify the structural features of popular media (for example, newspapers, magazines, online information).

Reading Standard 3.4 Analyze the relevance of the setting (for example, place, time, customs) to the mood, tone, and meaning of the text.

Practice Read

One of the first questions that will probably pop into your mind as you read this story is "Where are we?" The questions and comments in the side columns will help you solve the puzzle presented by the setting. After you read the story, you will use the "Sketch to Stretch" strategy to suggest the meaning or feeling of the story—as you see it. So, as you read, think about what the setting is and how *you* would feel if you were in that place and time.

Lost and Found

Ed Combs

PREDICT

Circle the name of the character in the first paragraph. What does this name tell you about the kind of story this will be?

_____

_____

_____

_____

_____

VOCABULARY DEVELOPMENT

catapulted (cat′ə·pult′əd) *v.*: shot or launched from.

Circle the context clues that help you define *catapulted*.

After lunch on the day before we arrived home, Sander7 walked out of the public library and was nearly hit on the head by a wallet falling out of the sky.

Sander7 stared at the wallet lying on the ground. It was a perfectly normal-looking wallet of shiny green plastic, like the one his father tucked into his jacket pocket every morning as he got ready for work. Why did a wallet fall out of the sky as if it had been **catapulted** from another planet? Nothing ever fell out of the sky here. Nothing was
10 even in the sky.

Looking around to see if anyone was watching, Sander7 quickly reached down and picked up the wallet. It fell open in his hands, revealing an identification card that read, "Christo4. Lookout. Crow's Nest Position. First shift. Contact number 4978." Well, nothing out of the ordinary, thought Sander7 as he heard the town's air circulation

generator turn itself on. Why can't anything interesting ever happen around here? It's the same thing day after day— same temperature, same people, same routine. Even a
20 wallet falling out of the sky turns out to be boring.

Sander7 wound through the neat sidewalks and streets until he got home. He slipped his cardkey into the door lock, waited for the beep that signaled the door to slide open, and stepped inside. The door slid shut after him, locking automatically like a prison cell. He headed to the kitchen and plucked a postage stamp-sized dry square out of a box. Even the food is boring, he thought as he tossed the square into the hydration machine. Seconds later the machine door popped open, and Sander7 reached in and
30 pulled out a loaf of steaming bread.

Taking the bread over to the telephone, Sander7 dialed the contact number on the identification card of Christo4. After four rings, a shaky-sounding voice picked up. "Yes?"

"Hello, sir, my name is Sander7, and I think I just found your wallet. Christo4, right? Actually, it just fell in front of me out of nowhere." There was a long pause at the other end and the sound of things being shuffled around.

"Oh! Oh, I see. Yes, well, I guess that makes sense. I didn't even know my wallet was missing, but I can certainly
40 guess how it might have happened."

Sander7 frowned. "Really? I'm glad you can, because I can't figure it out at all!"

Again, there was a long pause at the other end of the line. Finally, Christo4 said, "Um, look. My shift is over in about twenty minutes. Would you meet me at the USA Park near France Street? I'd like to buy you a snow cone for returning my wallet."

IDENTIFY

Re-read lines 9–20. Underline the words and phrases that give you clues about the **setting**.

INFER

Underline the words in the paragraph beginning on line 21 that suggest that the **setting** is a prison. Underline other clues in this paragraph that tell you something about the setting. Is it a pleasant place?

_____

_____

_____

WORD KNOWLEDGE

Use clues in the story to figure out what a *hydration* (hī·drā′shən) *machine* (line 28) is.

_____

_____

_____

WORD KNOWLEDGE

Hydration is built on the Greek word *hydor,* meaning "water." What other English words are built on *hydor*?

_____

_____

_____

distressed (di·strest′) *adj.:* troubled; anxious.

Circle the context clues that help you figure out the meaning of *distressed*.

Although a park is usually a happy place, this one has a different mood. Underline the words and phrases that suggest something strange about this park. Can you guess what these statues are?

_____

_____

_____

_____

_____

_____

_____

Underline the detail that tells you where Christo4 gets the snow cones from.

Sander7 frowned. Something seemed strange about this whole thing. Why did this guy sound so flustered? Why

50 didn't he know his wallet was missing? And why was he offering to buy him a snow cone, the most expensive food on the planet? But anything would be better than hanging around here, so Sander7 said, "I'll be there."

When Sander7 arrived at USA Park, he saw a man sitting alone on a bench in front of the sculpture of a man and a woman riding something called an automobile. That must be Christo4, he thought. Christo4 looked **distressed,** his body hunched over, his head in his hands. The other sculptures in the park stood like silent ghosts: the one of

60 men and women flying in some machine called an airplane, the one of a track that looped around and around with a cart with lots of wheels attached to it. The figures in the cart appeared to be smiling and screaming, some with their hands held up in the air.

But Christo4 wasn't smiling. Sander7 approached him. "Hi," he said.

Christo4 finally spoke, as if to the air. "You know, I never thought I'd see the day. . . ."

"The day when what?" replied Sander7.

70 Christo4 looked him in the eye without saying anything for a moment. Then he said quietly, "Sander7, how old are you?"

"Almost twelve, sir."

"Well, I think 'almost twelve' will have to do in this case." Christo4 walked over to the snow cone vault and bought two snow cones. "Let's walk, shall we?" Sander7 followed as Christo4 began to wander among the statues.

"Sander7, tomorrow Mayor Ang4 will make a speech. He will tell everyone that we have arrived at the end of a

80 very long trip—a trip across billions of miles and hundreds of years." Christo4 stopped and stared at the ground. "We've finally found a new home," he said.

Sander7 looked at him, not understanding. "What do you mean, 'a new home'? We all have homes already."

"Yes, but. . . ." Christo4 didn't know what to say. "Come with me." He began to walk quickly toward Switzerland Street. Sander7 almost had to run to keep up. When they got to the edge of the park, Christo4 pulled out a small metal wedge and put it into what looked like a tiny hole in

90 the wall of the nearest building.

"What's that?" Sander7 asked.

"It's an old-fashioned, earlier version of your cardkey," said Christo4. "It's just called a key."

Christo4 turned the key, and a part of the wall opened. Inside was a hidden stairway. They both entered. Sander7 jumped as the wall closed behind them. It made a squeaking sound he had never heard before. "That's just the sound of rusty metal scraping against metal," explained Christo4. Sander7 had no idea what the word "rusty" meant, but he

100 kept silent as he followed behind Christo4, stepping first quickly up the stairs, then slowing down as he **ascended** higher and higher. Finally, they reached the top. This time, Christo4 held his ID up to a small camera. The door slid open.

What Sander7 saw was anything but boring. It was a control room like the one he had seen at the town's power station. The center of the room was filled with lit-up computers that seemed as if they were people silently thinking. Windows covered the walls, looking out like the

110 eyes of the universe. Beyond those windows was the blackness of space.

IDENTIFY

What have you noticed about the street names? Check back through the story, and underline them.

_____

_____

_____

_____

_____

IDENTIFY

What do you think it means that Sander7 does not know what *rusty* means (line 99)?

_____

_____

_____

_____

_____

_____

VOCABULARY DEVELOPMENT

ascended (ə·send′əd) v.: moved upward; climbed.

Sometimes the words in the sentence just go right ahead and tell you what a more difficult word means. Circle the words that define the word *ascended*.

IDENTIFY

Finally we know the setting of this story. What is it?

_____

_____

_____

_____

_____

_____

INTERPRET

How do you interpret the last line of the story?

_____

_____

_____

_____

_____

_____

IDENTIFY

Go back over the story, and list all the clues that hint at what the setting is. How do you know water is a major problem?

_____

_____

_____

_____

_____

_____

"What is this?" Sander7 asked.

"This," said Christo4, "is the Crow's Nest. This is where I work." He looked down at Sander7 and took a deep breath. "Sander7, we're on a spaceship. We—you and your parents and your grandparents and their parents and grandparents—have all been riding on a spaceship for generations. Our home planet, which was called Earth, was destroyed. Our ancestors built three spaceships designed to

120   carry us to a new planet. Now we've finally found one. I was so surprised when I spotted the new planet that I almost jumped out of my own skin. I think that must be when I lost my wallet. It must have fallen through a hole in a floor panel and dropped in front of you at the library."

Sander7 couldn't believe it. Everything he had known as his home was fake. "Why didn't anyone tell me? This is so unfair. So my life has been like a scene from a movie, complete with a stage set. Nothing has been real. Did my parents know? Why didn't they teach us this in school?

130   Why. . . ?"

"The commander thought that keeping all of this secret would keep people from becoming unhappy during the trip. Only those who had to know were told. Now, since we've almost arrived at our new home, you can know the truth."

"And what is the truth?" asked Sander7.

"What we had lost is now found."

OWN THE STORY

Setting Throughout most of this story, Sander7 thinks he knows when and where he is living. We, the readers, aren't so sure. This story's suspense and mood come from the element of setting. What is Sander7's reaction when he learns where his home really is? Quote a line from the story in your answer.

_____

_____

_____

_____

Setting Sketch Show what the setting of "Lost and Found" suggests to you by filling in the "Sketch to Stretch" that follows on the next page.

KEEPING TRACK

Personal Word List Record the words you learned from this story in your Personal Word List.

Personal Reading Log As you record the title of this story in your Personal Reading Log, indicate how you feel about science fiction stories. Give yourself 3 points on the Reading Meter for reading "Lost and Found."

Checklist for Standards Mastery Use the Checklist for Standards Mastery to chart your progress in mastering the reading standards.

Lost and Found ■ *Interactive Reading,* page 90

Interact with a Literary Text

"Sketch to Stretch"   Make a list of the words that describe the setting of "Lost and Found." Use specific details from the story.

Draw a sketch that represents how the story and its settings affected you. Think of symbols that represent the feeling you have about the story's setting. Before you draw, review the notes you made as you read the story. At the bottom of your sketch, explain briefly what you intended to show in your sketch.

Setting Words

Sketch to Stretch

Write an explanation of your sketch.

_____

_____

_____

_____

_____

In Trouble

Interact with a Literary Text

"Follow the Setting" Chart   Many stories have more than one
setting. As the reader, you have to follow the story wherever it takes
you. Remember that when the story takes you to different settings,
the whole mood of the story can change. In this selection, Gary
Paulsen takes you to four different settings, ranging from steel-
breaking cold parts of Alaska to a toasty-warm cabin.

Use this chart to follow the setting. The first column is filled in
for you. Fill in the rest of the chart, and you'll have a path to the
story's settings.

Setting: Where	When story occurs	Setting words from the story	Mood the setting creates
a river in Alaska	probably winter	"whirlpool frozen into a cone," "water roaring through it at the bottom"	beautiful, but scary
the kennel area			
a "trapping" run			
Paulsen's cabin			

Fast, Strong, and Friendly Too

Interact with an Informational Text

"It Makes a Difference" Chart   The inability to see similarities and differences is a skill that can dog you throughout your life. Situations occur every day at work and in life that require your brain to compare things. Here's one example. Imagine you are an animal consultant. Part of your job is to recommend certain breeds of dogs to people. For example, if a person has a two-year-old child, you wouldn't want to recommend a breed that has a tendency toward aggression.

Read each person's situation below. Then, write down your recommendation for the breed of dog the person needs. You have only four choices (you can make more than one recommendation per person): Siberian husky, Samoyed, Alaskan malamute, or American Eskimo dog.

Situation	Breed You Recommend
1. This man has very limited space in his home, but he wants a husky.	
2. This woman wants a dog that is good with children, but she enjoys racing, so she also wants the dog to be able to win races.	
3. This man lives in rough tundra. He needs a very large dog that can endure extreme temperatures and rugged land.	
4. This popular man, Mr. Claus, needs a dog to guard his reindeer.	

Now for each recommendation you made, tell why you decided on that breed.

1. _____

_____

2. _____

_____

3. _____

_____

_____

4. _____

_____

There Will Come Soft Rains

Interact with a Literary Text

"What's *Really* Going On?" Chart   In this story, Ray Bradbury describes some hideous events. But as the reader, you have to keep asking yourself the question "What's *really* going on here?" It is not always clear what is actually happening. For help following the story, use this time chart as you read. Each tinted row contains a time and a main story event that the writer tells us happened at that time. Fill in each untinted box with what *you* think is really happening at that time. The first one is done for you.

Summary of Main Events — **What's *Really* Going On?**

7:00 A clock announces the time. A stove fixes breakfast automatically.	
It seems as if the house has been abandoned by people, but it's still operating as if it's alive.	
8:01 Garage door opens, but no one comes out. House is cleaned by robot mice.	
10:00 House is the only one in the city. Rest of city is in ashes and glows as if from radiation. Images of people are on the wall of the house.	
12:00 A starving dog walks into the house and searches for people. Dog dies in house.	
2:00 Bridge tables pop out from the walls. Nursery walls seem to come alive.	
5:00 Bath fills with water, and dinner dishes are washed. The house prepares for bedtime.	
10:00 House catches fire. Robots try to put out fire. The house burns down.	

Destination: Mars

Interact with an Informational Text

Matching Chart   Magazines are built around design features that make it easy for the reader to see the highlights quickly. If done well by the publisher, those same design features can increase sales of the magazine.

Read the following definitions of design features. Then, match the design feature to its use in "Destination: Mars." Write the letter of the example from the right column next to the correct label in the left column.

Design

___ **Decorative typefaces** have elaborately designed characters that convey a distinct mood. They are often used in titles.

___ **Contrast** refers to the visual effect of using different typefaces in an article. There might be one kind of typeface in the body of the article and another typeface with more emphasis in the beginning.

___ **Symbols** help draw the eye to special features like charts or drawings.

___ **Rule lines** draw your eye to something on the page. Rule lines can be thick or thin, plain or fancy, vertical or horizontal.

___ Another kind of graphic is a **table** that provides information in an organized way.

Design Examples from "Destination: Mars"

a. **SO FAR** only robots have visited Mars.

b. ◀ Inside the "can," the nickname for the simulated capsule, the crew

c. *Destination: MARS*

d. **The Earthlings are coming! The Earthlings are coming!**

e. **EARTH**

Nickname: the Blue Planet
Length of day: 23 hours, 56 minutes
Length of year: 365 days
Moons: one
Planet surface: mostly wet and warm
Atmosphere: 98 percent oxygen and nitrogen mix

The Circuit

for use with
Holt Literature and Language Arts,
page 183

MAKING
INFERENCES

Interact with a Literary Text

"Thought Bubbles" Frames   Creating thought bubbles can help
you make inferences about what a character is feeling about a
setting, an event, or another character.

Fill out a thought bubble for each of the following moments from
"The Circuit." In the bubbles, sketch or write what Panchito is
seeing, feeling, or thinking during the scene.

**The family leaves their "little shack" to go
on the road in search of work.**

**Panchito hides while watching
the schoolboys get off the bus.**

**Panchito enters his new
school for the first time.**

**Returning home, Panchito sees
the packed cardboard boxes again.**

Cesar Chavez: He Made a Difference

for use with
Holt Literature and Language Arts,
page 192

Interact with an Informational Text

What If? Chart   Reading about events in history gives us a chance to ask the question, "What would have happened if . . . ?" After you read "Cesar Chavez: He Made a Difference," think about what would have happened if certain events had not taken place. Write your responses in the boxes provided.

What If? (Cause)   **Possible Effects**

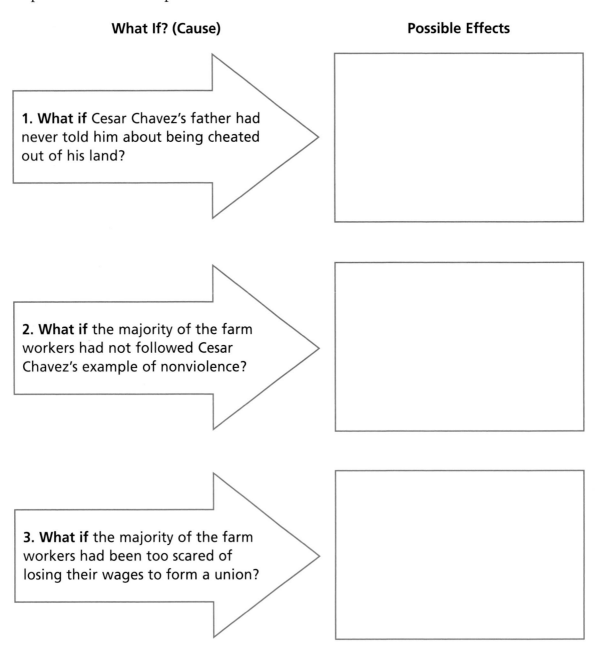

1. What if Cesar Chavez's father had never told him about being cheated out of his land?

2. What if the majority of the farm workers had not followed Cesar Chavez's example of nonviolence?

3. What if the majority of the farm workers had been too scared of losing their wages to form a union?

Picking Strawberries: Could You Do It?

Interact with an Informational Text

Conclusions Chart   When you reach a conclusion about something, your conclusion should be supported by evidence. For example, if there is a suspicious character in a murder mystery with no alibi but a huge motive, you would conclude that she is guilty. A conclusions chart can help you evaluate evidence and lead you to a logical conclusion.

After you read "Picking Strawberries: Could You Do It?" think about the conclusion you would draw about strawberry picking. Write your conclusion in the last box below. In the evidence boxes, write four pieces of evidence that lead you to this conclusion.

Evidence	Evidence	Evidence	Evidence

Conclusion

Literature

AUTHOR STUDY

 If you've read the science fiction story by **Ray Bradbury** called "There Will Come Soft Rains" (*Holt Literature and Language Arts,* page 168), you have an idea of the kind of writer Ray Bradbury is. You also have a glimmer of why he's such a popular writer. Sitting in his office surrounded by interesting toys, Bradbury creates science fiction and fantasy stories that keep us reading. But his stories do more than entertain. After you've read a Bradbury story, you might find yourself wondering if there is more to the story than an exciting plot.

BEFORE YOU READ

You can look up "fog horn" on the Internet and actually hear one. But it's not the same as being there. If you've ever heard a fog horn blast in the dead of a dark, foggy night, you may agree that it's the sound of loneliness. The following facts about fog horns and lighthouses may help you understand Bradbury's mysterious story. But don't be surprised if you have more questions at the end of the story than you do at the beginning.

> ### Lighthouse Facts
> - Lighthouses were built to save lives. They were built along coastlines that pose hazards to ships. With intense light beams, lighthouses warn ships of dangers, such as rocky ledges. Before lighthouses were built, many seamen went to their deaths because their ships crashed into land.
> - The fog horn helps to guide ships in foggy weather. The sound is made by quickly releasing compressed air.
> - Most lighthouses range in height from 33 feet to 208 feet and are built from wood, stone, brick, reinforced concrete, iron, or steel. They are not easy to destroy.
> - Until recently, lighthouse keepers lived and worked at lighthouses to operate the signals. Now most lighthouses are automated.

Reading Standard 3.4 Analyze the relevance of the setting (for example, place, time, customs) to the mood, tone, and meaning of the text.

The Fog Horn

Ray Bradbury

Out there in the cold water, far from land, we waited every night for the coming of the fog, and it came, and we oiled the brass machinery and lit the fog light up in the stone tower. Feeling like two birds in the gray sky, McDunn and I sent the light touching out, red, then white, then red again, to eye the lonely ships. And if they did not see our light, then there was always our Voice, the great deep cry of our Fog Horn shuddering through the rags of mist to startle the gulls away like decks of scattered cards and make the waves
10   turn high and foam.

"It's a lonely life, but you're used to it now, aren't you?" asked McDunn.

"Yes," I said. "You're a good talker, thank the Lord."

"Well, it's your turn on land tomorrow," he said, smiling, "to dance the ladies and drink gin."

"What do you think, McDunn, when I leave you out here alone?"

"On the mysteries of the sea." McDunn lit his pipe. It was a quarter past seven of a cold November evening, the
20   heat on, the light switching its tail in two hundred directions, the Fog Horn bumbling in the high throat of the tower. There wasn't a town for a hundred miles down the coast, just a road which came lonely through dead country to the sea, with few cars on it, a stretch of two miles of cold water out to our rock, and rare few ships.

"The mysteries of the sea," said McDunn thoughtfully. "You know, the ocean's the most confounded big snowflake

---

IDENTIFY

The box about lighthouses and fog horns in the Before You Read section gave you factual information. As you read this first page, you get more of a feel for what this particular lighthouse setting is like. Underline phrases and words that create the mood for this **setting**.

_____

_____

_____

_____

_____

_____

_____

_____

_____

_____

_____

_____

Bradbury is known for his descriptive language. In line 34, underline the **simile** (a comparison using *like* or *as*) that helps you picture the fishes' eyes.

IDENTIFY

McDunn is good at telling a story. He makes the tower seem like a person. Underline the parts of his story that make us feel that the tower has a life of its own.

INFER

Underline the words that tell how McDunn's story of the fish affects the narrator.

INTERPRET

Writers use **foreshadowing** to hint at events that might happen later. What could be foreshadowed in the paragraph beginning "Oh, the sea's full"?

_____

_____

_____

_____

_____

_____

_____

_____

ever? It rolls and swells a thousand shapes and colors, no two alike. Strange. One night, years ago, I was here alone,
30 when all of the fish of the sea surfaced out there. Something made them swim in and lie in the bay, sort of trembling and staring up at the tower light going red, white, red, white across them so I could see their funny eyes. I turned cold. They were like a big peacock's tail, moving out there until midnight. Then, without so much as a sound, they slipped away, the million of them was gone. I kind of think maybe, in some sort of way, they came all those miles to worship. Strange. But think how the tower must look to them, standing seventy feet above the water,
40 the God-light flashing out from it, and the tower declaring itself with a monster voice. They never came back, those fish, but don't you think for a while they thought they were in the Presence?"

I shivered. I looked out at the long gray lawn of the sea stretching away into nothing and nowhere.

"Oh, the sea's full." McDunn puffed his pipe nervously, blinking. He had been nervous all day and hadn't said why. "For all our engines and so-called submarines, it'll be ten thousand centuries before we set foot on the real bottom of
50 the sunken lands, in the fairy kingdoms there, and know *real* terror. Think of it, it's still the year 300,000 Before Christ down under there. While we've paraded around with trumpets, lopping off each other's countries and heads, they have been living beneath the sea twelve miles deep and cold in a time as old as the beard of a comet."

"Yes, it's an old world."

"Come on. I got something special I been saving up to tell you."

We ascended the eighty steps, talking and taking
60   our time. At the top, McDunn switched off the room
lights so there'd be no reflection in the plate glass. The
great eye of the light was humming, turning easily in its
oiled socket. The Fog Horn was blowing steadily, once
every fifteen seconds.

"Sounds like an animal, don't it?" McDunn nodded to
himself. "A big lonely animal crying in the night. Sitting
here on the edge of ten billion years called out to the
Deeps, I'm here, I'm here, I'm here. And the Deeps do
answer, yes, they do. You been here now for three months,
70   Johnny, so I better prepare you. About this time of year,"
he said, studying the murk and fog, "something comes to
visit the lighthouse."

"The swarms of fish like you said?"

"No, this is something else. I've put off telling you
because you might think I'm daft. But tonight's the latest I
can put it off, for if my calendar's marked right from last
year, tonight's the night it comes. I won't go into detail,
you'll have to see it yourself. Just sit down there. If you
want, tomorrow you can pack your duffel and take the
80   motorboat in to land and get your car parked there at the
dinghy pier on the cape and drive on back to some little
inland town and keep your lights burning nights. I won't
question or blame you. It's happened three years now, and
this is the only time anyone's been here with me to **verify**
it. You wait and watch."

Half an hour passed with only a few whispers
between us. When we grew tired of waiting, McDunn
began describing some of his ideas to me. He had some
theories about the Fog Horn itself.

IDENTIFY

Underline McDunn's line in the second paragraph that tells what the problem in the story will probably be.

WORD KNOWLEDGE

A *dinghy* (diŋ'ē) (line 81) is a small rowboat.

Don't confuse the noun *dinghy,* a boat, with the adjective *dingy* (din'jē), which means "shabby; not clean; grimy."

VOCABULARY DEVELOPMENT

verify (ver'ə·fī) *v.:* confirm; prove to be true.

PREDICT

What do you predict will happen tonight?

What one word would
you use to describe the
Fog Horn? Write the
word, and draw a symbol
to represent that word.

_____

_____

_____

_____

_____

_____

_____

INFER

What question do you think
the narrator was going to
ask in line 110?

_____

_____

_____

_____

_____

_____

90 "One day many years ago a man walked along and stood in the sound of the ocean on a cold sunless shore and said, "We need a voice to call across the water, to warn ships. I'll make one. I'll make a voice like all of time and all of that fog that ever was; I'll make a voice that is like an empty bed beside you all night long, and like an empty house when you open the door, and like trees in autumn with no leaves. A sound like the birds flying south, crying, and a sound like November wind and the sea on the hard, cold shore. I'll make a sound that's so alone that no one can

100 miss it, that whoever hears it will weep in their souls, and hearths will seem warmer, and being inside will seem better to all who hear it in the distant towns. I'll make me a sound and an apparatus and they'll call it a Fog Horn and whoever hears it will know the sadness of eternity and the briefness of life."

The Fog Horn blew.

"I made up that story," said McDunn quietly, "to try to explain why this thing keeps coming back to the lighthouse every year. The Fog Horn calls it, I think, and it comes. . . ."

110 "But—" I said.

"Sssst!" said McDunn. "There!" He nodded out to the Deeps.

Something was swimming toward the lighthouse tower.

It was a cold night, as I have said; the high tower was cold, the light coming and going, and the Fog Horn calling and calling through the raveling mist. You couldn't see far and you couldn't see plain, but there was the deep sea moving on its way about the night earth, flat and quiet, the

120 color of gray mud, and here were the two of us alone in the high tower, and there, far out at first, was a ripple, followed

by a wave, a rising, a bubble, a bit of froth. And then, from the surface of the cold sea came a head, a large head, dark-colored, with **immense** eyes, and then a neck. And then— not a body—but more neck and more! The head rose a full forty feet above the water on a slender and beautiful dark neck. Only then did the body, like a little island of black coral and shells and crayfish, drip up from the **subterranean.** There was a flicker of tail. In all, from

130 head to tip of tail, I estimated the monster at ninety or a hundred feet.

I don't know what I said. I said something.

"Steady, boy, steady," whispered McDunn.

"It's impossible!" I said.

"No, Johnny, *we're* impossible. *It's* like it always was ten million years ago. *It* hasn't changed. It's *us* and the land that've changed, become impossible. *Us!*"

It swam slowly and with a great dark majesty out in the icy waters, far away. The fog came and went about it,

140 momentarily erasing its shape. One of the monster eyes caught and held and flashed back our immense light, red, white, red, white, like a disk held high and sending a message in **primeval** code. It was as silent as the fog through which it swam.

"It's a dinosaur of some sort!" I crouched down, holding to the stair rail.

"Yes, one of the tribe."

"But they died out!"

"No, only hid away in the Deeps. Deep, deep down

150 in the deepest Deeps. Isn't *that* a word now, Johnny, a real word, it says so much: the Deeps. There's all the coldness and darkness and deepness in a word like that."

VOCABULARY
DEVELOPMENT

immense (i·mens') *adj.*: extremely large; vast; huge.

subterranean (sub'tə·rā'ē·ən) *n.*: place beneath the earth's surface; underground.

Subterranean is usually used as an adjective, meaning "underground."

Sub- is a prefix meaning "under." *Terra* is the Latin word for "earth."

What does *substandard* mean? What is a *terrestrial*?

_____

_____

_____

_____

_____

_____

primeval (prī·mē'vəl) *adj.*: of the earliest times and ages; ancient.

INTERPRET

Circle the word *deep* each time it appears in the paragraph beginning at line 149. What mood does this repeated word create?

_____

_____

_____

_____

_____

_____

_____

_____

_____

COMPARE & CONTRAST

The monster and the Fog Horn seem as if they're speaking the same language. Underline the words in the paragraph beginning on line 162 that show the similarities between the sounds they make.

IDENTIFY

McDunn asks a question in lines 170–171. How does he go on to answer it?

_____

_____

_____

_____

_____

_____

_____

_____

"What'll we do?"

"Do? We got our job, we can't leave. Besides, we're safer here than in any boat trying to get to land. That thing's as big as a destroyer and almost as swift."

"But here, why does it come *here*?"

The next moment I had my answer.

160   The Fog Horn blew.

And the monster answered.

A cry came across a million years of water and mist. A cry so anguished and alone that it shuddered in my head and my body. The monster cried out at the tower. The Fog Horn blew. The monster roared again. The Fog Horn blew. The monster opened its great toothed mouth and the sound that came from it was the sound of the Fog Horn itself. Lonely and vast and far away. The sound of isolation, a viewless sea, a cold night, apartness. That was the sound.

170   "Now," whispered McDunn, "do you know why it comes here?"

I nodded.

"All year long, Johnny, that poor monster there lying far out, a thousand miles at sea, and twenty miles deep maybe, biding its time, perhaps it's a million years old, this one creature. Think of it, waiting a million years; could *you* wait that long? Maybe it's the last of its kind. I sort of think that's true. Anyway, here come men on land and build this lighthouse, five years ago. And set up their Fog Horn and

180   sound it and sound it out toward the place where you bury yourself in sleep and sea memories of a world where there were thousands like yourself, but now you're alone, all alone in a world not made for you, a world where you have to hide.

"But the sound of the Fog Horn comes and goes, comes and goes, and you stir from the muddy bottom of the Deeps, and your eyes open like the lenses of two-foot cameras and you move, slow, slow, for you have the ocean sea on your shoulders, heavy. But that Fog Horn comes

190 through a thousand miles of water, faint and familiar, and the furnace in your belly stokes up, and you begin to rise, slow, slow. You feed yourself on great slakes of cod and minnow, on rivers of jellyfish, and you rise slow through the autumn months, through September when the fogs started, through October with more fog and the horn still calling you on, and then, late in November, after pressurizing yourself day by day, a few feet higher every hour, you are near the surface and still alive. You've got to go slow; if you surfaced all at once you'd explode. So it takes you all of

200 three months to surface, and then a number of days to swim through the cold waters to the lighthouse. And there you are, out there, in the night, Johnny, the biggest monster in creation. And here's the lighthouse calling to you, with a long neck like your neck sticking way up out of the water, and a body like your body, and, most important of all, a voice like your voice. Do you understand now, Johnny, do you understand?"

The Fog Horn blew.

The monster answered.

210 I saw it all, I knew it all—the million years of waiting alone, for someone to come back who never came back. The million years of isolation at the bottom of the sea, the insanity of time there, while the skies cleared of reptile-birds, the swamps dried on the continental lands, the sloths and saber-tooths had their day and sank in tar pits, and men ran like white ants upon the hills.

CONNECT

McDunn has an explanation for the fact that the monster appears in November. What is it? How might a marine biologist respond to his story? What might an expert in mythology say?

_____

_____

_____

_____

_____

_____

_____

_____

_____

_____

INFER

What episodes in natural history are hinted at in this paragraph? Underline them.

_____

_____

_____

_____

Pause at line 234. What do you predict is going to happen next?

_____

_____

_____

_____

_____

_____

Pause at line 248. Which word or words would you use to describe the monster's feelings: _angry, desperate, bewildered,_ or _sad_ (or any other word you think of)? Underline the text that reveals the monster's feelings.

_____

_____

_____

_____

_____

The Fog Horn blew.

"Last year," said McDunn, "that creature swam round and round, round and round, all night. Not coming too 220 near, puzzled, I'd say. Afraid, maybe. And a bit angry after coming all this way. But the next day, unexpectedly, the fog lifted, the sun came out fresh, the sky was as blue as a painting. And the monster swam off away from the heat and the silence and didn't come back. I suppose it's been brooding on it for a year now, thinking it over from every which way."

The monster was only a hundred yards off now, it and the Fog Horn crying at each other. As the lights hit them, the monster's eyes were fire and ice, fire and ice.

230 "That's life for you," said McDunn. "Someone always waiting for someone who never comes home. Always someone loving some thing more than that thing loves them. And after a while, you want to destroy whatever that thing is, so it can't hurt you no more."

The monster was rushing at the lighthouse.

The Fog Horn blew.

"Let's see what happens," said McDunn.

He switched the Fog Horn off.

The ensuing minute of silence was so intense that we 240 could hear our hearts pounding in the glassed area of the tower, could hear the slow greased turn of the light.

The monster stopped and froze. Its great lantern eyes blinked. Its mouth gaped. It gave a sort of rumble, like a volcano. It twitched its head this way and that, as if to seek the sounds now dwindled off into the fog. It peered at the lighthouse. It rumbled again. Then its eyes caught fire. It reared up, threshed the water, and rushed at the tower, its eyes filled with angry torment.

"McDunn!" I cried. "Switch on the horn!"

250   McDunn fumbled with the switch. But even as he
flicked it on, the monster was rearing up. I had a glimpse of
its gigantic paws, fishskin glittering in webs between the
finger-like projections, clawing at the tower. The huge eyes
on the right side of its anguished head glittered before me
like a caldron into which I might drop, screaming. The
tower shook. The Fog Horn cried; the monster cried. It
seized the tower and gnashed at the glass, which shattered
in upon us.

McDunn seized my arm. "Downstairs!"

260   The tower rocked, trembled, and started to give. The
Fog Horn and the monster roared. We stumbled and half
fell down the stairs. "Quick!"

We reached the bottom as the tower buckled down
toward us. We ducked under the stairs into the small stone
cellar. There were a thousand concussions as the rocks
rained down; the Fog Horn stopped **abruptly.** The monster
crashed upon the tower. The tower fell. We knelt together,
McDunn and I, holding tight, while our world exploded.

Then it was over, and there was nothing but darkness
270   and the wash of the sea on the raw stones.

That and the other sound.

"Listen," said McDunn quietly. "Listen."

We waited a moment. And then I began to hear it. First
a great vacuumed sucking of air, and then the lament, the
bewilderment, the loneliness of the great monster, folded
over and upon us, above us, so that the sickening reek of its
body filled the air, a stone's thickness away from our cellar.
The monster gasped and cried. The tower was gone. The
light was gone. The thing that had called to it across a
280   million years was gone. And the monster was opening its

INFER

Why is the monster
anguished (line 254)?

_____

_____

_____

_____

_____

**VOCABULARY
DEVELOPMENT**

abruptly (ə·brupt′lē) adv.:
suddenly; unexpectedly.

INFER

Which scene on this page
do you think is the climax of
the plot—the most exciting
moment when the outcome
of the hero's quest is determined? Who or what is the
hero in this story?

_____

_____

_____

_____

**WORD
KNOWLEDGE**

Underline context clues that
help you understand that
reek in line 276 means
"stench" or "stink."

INTERPRET

Pause at line 291. Why do you think McDunn doesn't tell the rescuers what really happened?

_____

_____

_____

_____

_____

_____

_____

_____

_____

_____

_____

_____

_____

_____

_____

_____

_____

_____

_____

_____

_____

_____

_____

mouth and sending out great sounds. The sounds of a Fog Horn, again and again. And ships far at sea, not finding the light, not seeing anything, but passing and hearing late that night, must've thought: There it is, the lonely sound, the Lonesome Bay horn. All's well. We've rounded the cape.

And so it went for the rest of that night.

The sun was hot and yellow the next afternoon when the rescuers came out to dig us from our stoned-under cellar.

"It fell apart, is all," said Mr. McDunn gravely. "We had
290 a few bad knocks from the waves and it just crumbled." He pinched my arm.

There was nothing to see. The ocean was calm, the sky blue. The only thing was a great algaic stink from the green matter that covered the fallen tower stones and the shore rocks. Flies buzzed about. The ocean washed empty on the shore.

The next year they built a new lighthouse, but by that time I had a job in the little town and a wife and a good small warm house that glowed yellow on autumn nights,
300 the doors locked, the chimney puffing smoke. As for McDunn, he was master of the new lighthouse, built to his own specifications, out of still-reinforced concrete. "Just in case," he said.

The new lighthouse was ready in November. I drove down alone one evening late and parked my car and looked across the gray waters and listened to the new horn sounding, once, twice, three, four times a minute far out there, by itself.

The monster?
310 It never came back.

"It's gone away," said McDunn. "It's gone back to the Deeps. It's learned you can't love anything too much in this world. It's gone into the deepest Deeps to wait another million years. Ah, the poor thing! Waiting out there, and waiting out there, while man comes and goes on this pitiful little planet. Waiting and waiting."

I sat in my car, listening. I couldn't see the lighthouse or the light standing out in Lonesome Bay. I could only hear the Horn, the Horn, the Horn. It sounded like the monster calling.

320

I sat there wishing there was something I could say.

EVALUATE

Underline the part of McDunn's remarks that seems to suggest the message of the story. Do you agree with it?

_____

_____

_____

_____

_____

_____

SKETCH TO STRETCH

Sketch a symbol of how you see the monster living out in the Deeps, "waiting and waiting."

_____

_____

_____

_____

_____

_____

_____

_____

_____

_____

_____

_____

OWN THE STORY

Setting   Write a paragraph in which you describe the **mood** of "The Fog Horn." Use details from the story to show how the **setting** contributes to that mood. Before you write, gather details about the smells, sounds, sights, temperature, time of year, and so on, revealed in the story.

_____

_____

_____

_____

_____

_____

_____

Sketch to Stretch   On a separate sheet of paper, create a sketch that suggests the mood or message of "The Fog Horn." Don't try to capture a scene described in the story. Try to capture the story's mood or message with your sketch. On the back of your sketch, write an explanation of your drawing. Share your finished sketch with a classmate. See if you can interpret each other's sketches.

Personal Word List   Record the words you learned from this story in your Personal Word List. Then, use one of the words in conversation today with some friends.

Personal Reading Log   As you record the title of this story in your Personal Reading Log, explain what you like about Bradbury's story. Give yourself 6 points on the Reading Meter.

Checklist for Standards Mastery   Check your progress toward understanding the power of setting. Record your progress in the Checklist for Standards Mastery.

The Fog Horn ▪ *Interactive Reading,* page 105

Go Beyond a Literary Text

Author Profile   Use your library and the Internet to find out more about Ray Bradbury. Then, fill out this author profile.

Profile: Ray Bradbury _____

Birth date: _____

Birthplace: _____

Parents: _____

Early life: _____

_____

_____

How he became a writer: _____

_____

_____

_____

Later achievements: _____

_____

_____

_____

_____

_____

_____

Major works: _____

_____

_____

_____

_____

_____

_____

_____

_____

ARTICLE

Reading Standard 2.1 (Grade 6 Review) Identify the structural features of popular media (for example, newspapers, magazines, online information).

BEFORE YOU READ

This article about the world's most famous monster is from a Web site called *NOVA Online.* In Scotland and Ireland a lough, or loch (läkh), is a lake. Loch Ness is a lake in Scotland that has earned fame from a monster that might not really live there at all. The search for the monster has gone on for years. As you read, see if Nessie reminds you of Bradbury's lonely monster.

from NOVA Online

Birth of a Legend

Stephen Lyons

TEXT STRUCTURE

Circle the quotation of G. K. Chesterton. A clever quotation at the beginning of an article can grab our attention and focus our thinking on the article's topic.

Does Chesterton believe in the monster? Explain.

_____

_____

_____

_____

_____

_____

"Many a man has been hanged on less evidence than there is for the Loch Ness Monster."
—G. K. Chesterton

Residents at the coast of Loch Ness.

When the Romans first came to northern Scotland in the
first century A.D., they found the Highlands occupied by
fierce, tattoo-covered tribes they called the Picts, or painted
people. From the carved, standing stones still found in the
region around Loch Ness, it is clear the Picts were fascinated
by animals and careful to render them with great fidelity. All
the animals depicted on the Pictish stones are lifelike and
easily recognizable—all but one. The exception is a strange
beast with an elongated beak or muzzle, a head locket or
spout, and flippers instead of feet. Described by some scholars as a swimming elephant, the Pictish beast is the earliest
known evidence for an idea that has held sway in the
Scottish Highlands for at least 1,500 years—that Loch Ness
is home to a mysterious aquatic animal.

In Scottish folklore, large animals have been associated
with many bodies of water, from small streams to the
largest lakes, often labeled Loch-na-Beistie on old maps.
These water-horses, or water-kelpies, are said to have
magical powers and malevolent intentions. According to
one version of the legend, the water-horse lures small
children into the water by offering them rides on its back.
Once the children are aboard, their hands become stuck
to the beast and they are dragged to a watery death, their
livers washing ashore the following day.

The earliest written reference linking such creatures to
Loch Ness is in the biography of Saint Columba, the man
credited with introducing Christianity to Scotland. In A.D.
565, according to this account, Columba was on his way to
visit a Pictish king when he stopped along the shore of
Loch Ness. Seeing a large beast about to attack a man who
was swimming in the lake, Columba raised his hand,
invoking the name of God and commanding the monster

WORD KNOWLEDGE

The words *beak* and *locket*
(line 12) are defined in context by restatement. Underline the two restatements.

INFER

To be *malevolent*
(mə·lev′ə·lənt) means "wishing someone harm" (line 22).
Even if you didn't know the
definition of *malevolent,* the
context would give you a
clue about the word's meaning. The description of what
the water horse does to children should tell you that
whatever *malevolent* means,
it isn't very good.

The Latin prefix *mal-* means
"wrong or bad." What does
maladjusted mean?

VOCABULARY DEVELOPMENT

complied (kəm·plīd') *v.*:
agreed; went along with.

How does the context
tell you what the word
complied means?

_____

_____

_____

_____

_____

_____

_____

_____

_____

· · · · · · **Notes** · · · · · ·

_____

_____

_____

_____

_____

_____

_____

_____

_____

_____

to "go back with all speed." The beast **complied,** and the swimmer was saved.

　　When Nicholas Witchell, a future BBC correspondent, researched the history of the legend for his 1974 book *The*
40 *Loch Ness Story,* he found about a dozen pre-20th-century references to large animals in Loch Ness, gradually shifting in character from these clearly mythical accounts to something more like eyewitness descriptions.

　　But the modern legend of Loch Ness dates from 1933, when a new road was completed along the shore, offering the first clear views of the loch from the northern side. One April afternoon, a local couple was driving home along this road when they spotted "an enormous animal rolling and plunging on the surface." Their account was written up by a
50 correspondent for the *Inverness Courier,* whose editor used the word "monster" to describe the animal. The Loch Ness Monster has been a media phenomenon ever since.

Is this the Loch Ness Monster?

Submarine used in the search for the Loch Ness Monster.

Public interest built gradually during the spring of 1933, then picked up sharply after a couple reported seeing one of the creatures on land, lumbering across the shore road. By October, several London newspapers had sent correspondents to Scotland, and radio programs were being interrupted to bring listeners the latest news from the loch. A British circus offered a reward of £20,000 for the capture of the beast. Hundreds of Boy Scouts and outdoorsmen arrived, some venturing out in small boats, others setting up deck chairs and waiting expectantly for the monster to appear.

The excitement over the monster reached a fever pitch in December, when the *London Daily Mail* hired an actor, film director, and big-game hunter named Marmaduke Wetherell to track down the beast. After only a few days at the loch, Wetherell reported finding the fresh footprints of a large, four-toed animal. He estimated it to be 20 feet long. With great fanfare, Wetherell made plaster casts of the footprints and, just before Christmas, sent them off to

60

70

WORD KNOWLEDGE

The word *perpetrator* (pʉr′pə·trā′tər) in line 82 means "one who commits something or originates something (something evil or offensive)." What is the "perpetrator of a hoax"?

_____

_____

WORD KNOWLEDGE

Optical (äp′ti·kəl) in line 88 is related to the words *optician* and *myopic.* They share the Greek root word *ops,* meaning "eye." What does *optical* mean?

_____

_____

TEXT STRUCTURE

How would you sum up the main point of the first part of this article, lines 1–90?

_____

_____

_____

WORD KNOWLEDGE

You can get an idea of what *protruding* (line 96) means by looking at the way it is used in the sentence. The "humps" were "protruding above the surface."

the Natural History Museum in London for analysis. While the world waited for the museum zoologists to return from holiday, legions of monster hunters descended on Loch Ness, filling the local hotels. Inverness was floodlit for the occasion, and traffic jammed the shoreline roads in both directions.

The bubble burst in early January, when museum zoologists announced that the footprints were those of a
80 hippopotamus. They had been made with a stuffed hippo foot—the base of an umbrella stand or ashtray. It wasn't clear whether Wetherell was the perpetrator of the hoax or its gullible victim. Either way, the incident tainted the image of the Loch Ness Monster and discouraged serious investigation of the phenomenon. For the next three decades, most scientists scornfully dismissed reports of strange animals in the loch. Those sightings that weren't outright hoaxes, they said, were the result of optical illusions caused by boat wakes, wind slicks, floating logs,
90 otters, ducks, or swimming deer.

Saw Something, They Did

Nevertheless, eyewitnesses continued to come forward with accounts of their sightings—more than 4,000 of them, according to Witchell's estimate. Most of the witnesses described a large creature with one or more humps protruding above the surface like the hull of an upturned boat. Others reported seeing a long neck or flippers. What was most remarkable, however, was that many of the eyewitnesses were sober, level-headed people:
100 lawyers and priests, scientists and schoolteachers, policemen and fishermen—even a Nobel Prize winner.

Wide view of Loch Ness.

WORD KNOWLEDGE

An *anecdote* (an′ik·dōt) is a short, entertaining story used to make a point. Anecdotes are often personal. What would you say *anecdotal evidence* is (line 104)?

_____

_____

_____

_____

_____

_____

Eyewitness Accounts

While no hard evidence for the existence of the Loch Ness Monster has yet turned up, heaps of anecdotal evidence exist. Although such eyewitness accounts are of little value scientifically, they can be compelling nevertheless. Below, lend an ear to several native Scots who swear they saw something in the loch. These tales were collected by the producers of the NOVA film *The Beast of Loch Ness.*

TEXT STRUCTURE

Circle the subheading for the first eyewitness account. What purpose does this heading have?

_____

_____

_____

_____

110   "I saw it, and nothing can take that away."

Well, we're talking about an incident that happened approximately 32 years ago, almost to the very day— mid-summer, June 1965. I, along with a friend, was on the south shore of Loch Ness, fishing for brown trout, looking almost directly into Urquhart Bay, when I saw something break the surface of the water. I glanced there, and I saw it, and then it wasn't there, it had disappeared.

TEXT STRUCTURE

Who is speaking now? Turn to the next page to find out.

_____

_____

_____

**VOCABULARY
DEVELOPMENT**

submerged (səb·mʉrjd′) v.:
plunged into water; sank.

TEXT STRUCTURE

Why do you think a description of the eyewitness is
included at the end of this
anecdote? (See line 140.)

_____

_____

_____

_____

_____

_____

TEXT STRUCTURE

Who is talking now (line
145)? Where can you find
out?

_____

_____

_____

**WORD
KNOWLEDGE**

Gobsmacked (line 145) is
British slang. What do you
guess it means?

_____

_____

_____

_____

But while watching, keeping an eye, and fishing gently,
I saw an object surface. It was a large, black object—a
120 whale-like object, going from infinity up, and came round
onto a block end—and it **submerged,** to reappear a matter
of seconds later. But on this occasion, the block end, which
had been on my right, was now on my left, so I realized
immediately that while in the process of surfacing, as it
may, it had rotated. And with the predominant wind, the
south-west wind, it appeared to be, I would say, at that
stage drifting easily across.

So I called to my friend Willie Frazer, who incidentally
had a sighting of an object on the loch almost a year ago to
130 the very day. I called him, and he come up and joined me.
We realized that it was drifting towards us, and, in fact, it
came to within I would say about 250, 300 yards.

In no way am I even attempting to convert anybody to
the religion of the object of Loch Ness. I mean, they can
believe it, but it doesn't upset me if they don't believe it.
Because I would question very much if I hadn't the extraordinary experience of seeing this object. If I hadn't seen it
I would have without question given a lot of skepticism to
what it was. But I saw it, and nothing can take that away.

140   —Ian Cameron, a retired superintendent of
                                  the Northern Police Force, lives with his
                                  wife Jessie in Inverness, Scotland, at the
                                  head of the loch. A keen angler, he is an
                                  authority on the Atlantic salmon.

"I'm gobsmacked, I just didn't know what it was."

Right, I'm driving along the loch side, glancing out of the
window. You can see the rock formation, I was just down
on the road there, it just rises. I saw this boiling in the

water. I thought, "No, it can't be anything," and I carried on
150 a wee bit. Then I looked again, and I saw three black
humps. I mean, you know, there's the chance, I've seen
something in the water. But what is it?

So I'm gobsmacked, I'm looking out the window, I
just didn't know what it was. Then the people came
behind me, and they obviously wanted me to move. But I
didn't want to lose sight of this thing. So I just pulled over
to the side, grabbed my camera, and I thought I was being
very cool and very **nonchalant** and took two or three
photos. In fact, as I say, I had taken nine or ten, without
160 realizing, I just punched the button. It was just a pity it
was a small camera.

NOVA: Did anybody else see anything?

WHITE: Yeah, the other two people who were there—
I was just so excited I didn't get their name and address or
anything—they saw it exactly the same as me. Because the
wee wifey, who would have been a lady in her fifties, on
holiday, she was Scottish, she said to me, "I've not been in
the bar this morning!" And her husband said, "Ach, it's an
eel! It's an eel!" And I said, "There's no eels that big!" And
170 he said, "Ach, it's otters!" And I said, "You don't get otters
swimming out like that!"

I saw what I saw, and I'm not going to be dissuaded.
It wasn't just an imagination. I'm a sane guy, and I've got
no ax to grind. As I say I sell pet food! What use to me is
the Loch Ness Monster? Unless I can invent a food called,
I don't know, Monster Munchies perhaps?

> —Richard White lives in the village of Muir
> of Ord, north of Inverness. He runs his
> own business selling pet food.

VOCABULARY
DEVELOPMENT

nonchalant (nän′shə·länt′)
adj.: matter-of-fact; showing
no concern or worry.

How can you tell from the
sentence the meaning of the
word *nonchalant* (line 158)?

_____

_____

_____

_____

_____

_____

_____

_____

_____

_____

TEXT STRUCTURE

Circle the words *NOVA* and
WHITE in lines 162 and 163.
What does this text format
indicate?

_____

_____

_____

_____

_____

_____

OWN THE TEXT

Practicing the Standards   Create an outline showing the main topics and supporting details of this article. On your outline, indicate the article's basic sections and its anecdotal features. Filling out the time line on the next page will help you write your outline.

_____

_____

_____

_____

_____

_____

_____

_____

_____

_____

_____

_____

_____

_____

_____

KEEPING TRACK

Personal Word List   In your Personal Word List, record the words in this article whose meanings can be found from the context.

Personal Reading Log   Add this article to your Personal Reading Log. You may want to include your own ideas about the Loch Ness Monster. Give yourself 4 points on the Reading Meter.

Checklist for Standards Mastery   Use the Checklist for Standards Mastery to see how much progress you have made in understanding informational texts.

Birth of a Legend  ■ *Interactive Reading,* page 118

Interact with an Informational Text

Time Line   Creating a time line can be a good way to understand certain kinds of informational text. Fill in the vertical time line below to show the events described in "Birth of a Legend." The dates and time periods have been filled in for you. Next to each date, write a summary of what happened during that time period.

First century A.D. _____

_____

_____

_____

A.D. **565** _____

_____

_____

_____

1933, Spring _____

_____

_____

_____

1934, January _____

_____

_____

_____

_____

1974 _____

_____

_____

_____

1974–present _____

_____

_____

_____

BEFORE YOU READ

"Greyling," a story based on an old legend, has something in common with the many other tales passed down through the ages. First, a **metamorphosis,** or transformation, takes place, as in the story of the frog who turns into a handsome prince. Second, things are counted in threes, like the three stepsisters in "Cinderella" or the three little pigs.

Before you read, you might want to know that according to legend, *selchies* (sel'kēz) are seals who rise from the waves, change into humans, and come ashore. Selchies are great friends of the mermaids. Legend has it that a mermaid once died to save a seal's life and that ever since then, selchies have done all they could to help mermaids.

Reading Standard 3.4 Analyze the relevance of the setting (for example, place, time, customs) to the mood, tone, and meaning of the text.

Greyling

Jane Yolen

VISUALIZE

Pause at line 13. Describe the **setting** of this story.

_____

_____

_____

_____

_____

_____

IDENTIFY

What does the couple want?

_____

Once on a time when wishes were aplenty, a fisherman and his wife lived by the side of the sea. All that they ate came out of the sea. Their hut was covered with the finest mosses that kept them cool in the summer and warm in the winter. And there was nothing they needed or wanted except a child.

Each morning, when the moon touched down behind the water and the sun rose up behind the plains, the wife would say to the fisherman, "You have your boat and your
10 nets and your lines. But I have no baby to hold in my arms." And again, in the evening, it was the same. She would weep and wail and rock the cradle that stood by the hearth. But year in and year out the cradle stayed empty.

Now the fisherman was also sad that they had no child. But he kept his sorrow to himself so that his wife would not know his grief and thus double her own. Indeed, he would leave the hut each morning with a breath of song and return each night with a whistle on his lips. His nets were full but his heart was empty, yet he never told his wife.

20 One sunny day, when the beach was a tan thread spun between sea and plain, the fisherman as usual went down to his boat. But this day he found a small grey seal stranded on the sandbar, crying for its own.

The fisherman looked up the beach and down. He looked in front of him and behind. And he looked to the town on the great grey cliffs that sheared off into the sea. But there were no other seals in sight.

So he shrugged his shoulders and took off his shirt. Then he dipped it into the water and wrapped the seal pup 30 carefully in its folds.

"You have no father and you have no mother," he said. "And I have no child. So you shall come home with me."

And the fisherman did no fishing that day but brought the seal pup, wrapped in his shirt, straight home to his wife.

When she saw him coming home early with no shirt on, the fisherman's wife ran out of the hut, fear riding in her heart. Then she looked wonderingly at the bundle which he held in his arms.

40 "It's nothing," he said, "but a seal pup I found stranded in the shallows and longing for its own. I thought we could give it love and care until it is old enough to seek its **kin.**"

The fisherman's wife nodded and took the bundle. Then she uncovered the wrapping and gave a loud cry. "Nothing!" she said. "You call this nothing?"

PREDICT

Pause at line 35. What do you think will happen when the fisherman brings the seal pup home?

_____
_____
_____
_____
_____
_____
_____
_____
_____
_____

VOCABULARY DEVELOPMENT

kin (kin) *n.:* relatives.

How can you figure out the meaning of *kin* (line 42)? Look in the previous sentence to find a context clue.

_____
_____
_____
_____
_____

WORD KNOWLEDGE

A *mantel* (line 67) is the shelf above a fireplace.

A *mantle* can also be a cloak or a shawl. The words are pronounced the same.

FLUENCY

This boxed paragraph reflects a dramatic shift in mood and contains strong images. Read this paragraph aloud several times. With each reading, try to improve the speed and smoothness of your delivery.

The fisherman looked. Instead of a seal lying in the folds, there was a strange child with great grey eyes and silvery grey hair, smiling up at him.

The fisherman wrung his hands. "It is a selchie," he
50 cried. "I have heard of them. They are men upon the land and seals in the sea. I thought it was but a tale."

"Then he shall remain a man upon the land," said the fisherman's wife, clasping the child in her arms, "for I shall never let him return to the sea."

"Never," agreed the fisherman, for he knew how his wife had wanted a child. And in his secret heart, he wanted one, too. Yet he felt, somehow, it was wrong.

"We shall call him Greyling," said the fisherman's wife, "for his eyes and hair are the color of a storm-coming sky.
60 Greyling, though he has brought sunlight into our home."

And though they still lived by the side of the water in a hut covered with mosses that kept them warm in the winter and cool in the summer, the boy Greyling was never allowed into the sea.

He grew from a child to a lad. He grew from a lad to a young man. He gathered driftwood for his mother's hearth and searched the tide pools for shells for her mantel. He mended his father's nets and tended his father's boat. But though he often stood by the shore or high in the town on
70 the great grey cliffs, looking and longing and grieving his heart for what he did not really know, he never went into the sea.

Then one wind-wailing morning just fifteen years from the day that Greyling had been found, a great storm blew up suddenly in the North. It was such a storm as had never been seen before: The sky turned nearly black and even the fish had trouble swimming. The wind pushed huge waves onto the shore. The waters gobbled up the little hut on the beach. And Greyling and the fisherman's

80 wife were forced to flee to the town high on the great grey cliffs. There they looked down at the **roiling,** boiling sea. Far from shore they spied the fisherman's boat, its sails flapping like the wings of a wounded gull. And clinging to the broken mast was the fisherman himself, sinking deeper with every wave.

The fisherman's wife gave a terrible cry. "Will no one save him?" she called to the people of the town who had gathered on the edge of the cliff. "Will no one save my own dear husband who is all of life to me?'"

90 But the townsmen looked away. There was no man there who dared risk his life in that sea, even to save a drowning soul.

"Will no one at all save him?" she cried out again.

"Let the boy go," said one old man, pointing at Greyling with his stick. "He looks strong enough."

But the fisherman's wife clasped Greyling in her arms and held his ears with her hands. She did not want him to go into the sea. She was afraid he would never return.

"Will no one save my own dear heart?" cried the

100 fisherman's wife for a third and last time.

But shaking their heads, the people of the town edged to their houses and shut their doors and locked their windows and set their backs to the ocean and their faces to the fires that glowed in every hearth.

"I will save him, Mother," cried Greyling, "or die as I try."

And before she could tell him no, he broke from her grasp and dived from the top of the great cliffs, down, down, down into the tumbling sea.

VOCABULARY
DEVELOPMENT

roiling (roil'in) *adj.:* stirred up; agitated.

Imaginative writers choose words for their sounds as well as for their meanings. What words in this passage rhyme?

_____

_____

_____

_____

_____

_____

PREDICT

What do you predict will happen when Greyling returns to the sea?

_____

_____

_____

_____

_____

_____

_____

_____

_____

110   "He will surely sink," whispered the women as they ran
from their warm fires to watch.

"He will certainly drown," called the men as they took
down their spyglasses from the shelves.

They gathered on the cliffs and watched the boy dive
down into the sea.

As Greyling disappeared beneath the waves, little
fingers of foam tore at his clothes. They snatched his shirt
and his pants and his shoes and sent them bubbling away
to the shore. And as Greyling went deeper beneath the

120   waves, even his skin seemed to **slough** off till he swam,
free at last, in the sleek grey coat of a great grey seal.

The selchie had returned to the sea.

But the people of the town did not see this. All they
saw was the diving boy disappearing under the waves and
then, farther out, a large seal swimming toward the boat
that **wallowed** in the sea. The sleek grey seal, with no effort
at all, eased the fisherman to the shore though the waves
were wild and bright with foam. And then, with a final
salute, it turned its back on the land and headed joyously

130   out to sea.

The fisherman's wife hurried down to the sand. And
behind her followed the people of the town. They searched
up the beach and down, but they did not find the boy.

"A brave son," said the men when they found his shirt,
for they thought he was certainly drowned.

"A very brave son," said the women when they found
his shoes, for they thought him lost for sure.

"Has he really gone?" asked the fisherman's wife of her
husband when at last they were alone.

140   "Yes, quite gone," the fisherman said to her. "Gone
where his heart calls, gone to the great wide sea. And

though my heart grieves at his leaving, it tells me this way is best."

The fisherman's wife sighed. And then she cried. But at last she agreed that, perhaps, it was best. "For he is both man and seal," she said. "And though we cared for him for a while, now he must care for himself." And she never cried again.

So once more they lived alone by the side of the sea in a new little hut which was covered with mosses to keep them warm in the winter and cool in the summer.

Yet, once a year, a great grey seal is seen at night near the fisherman's home. And the people in the town talk of it, and wonder. But seals do come to the shore and men do go to the sea, and so the townfolk do not dwell upon it very long.

But it is no ordinary seal. It is Greyling himself come home—come to tell his parents tales of the lands that lie far beyond the waters, and to sing them songs of the wonders that lie far beneath the sea.

150

160

INTERPRET

How would you state the **theme** of this folk tale? What does it tell you about our lives—about love and acceptance?

_____

_____

_____

_____

_____

_____

_____

_____

SKETCH TO STRETCH

Do you think this ending is happy or sad? In a sketch, draw a symbol of what the story suggests to you.

_____

_____

_____

_____

_____

_____

_____

_____

_____

_____

OWN THE STORY

Setting   What part does this story's setting—the sea—play in its plot? Write your answer in at least two sentences.

_____

_____

_____

_____

_____

Movie Setting   If you were to direct a movie based on "Greyling," what overall mood might you want the film to evoke? Write a description of the movie's settings, and describe how you would use costumes, sound effects, and lighting to enhance the mood of the narrative.

_____

_____

_____

_____

_____

_____

KEEPING TRACK

Personal Word List   List in your Personal Word List the words you learned from this story.

Personal Reading Log   As you record "Greyling" in your Personal Reading Log, write a few sentences about it for a book-review segment on a TV talk show. Give yourself 3 points on the Reading Meter.

Checklist for Standards Mastery   You've just completed activities having to do with setting. Now, use the Checklist for Standards Mastery to see how well you've mastered the related reading standards.

Greyling ■ *Interactive Reading,* **page 128**

PROJECT

Go Beyond a Literary Text

Retelling Chart "Greyling" is a retelling of an old legend. Suppose *you* were the storyteller. How would you tell the story?

You would have to consider the basic story elements in a retelling. Write your ideas for a retelling of this tale on the lines below. Here are the story elements to consider:

1. **Setting,** including place and time

2. **Characters,** including the seal

3. **Conflict**

4. **Climax**

5. **Resolution**

6. **Theme**

Retelling of "Greyling"

Chapter 4

We Still Believe

Chapter Preview In this chapter you will—

Strategy Launch:
"Save the Last Word for Me"

LITERARY FOCUS: THEME

The **theme** of a work of literature is its revelation or observation about life. A story's or poem's theme is not the same as its subject. Theme is what the story or poem or play *says about* the subject. For example, a story may be about a person who struggles to win a contest. The story's theme may be "Winning isn't everything."

Most themes are not stated directly. We must use key details in the story to arrive at a statement of theme. To do this, we make inferences. There is no one correct theme in a work of literature: Different readers may come up with different themes.

A STRATEGY THAT WORKS: "SAVE THE LAST WORD FOR ME"

Everyone's got something to say about what they read. But since no two people read a story in exactly the same way, you may feel unsure about your conclusions. One way to feel more confident about your ideas is to relate them to a very specific passage in what you've read. To do this, use the "Save the Last Word for Me" strategy.

POINTERS FOR USING "SAVE THE LAST WORD FOR ME"

)))) Read the text; mark passages you find interesting or important.

)))) When you're finished reading, re-read and identify what you think is the most important passage. Write it down.

)))) Then, write why you chose that passage. Include at least two reasons for your choice.

)))) Read the passage you selected to a small group, and let the group discuss it. Then, read to the group the reasons you chose that passage. If you wish, after your discussion, rewrite your reasons, or add to them. This is your last word! No one can disagree, add to, or change what you finally write.

Reading Standard 1.3 Use word meanings within the appropriate context, and show ability to verify those meanings by definition, restatement, example, comparison, or contrast.

Reading Standard 2.3 (Grade 6 Review) Connect and clarify main ideas by identifying their relationships to other sources and related topics.

Reading Standard 3.5 Identify and analyze recurring themes (e.g., good versus evil) across traditional and contemporary works.

BEFORE YOU READ

Times change: What we wear, where we live, how we travel, the language we use—all change. At heart, though, humanity seems to change very little. Ideas about right and wrong, cowardice and courage, and hope and despair, occupy much of our thoughts, just as they occupied the thoughts of people living hundreds and even thousands of years ago.

The essence of humanity is reflected in literature. You can read a love poem by Petrarch, an Italian poet who lived hundreds of years ago, and be struck by how similar its message is to the message of a poem written just last year.

After you read this folk tale, "The Wise Old Woman" by Yoshiko Uchida, you'll read a contemporary poem, "Legacy II" by Leroy V. Quintana. You'll see how the two selections reflect similar **themes**.

The Wise Old Woman

Yoshiko Uchida

IDENTIFY

Where and when does this story take place? Underline the passages revealing this information.

VOCABULARY DEVELOPMENT

decree (dē·krē′) v.: order; rule.

Many long years ago, there lived an arrogant and cruel young lord who ruled over a small village in the western hills of Japan.

"I have no use for old people in my village," he said haughtily. "They are neither useful nor able to work for a living. I therefore **decree** that anyone over seventy-one must be banished from the village and left in the mountains to die."

10   "What a dreadful decree! What a cruel and unreasonable lord we have," the people of the village murmured. But the lord fearfully punished anyone who disobeyed him, and

Text from "The Wise Old Woman" from *The Sea of Gold and Other Tales from Japan,* adapted by Yoshiko Uchida. Copyright © 1965 by Yoshiko Uchida. Reprinted by permission of *The Bancroft Library.*

so villagers who turned seventy-one were tearfully carried into the mountains, never to return.

Gradually there were fewer and fewer old people in the village and soon they disappeared altogether. Then the young lord was pleased.

"What a fine village of young, healthy, and hard-working people I have," he bragged. "Soon it will be the finest village in all of Japan."

20 Now, there lived in this village a kind young farmer and his aged mother. They were poor, but the farmer was good to his mother, and the two of them lived happily together. However, as the years went by, the mother grew older, and before long she reached the terrible age of seventy-one.

"If only I could somehow deceive the cruel lord," the farmer thought. But there were records in the village books and everyone knew that his mother had turned seventy-one.

30 Each day the son put off telling his mother that he must take her into the mountains to die, but the people of the village began to talk. The farmer knew that if he did not take his mother away soon, the lord would send his soldiers and throw them both into a dark dungeon to die a terrible death.

"Mother—" he would begin, as he tried to tell her what he must do, but he could not go on.

Then one day the mother herself spoke of the lord's dread decree. "Well, my son," she said, "the time has come
40 for you to take me to the mountains. We must hurry before the lord sends his soldiers for you." And she did not seem worried at all that she must go to the mountains to die.

IDENTIFY

Pause at line 13. What do the villagers and the young lord disagree about?

_____

_____

_____

_____

_____

_____

INTERPRET

Pause at line 29. What **conflict** does the young farmer face?

_____

_____

_____

_____

_____

_____

_____

_____

_____

_____

_____

_____

_____

_____

VOCABULARY DEVELOPMENT

clustered (klus'tərd) *v.*: gathered in a group.

Circle the word in the sentence that helps you figure out the meaning of *clustered*.

INTERPRET

Pause at line 62. What do the mother's actions reveal about her **character**?

_____

_____

_____

_____

_____

_____

_____

_____

_____

_____

_____

_____

_____

_____

_____

_____

"Forgive me, dear mother, for what I must do," the farmer said sadly, and the next morning he lifted his mother to his shoulders and set off on the steep path toward the mountains. Up and up he climbed, until the trees **clustered** close and the path was gone. There was no longer even the sound of birds, and they heard only the soft wail of the wind in the trees. The son walked slowly, for he

50   could not bear to think of leaving his old mother in the mountains. On and on he climbed, not wanting to stop and leave her behind. Soon, he heard his mother breaking off small twigs from the trees that they passed.

"Mother, what are you doing?" he asked.

"Do not worry, my son," she answered gently. "I am just marking the way so you will not get lost returning to the village."

The son stopped. "Even now you are thinking of me?" he asked, wonderingly.

60   The mother nodded. "Of course, my son," she replied. "You will always be in my thoughts. How could it be otherwise?"

At that, the young farmer could bear it no longer. "Mother, I cannot leave you in the mountains to die all alone," he said. "We are going home and no matter what the lord does to punish me, I will never desert you again."

So they waited until the sun had set and a lone star crept into the silent sky. Then, in the dark shadows of night, the farmer carried his mother down the hill and they

70   returned quietly to their little house. The farmer dug a deep hole in the floor of his kitchen and made a small room where he could hide his mother. From that day, she spent all her time in the secret room and the farmer carried meals to her there. The rest of the time, he was careful to

work in the fields and act as though he lived alone. In this way, for almost two years he kept his mother safely hidden and no one in the village knew that she was there.

Then one day there was a terrible commotion among the villagers, for Lord Higa of the town beyond the hills threatened to **conquer** their village and make it his own.

80

"Only one thing can spare you," Lord Higa announced. "Bring me a box containing one thousand ropes of ash and I will spare your village."

The cruel young lord quickly gathered together all the wise men of his village. "You are men of wisdom," he said. "Surely you can tell me how to meet Lord Higa's demands so our village can be spared."

But the wise men shook their heads. "It is impossible to make even one rope of ash, sire," they answered. "How can we ever make one thousand?"

90

"Fools!" the lord cried angrily. "What good is your wisdom if you cannot help me now?"

And he posted a notice in the village square offering a great reward of gold to any villager who could help him save their village.

But all the people in the village whispered, "Surely, it is an impossible thing, for ash crumbles at the touch of the finger. How could anyone ever make a rope of ash?" They shook their heads and sighed, "Alas, alas, we must be conquered by yet another cruel lord."

100

The young farmer, too, supposed that this must be, and he wondered what would happen to his mother if a new lord even more terrible than their own came to rule over them.

When his mother saw the troubled look on his face, she asked, "Why are you so worried, my son?"

VOCABULARY DEVELOPMENT

conquer (kaŋ'kər) v.: defeat; get control of by winning.

Underline the words in line 80 that help you understand what *conquer* means.

INTERPRET

Re-read lines 84–92, and circle the words *wise* and *wisdom* whenever they appear. Why might the writer have chosen to repeat this idea so often?

_____

_____

_____

_____

_____

_____

_____

_____

_____

_____

_____

_____

_____

_____

_____

_____

_____

INTERPRET

How does the mother's response to the problem (lines 110–114) reveal her worth?

_____

_____

_____

_____

_____

_____

_____

_____

_____

_____

_____

IDENTIFY

Underline the second impossible task (lines 124–126).

VOCABULARY DEVELOPMENT

bewilderment
(bə·wil′dər·mənt) n.: state of confusion; puzzlement.

Which words in line 130 help you figure out the meaning of bewilderment? Underline those words.

So the farmer told her of the impossible demand made by Lord Higa if the village was to be spared, but his mother did not seem troubled at all. Instead she laughed softly and said, "Why, that is not such an impossible task. All one has to do is soak ordinary rope in salt water and dry it well. When it is burned, it will hold its shape and there is your rope of ash! Tell the villagers to hurry and find one thousand pieces of rope."

The farmer shook his head in amazement. "Mother, you are wonderfully wise," he said, and he rushed to tell the young lord what he must do.

"You are wiser than all the wise men of the village," the lord said when he heard the farmer's solution, and he rewarded him with many pieces of gold. The thousand ropes of ash were quickly made and the village was spared.

In a few days, however, there was another great commotion in the village as Lord Higa sent another threat. This time he sent a log with a small hole that curved and bent seven times through its length, and he demanded that a single piece of silk thread be threaded through the hole. "If you cannot perform this task," the lord threatened, "I shall come to conquer your village."

The young lord hurried once more to his wise men, but they all shook their heads in **bewilderment.** "A needle cannot bend its way through such curves," they moaned. "Again we are faced with an impossible demand."

"And again you are stupid fools!" the lord said, stamping his foot impatiently. He then posted a second notice in the village square asking the villagers for their help.

Once more the young farmer hurried with the problem to his mother in her secret room.

"Why, that is not so difficult," his mother said with a quick smile. "Put some sugar at one end of the hole. Then tie an ant to a piece of silk thread and put it in at the other end. He will weave his way in and out of the curves to get to the sugar and he will take the silk thread with him."

"Mother, you are remarkable!" the son cried, and he hurried off to the lord with the solution to the second problem.

Once more the lord commended the young farmer and rewarded him with many pieces of gold. "You are a brilliant man and you have saved our village again," he said gratefully.

But the lord's troubles were not over even then, for a few days later Lord Higa sent still another demand. "This time you will undoubtedly fail and then I shall conquer your village," he threatened. "Bring me a drum that sounds without being beaten."

"But that is not possible," sighed the people of the village. "How can anyone make a drum sound without beating it?"

This time the wise men held their heads in their hands and moaned, "It is hopeless. It is hopeless. This time Lord Higa will conquer us all."

The young farmer hurried home breathlessly. "Mother, Mother, we must solve another terrible problem or Lord Higa will conquer our village!" And he quickly told his mother about the impossible drum.

His mother, however, smiled and answered, "Why, this is the easiest of them all. Make a drum with sides of paper and put a bumblebee inside. As it tries to escape, it will buzz and beat itself against the paper and you will have a drum that sounds without being beaten."

TEXT STRUCTURE

Pause at line 142. A story pattern has been established. How would you describe the pattern?

_____
_____
_____
_____
_____
_____
_____
_____
_____
_____
_____
_____
_____
_____
_____
_____
_____
_____
_____
_____
_____
_____
_____

PREDICT

Pause at line 177. Will the young farmer tell the young lord about his mother, or will he lie?

_____

_____

_____

_____

IDENTIFY

Circle the phrase in the paragraph beginning at line 183 that you feel is most important.

• • • • • • Notes • • • • • •

_____

_____

_____

_____

INTERPRET

What does the change in the young lord's behavior reveal about the **theme** of the story?

_____

_____

_____

_____

_____

170　　The young farmer was amazed at his mother's wisdom. "You are far wiser than any of the wise men of the village," he said, and he hurried to tell the young lord how to meet Lord Higa's third demand.

When the lord heard the answer, he was greatly impressed. "Surely a young man like you cannot be wiser than all my wise men," he said. "Tell me honestly, who has helped you solve all these difficult problems?"

The young farmer could not lie. "My lord," he began slowly, "for the past two years I have broken the law of the 180　land. I have kept my aged mother hidden beneath the floor of my house, and it is she who solved each of your problems and saved the village from Lord Higa."

He trembled as he spoke, for he feared the lord's displeasure and rage. Surely now the soldiers would be summoned to throw him into the dark dungeon. But when he glanced fearfully at the lord, he saw that the young ruler was not angry at all. Instead, he was silent and thoughtful, for at last he realized how much wisdom and knowledge old people possess.

190　　"I have been very wrong," he said finally. "And I must ask the forgiveness of your mother and of all my people. Never again will I demand that the old people of our village be sent to the mountains to die. Rather, they will be treated with the respect and honor they deserve and share with us the wisdom of their years."

And so it was. From that day, the villagers were no longer forced to abandon their parents in the mountains, and the village became once more a happy, cheerful place in which to live. The terrible Lord Higa stopped sending his

200   impossible demands and no longer threatened to conquer them, for he too was impressed. "Even in such a small village there is much wisdom," he declared, "and its people should be allowed to live in peace."

And that is exactly what the farmer and his mother and all the people of the village did for all the years thereafter.

SAVE THE LAST
WORD FOR ME

Re-read the story, and locate the passage you think is the most important. How would you translate that passage into a statement of the story's **theme**?

_____
_____
_____
_____
_____
_____
_____
_____
_____
_____
_____
_____
_____
_____
_____
_____
_____
_____

Fuji from the Mountains of Isu *by Hiroshige.*

IDENTIFY

Re-read lines 1–6, and under-line the words that describe the speaker's grandfather.

TEXT STRUCTURE

The Spanish words for *north, south, east,* and *west* are laid out on the page like a compass so the reader can tell what each word means. How do the directions trans-late into English?

_____

_____

_____

_____

_____

_____

SAVE THE LAST WORD FOR ME

Which lines of the poem hold the most meaning for you? How would you state the poem's **theme,** based on those lines?

_____

_____

_____

_____

_____

_____

_____

Legacy II

Leroy V. Quintana

Grandfather never went to school
spoke only a few words of English

a quiet man; when he talked
talked about simple things
5   planting corn or about the weather
sometimes about herding sheep as a child

One day pointed to the four directions
taught me their names
                    El Norte
10   Poniente   Oriente
                    El Sur

He spoke their names as if they were
one of only a handful of things
a man needed to know

15   Now I look back
only two generations removed
realize I am nothing but a poor fool
who went to college

trying to find my way back
20   to the center of the world
where Grandfather stood
that day

OWN THE SELECTIONS

Comparing Themes   Complete the "Save the Last Word for Me" cards on the next page. Then, get together with a group to compare the passages you chose and to discuss how the themes of these two selections are alike.

KEEPING TRACK

Personal Word List   Add any words you learned in the story and the poem to your Personal Word List. Note which Spanish and English words share *cognates* (käg′nāts)—that is, similar ancestors.

Personal Reading Log   Jot down your ideas about the themes of the story and the poem in your Personal Reading Log. Do you think the same themes are still found in the stories and poems of today? Give yourself 4 points on the Reading Meter.

Checklist for Standards Mastery   Track your progress in mastering the standards on the Checklist for Standards Mastery.

The Wise Old Woman;
Legacy II ▪ *Interactive Reading,* page 138

Interact with Literary Texts

"Save the Last Word for Me" Cards   To discover the theme of a work, fill out a "Save the Last Word for Me" card. On the front, copy the most important passage from the work as you see it. On the back, give two reasons for your choice, and state how the passage relates to the theme.

Fill out "Save the Last Word for Me" cards for "The Wise Old Woman" and "Legacy II." Then, sum up the similarities and differences between the themes in the space provided below.

"The Wise Old Woman": Most Important Passage	Two Reasons for My Choice
	What it says about theme:

"Legacy II": Most Important Passage	Two Reasons for My Choice
	What it says about theme:

Similarities and Differences Between Themes:

_____

_____

_____

_____

The Diary of Anne Frank

Interact with a Literary Text

Theme Chart   To find themes in a work of literature, you must look at the whole work and the details.

Find four (or more) details in *The Diary of Anne Frank* that suggest a theme to you. (Include direct quotations if you wish.) Write these details in the boxes on the theme chart. State what act and scene they come from, and briefly describe what happens. In the theme box, write down the idea that these details suggest to you. Be sure all the details relate to one theme.

Detail
Detail
Detail
Detail

Theme

CHARACTER

from The Diary of a Young Girl

Interact with a Literary Text

Words/Thoughts/Actions Chart   We get to know people from literature and from real life through what they say, how they think and feel, and what they do. Fill in the following chart with details from *The Diary of a Young Girl.* For each detail, tell what you learned about Anne.

Anne's Words, Thoughts, Actions	What I Learned About Anne

My Description of Anne:

_____

_____

_____

_____

Anne and Margot Frank

COMPARE & CONTRAST

Interact with an Informational Text

Main-Idea Chart   The essay on Anne and Margot Frank is a student work that might have been written as an assignment for a language arts class. To find the writer's main idea, use a graphic like the following one.

Topic of Essay
COMParison between Anne and Margot

Writer's Position on the Topic (Main Idea)
Characteristics Anne shares with Margot and different characteristics they have.

Supporting Details	**Supporting Details**	**Supporting Details**
Margot is mature, polite, helpful, quiet, and obedient. while Anne is loud, active curious and selfish,	Anne is childish, outgoing, cheerful, and peppy while Margot is charming, shy, not sociable, and has a hard time trusting others	In common, Anne and Margot are very brave and strong in the inside. They have the strength to survive through harsh times.

A Tragedy Revealed: A Heroine's Last Days

Interact with an Informational Text

"Main Idea and Examples" Chart   Fill in a "Main Idea and Examples" chart to understand how details in "A Tragedy Revealed" support the writer's main idea. The top box expresses a main idea from the text. In the boxes below, write examples from the article that support that main idea. If you can think of more than three examples, add them.

5/5

Main Idea from "A Tragedy Revealed"

"As we somehow knew she must be, Anne Frank, even in the most frightful extremity, was indomitable."

Supporting Detail 1

"It was almost impossible to not give up hope. and when a person gave up, his face became empty and dead." "Anne Frank, too, still had her face up to the very last she had never given up hope and was brave.

Supporting Detail 2

Anne Franks was more optimistic than scared in the camp. She was happy and felt like she had been liberated even through all the hard work.

Supporting Detail 3

Anne Frank was still encouraging Margot even through all the misery and hard times in the camp.

Walking with Living Feet

MAIN
IDEA

Interact with a Literary Text

Details Organizer   Use a details organizer to identify and make connections between details in informational writing. Fill in the organizer below to identify and connect the details in "Walking with Living Feet." First, write down the key details in each paragraph of "Walking with Living Feet." Then, use these details to make a statement about the main idea of the whole essay.

	Detail
Reading about the holocaust is nothing compared to seeing. It.	People scraped off the white paint trying to escape gas chambers.
Detail Majdanek stands right in the city of Lublin.	**Detail** About 5 of the barracks are filled with shoes of some people that were killed.
Detail There was over 850,000 pairs of different shoes.	**Detail** At the end of the camp was another gas chamber and the crematorium.
Detail Majdanek reeks of death everywhere	**Detail** There is no signs that life even existed in the cemetery.
Main Idea Seeing and reading about the Holocaust are different in many ways. People were tortured in the camps and over 850,000 people died. It was a harsh period for the jews.	

Camp Harmony;
In Response to Executive
Order 9066

4/5

Interact with Literary Texts

Side-by-Side Chart   The details in a literary selection work together to create a **theme,** or message about life. Different writers may explore the same theme but use different topics and details to convey that theme. Writers might also explore the same topic but convey very different themes.

Fill in the following chart with important details from "Camp Harmony" and "In Response to Executive Order 9066." Then, write the theme of each piece in the last cell of each column. Finally, write a general statement about the similarities and differences in the themes.

Important Details from "Camp Harmony"	Important Details from "In Response to Executive Order 9066"
Family were assigned their own apartment and not sepparated	She packed galoshes and three packs of tomato seeds.
Must be in rooms by 9 P.M and at 10 PM Lights must be off.	She has bad spelling and messy room
Japanese-Americans didn't have the rights to a fair trial	Favorite food is hot dog.
Wired fencing preventing escape.	Her best friend is white and her is Denise
Insufficient amount of ~~food~~ food for one family.	Denise doesn't trust her because she is Japanese
Theme The government had to do anything that would protect the nation	**Theme** Japanese Americans weren't trusted because of their race.

General Statement or Conclusion:

Even though the camps weren't as harsh as others, it was wrong to put them in camps because of their race.

The Gettysburg Address

LITERARY DEVICES

Interact with a Literary Text

Repetition Chart Nonfiction works like the Gettysburg Address often contain literary devices. Speeches, especially, use repetition of words, sounds, and structures. The use of repetition helps emphasize the writer's ideas and fixes those ideas in listeners' minds. Fill out the following repetition chart with details from the Gettysburg Address.

Repetition of Sounds	Repetition of Words	Repetition of Structures

from I Have a Dream

Interact with a Literary Text

Allusion Listing   Martin Luther King, Jr.'s, "I Have a Dream"
speech is full of allusions. **Allusions** are references to experiences
that people share. An allusion may refer to a person or a place or to
an event from literature, history, religion, politics, sports, or science.
Re-read King's famous speech, and fill in the chart below with
allusions you find. In the column to the right, explain where the
allusion comes from.

Allusion in "I Have a Dream"		Where the Allusion Comes From
	⟷	
	⟷	
	⟷	
	⟷	

from **The Power of Nonviolence**

for use with
Holt Literature and Language Arts,
page 339

LOGICAL NOTES

Interact with an Informational Text

Main-Idea Note Cards   Clarify your understanding of the excerpt from *The Power of Nonviolence* by taking notes on what you read. Fill in the note cards below with the main ideas from the text. Review your notes to clarify your understanding of the writer's ideas.

Note Card 1

Note Card 2

Note Card 3

Note Card 4

Note Card 5

Note Card 6

Literature

AUTHOR STUDY

Gerda Weissmann was a fifteen-year-old schoolgirl when Germany invaded Poland in 1939. Gradually, during the German occupation of Poland, the Weissmanns lost all their freedoms; each member of the family was eventually arrested by the Nazis. Gerda was the only member of her family who survived. Gerda spent three years in slave-labor camps. She survived a brutal "death march" from Germany to Czechoslovakia, through snow and freezing temperatures. When the Allies liberated Czechoslovakia, Gerda weighed only sixty-eight pounds. Among the American soldiers who saved her was her future husband, Kurt Klein. Gerda Weissmann Klein eventually settled in the United States, where she and her husband raised two daughters—who never had to experience the horrors that their mother miraculously survived.

BEFORE YOU READ

This excerpt from Gerda Weissmann Klein's book *All But My Life* opens when the Nazis are about to take her father to a slave-labor camp in Sucha. Her beloved brother Arthur has already been taken away. Gerda and her mother have orders to go to a slave-labor camp in Wadowitz the following Monday.

Here is what you need to know before you begin Gerda's story:
- World War II lasted from 1939 to 1945. Germany invaded Poland in 1939.
- The Nazis targeted Jews, Gypsies, and many other groups of people for extinction. Many victims of the Nazis were used for slave labor during the war. Millions of them died from disease, starvation, and freezing temperatures. Millions of others were killed in the death camps, which were designed to kill large numbers of people quickly and efficiently.
- SS troops were the main enforcers of Nazi policy. SS troopers were known for their brutality.

Reading Standard 3.5 Identify and analyze recurring themes (e.g., good versus evil) across traditional and contemporary works.

from All But My Life

Out of the Ghetto

Gerda Weissmann Klein

In the morning we did not talk about the train that was to leave a few hours hence. Silently we sat at the table. Then Papa picked up his Bible and started to read. Mama and I just sat looking at him. Then all of a sudden Papa looked up and asked Mama where my skiing shoes were.

"Why?" I asked, baffled.

"I want you to wear them tomorrow when you go to Wadowitz."

"But Papa, skiing shoes in June?"

10 He said steadily: "I want you to wear them tomorrow."

"Yes, Papa, I will," I said in a small voice.

I wonder why Papa insisted; how could he possibly have known? Those shoes played a vital part in saving my life. They were sturdy and strong, and when three years later they were taken off my frozen feet they were good still. . . .

When it came time to leave, Papa and Mama embraced. Then Papa put his hands on my head in **benediction**, as he had done for Arthur. His hands trem-

20 bled. He held me a while, then lifted my chin up and looked into my eyes. We were both weeping.

"My child," he managed. It was a question and a promise. I understood. I threw myself wildly into his embrace, clinging to him in **desperation** for the last time. I gave him my most sacred vow: "Yes, Papa." We had always understood each other, but never better than in that last hour.

From *All But My Life* by Gerda Weissmann Klein. Copyright © 1957, 1995 by Gerda Weissmann Klein. Reprinted by permission of **Hill and Wang, a division of Farrar, Straus and Giroux, LLC.**

INFER

Pause at line 10. Why does the father insist that Gerda wear skiing shoes?

_____

_____

_____

_____

_____

_____

_____

_____

_____

VOCABULARY DEVELOPMENT

benediction (ben′ə·dik′shən) *n.*: blessing.

desperation (des′pər·ā′shən) *n.*: state of hopelessness or despair.

Circle the word *ghetto* in line 50. A ghetto is a part of a city where a group of people lives because of social or economic pressure. Usually, a ghetto is a poor neighborhood.

reluctantly (ri·luk′tənt·lē) *adv.:* unwillingly.

Review the memoir up to this point, and identify a passage that has special meaning for you.

And so we went to the station, across the meadow, taking the longer way, trying to be together as long as possible. A crowd was already assembled. Papa was asked for his

30 identification. We went out onto the platform with him. The train would leave in a few minutes. People were saying their heartbreaking goodbyes.

Papa entered the last car and went to the open platform at the rear to see us as long as possible. There he stood in his good gray suit, his only one, his shoulders sloping, his hair steel gray in the sun, on his breast the yellow star and black word.

There he stood, already beyond my reach, my father, the center of my life, just labeled "Jew."

40 A shrill whistle blew through the peaceful afternoon. Like a puppet a conductor lifted a little red flag. Chug-chug-chug—puffs of smoke rose. The train began to creep away. Papa's eyes were fixed upon us. He did not move. He did not wave. He did not call farewell. Unseen hands were moving him farther and farther away from us.

We watched until the train was out of sight. I never saw my father again.

Only after several moments did I become conscious of the fact that Mama was with me. She took my hand like that of

50 a baby and we started to walk toward the ghetto. I didn't once look at her. Only after a while did I realize that she too was weeping.

That night she fixed me something to eat and I ate to please her. She asked me to sleep with her in Papa's bed. I did so **reluctantly.** I was half asleep when I felt her arms around me, clinging to me in desperation. All my life I shall be sorry that I did not feel more tender that night. When

Mama needed me most, I wanted to be alone. I pulled away
like a wounded animal that wants to lick its wounds in
60   peace. Finally I fell asleep—on a pillow soaked with my
mother's tears.

　　　We rose early. While I put on my skiing boots, Mama
made me a cup of cocoa—the precious cocoa which she
had saved for almost three years for a special occasion.

　　　"Aren't you eating, Mama?" I asked.

　　　"It's Monday," she answered. Mama had fasted every
Monday for half a day since Arthur had left.

　　　"But today," I said, "you should eat something."

　　　"Today especially not," she answered from the window,
70   holding the ivory-bound prayer book she had carried as a
bride. She prayed and watched me—and I watched her. The
chives were uprooted on the windowsill. Yesterday we had
taken out the few remaining jewels, sewed some into Papa's
jacket, Mama's corset, my coat.

　　　A shrill whistle blew through the ghetto. It was time to
leave.

　　　When we had made our way downstairs, we saw the
woman with the lovely complexion, Miss Pilzer, screaming
and begging to be allowed to go with her mother. The
80   dying old woman was thrown on a truck meant for the
aged and ill. Here the SS man kicked her and she screamed.
He kicked her again.

　　　On the same truck were Mr. Kolländer, the man with
paralyzed legs, and the mother with her little girls. The
twins were smiling; unaware of what was happening, they
were busy catching the raindrops. An epileptic woman was
put on the truck; her dog jumped after her. The SS man
kicked him away, but the dog kept on trying to get in the
truck. To our horror, the SS man pulled his gun and shot

Pause at line 74. What do
Gerda's mother's actions
reveal about her **character**?

_____

_____

_____

_____

_____

_____

_____

_____

_____

_____

_____

_____

_____

_____

_____

_____

_____

_____

_____

DECODING TIP

Underline the word *invalids* in line 93. In its singular form, *invalid,* the word has two pronunciations and two meanings. *Invalid* can be an adjective meaning "not valid" or "not acceptable." When an adjective, it is pronounced in·val'id. When *invalid* is a noun meaning "sick person," it is pronounced in'və·lid. Which way is *invalids* pronounced in line 93?

_____

_____

_____

INTERPRET

Pause at line 106. Why do you think Gerda still had faith in humanity, even though she had seen the brutality the Nazis carried out against the Jews?

_____

_____

_____

_____

_____

_____

_____

_____

the dog. I looked toward Mama. I wanted to run to her. I wanted to be held by her—to be comforted. Now it was too late.

Leaving the invalids behind, we assembled in a field in a suburb of Bielitz[1] called Lärchenfeld. Here we were left in the rain to wait. After about four hours the SS men finally came in a shiny black car, their high boots polished to perfection. A table was set up and covered with a cloth—a tablecloth in the rain!—and at that table they checked the lists of the people present.

100   We had all assembled.

Why? Why did we walk like meek sheep to the slaughterhouse? Why did we not fight back? What had we to lose? Nothing but our lives. Why did we not run away and hide? We might have had a chance to survive. Why did we walk deliberately and obediently into their clutches?

I know why. Because we had faith in humanity. Because we did not really think that human beings were capable of committing such crimes.

It cleared up and then it rained again. I was tired and
110   hungry, hot and cold, and still we stood at attention, losing track of time.

Finally, certain trucks were loaded and driven off amid crying and screaming. Mama kept looking into my eyes. Her courage gave me strength. Those of us who remained were lined up in rows of four and ordered to march to the station. Instead of marching us across the meadow directly to the station, we were marched all around town. Oh God, I asked, I prayed, oh God, are they going to do to us what

---

1. **Bielitz** (bye'litz) is Gerda's beloved hometown, in Poland.

they did to Erika's mother? Will we dig our own grave? Oh
God, no, no, NO! Don't let it happen—don't! I am afraid. I
don't want to die. Don't hurt Mama. Don't—

I saw Bielitz, my dear childhood town. Here and there
from behind a curtain a familiar face looked out. We kept
on marching. People went marketing. Guards beat strag-
glers with rubber truncheons.[2] Oh God, I prayed, don't let
it happen!

Someone pushed a baby carriage. Workmen were
repairing a street. On the butcher shop they were painting a
new sign. We were marching. A dry-goods store was deco-
rating its show window. We had bought the flowered fabric
for my dress there, but it was not colorfast. Oh God, don't
let it happen, don't, I prayed, don't! At the movie theater
they were putting up a sign announcing a new feature—
and we were marching.

I noticed Mama grow pale. She was gripping her
suitcase tightly. I jerked it out of her hand.

"You hurt my hand," she said in a whisper.

Finally we approached the railroad station on the
opposite side of town. Beyond the station were open
meadows where the annual circus set up its tents. There
we waited again.

From mouth to mouth the news traveled: "Merin!"
Merin was here. The king of the Jews, as he was called, had
arrived. His headquarters had been at Sosnowitz where
there were the biggest Jewish congregation, the largest
factories and shops in which Jews worked.

INFER

Pause at line 134. What do
you imagine the people
going through their everyday
activities were thinking while
their neighbors were being
forced to march?

---

2. **truncheons** (trun′chənz) *n*.: clubs.

**WORD
KNOWLEDGE**

The word *liquidate* (line 149)
means "wiping out or killing
off." When people are liquidated, they are killed. When
debts are liquidated, they are
cancelled.

INFER

What does Gerda mean
when she says that Merin
"was their kind" (line 160)?

_____

_____

_____

_____

_____

_____

_____

_____

_____

_____

_____

_____

_____

_____

_____

Customarily the Nazis established someone such as Merin as head of Jewish communities and gave him the job of liquidating them. It was said that Merin lived in luxury,

150 that he had visited Goebbels,[3] that he was the only Jew to own a car, that he was indescribably wealthy. I imagine these things were true. Certainly he was master of life and death.

I looked at him now. He was short, perhaps a bit over five feet, pale and thin; he had watery eyes, dull brown hair, and he was clad in a brown raincoat. He talked in a hoarse whisper. He pulled a bottle of schnapps from his pocket, drank first and then handed it to the SS men about him. They drank after him. I saw it all and marveled. Yes, he was

160 all right for them, he was their kind.

"I am glad you took the suitcase," Mama said very quietly. We were no longer standing at attention. "I would have fainted," she continued.

"Why didn't you throw it away?"

Her voice was without tone as she answered, "Arthur's picture is in it."

Merin was walking in our direction. Mama prompted me, "Go ask him if we are going to Wadowitz."

I asked him in Polish—it was known that his German

170 was very poor.

He looked at me, his eyes without expression.

"Are you crazy?" was his hoarse reply.

Mama asked me what he had said, but I had no time to answer, for "All march down this way" came the command.

---

3. **Joseph Goebbels** (gō′bəls) was the Nazi propagandist who helped pop-
ularize Hitler's philosophies.

In our clenched fists we held our working cards from the shop, those sacred cards that we thought meant security. As we marched along in pairs, we heard cries and screams ahead of us. Mama and I held hands tightly. A cane
180 hit our hands. They unclasped. The cane pointed at me, a voice shouted, "How old?" My answer came, "Eighteen." The cane shoved me aside. Like a puppet I went. I knew Mama was marching on—in the opposite direction. I did not turn around. I could not. I knew she was looking at me as Papa had looked at us from the platform of the train. I knew that if I turned around we would have to run to each other—and that they would beat us or shoot us. We had to go on alone.

I was herded toward a group where my friends Ilse,
190 Rita, and Ruth stood. Our parents were led to the other side of the meadow where a barbed-wire **enclosure** had been set up. I did not see Mama, but we saw how earrings were torn out of ears, rings from fingers, and all thrown into a pail. I pictured Mama's wide wedding band with Papa's inscription in it among them, and I pictured the SS men digging greedily into the gold. Digging into people's love and pledges. . . .

I saw a couple we knew. With their baby in their arms they walked up to the SS man, the judge of life and death.
200 He told them to give the baby to those marching to the right, and motioned them to the group to the left. I saw the couple look at each other. Then I turned away, feeling the wide field revolving around me. When I looked again, sick and limp, I saw the couple embracing their baby—and walking slowly toward the right. . . .

INTERPRET

Why did they think that their working cards (line 176) meant security?

_____

_____

_____

_____

_____

_____

_____

VOCABULARY DEVELOPMENT

enclosure (en·klō′zhər) n.: closed-in place; area surrounded by a boundary or fence.

· · · · · · Notes · · · · · ·

_____

_____

_____

_____

_____

_____

_____

_____

INFER

Pause at line 218. Why do you think Merin acts as he does?

_____

_____

_____

_____

_____

_____

_____

_____

_____

_____

_____

SAVE THE LAST WORD FOR ME

Just about any passage that you choose from this selection will be a powerful one. Choose the passage you feel is most powerful. Give two reasons for your choice.

_____

_____

_____

_____

_____

_____

_____

_____

_____

We had assumed all along that we were going on a train, but now a truck came for us. I was the last one to enter it. Then I screamed, "I want to go to my mother!" and jumped down. Just then Merin passed. He looked at me, and with strength unsuspected in that little man, he picked me up and threw me back on the truck.

"You are too young to die," he said tonelessly.

I glared at him. "I hate you," I screamed. "I hate you!"

His eyes were without expression; there was a faint smile on his pale, thin lips. It would have been easy for him to order me down and send me with my mother. Why did he not? Strange that the man who sent my mother to death had pushed me into the arms of life!

Someone fastened the canvas across the back of the truck and Merin walked away. Then above all the screams coming from behind the barbed wire I heard my mother. "Where to?" she called. I spread my arms and leaned out of the truck. I did not know the answer.

"Mama! Mama!" I called, as if the word could convey all I felt. Above all the confused, painful cries I heard Mama's voice again.

"Be strong!" And I heard it again like an echo: "Be strong!" Those were my mother's last words to me.

As the trucks pulled away, the late afternoon sun came through the gray clouds for a moment. Its rays touched the roof of the church, glistening wet. The church bells were ringing. And then the sun disappeared.

Once more Bielitz was gray and dark, and as the truck rolled on, the city disappeared before my misty eyes.

Theme   Get together with a partner, and discuss the theme of this selection. Compare your choices of important passages and your reasons for choosing them.

_____

_____

_____

_____

_____

_____

_____

_____

_____

_____

_____

_____

_____

_____

Personal Word List   Add to your Personal Word List any new words you learned in this story.

Personal Reading Log   This story deals with people trying to survive under terrifying conditions. Write your reaction to this story in your Personal Reading Log. React to any single event that stands out for you, or if you prefer, react to the story as a whole. Give yourself 5 points on the Reading Meter.

Checklist for Standards Mastery   What have you learned about themes? Use the Checklist for Standards Mastery to see how far you have come in mastering the standards.

Out of the Ghetto ▪ *Interactive Reading,* page 159

Go Beyond a Literary Text

Museum Brochure   The U.S. Holocaust Memorial Museum was chartered by Congress in 1980. It is dedicated to educating the public about the Holocaust and to providing a memorial to all those who suffered and died at the hands of the Nazi regime. Research this museum, and create a brochure for visitors. Use the template that follows to help guide your research.

The Museum and Its Mission: _____

_____

_____

_____

Museum Location: _____

_____

_____

Hours/Tours: _____

_____

_____

Collections and Archives: _____

_____

_____

Online Exhibits: _____

_____

_____

Other: _____

_____

_____

_____

_____

_____

Information

Reading Standard 2.3 (Grade 6 Review) Connect and clarify main ideas by identifying their relationships to other sources and related topics.

BEFORE YOU READ

The following text is taken from parts of a Web site dedicated to the memory of Anne Frank and her family. When online, users can navigate the site by clicking buttons. Here, you'll turn the pages to learn about the Franks.

An Anne Frank Scrapbook

Frankfurt, Germany ■ 1929–1933

Anne Frank, born on June 12, 1929, was the second daughter of Otto and Edith Frank, both from respected German-Jewish families.

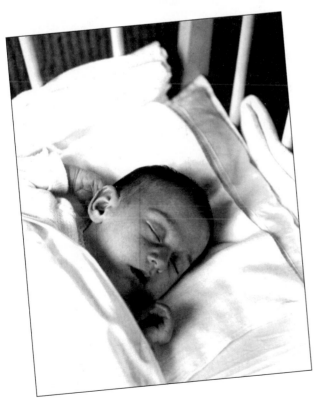

Anneliese Frank sleeping in a crib shortly after her birth.

TEXT STRUCTURE

Skim through this selection, paying close attention to the headings. How is this selection organized?

_____

_____

_____

_____

_____

_____

_____

_____

_____

_____

_____

From *Anne Frank: Her Life and Times,* accessed May 23, 2001, at
http://www.annefrank.com/site/af_life/af_scrpbk/af_scrpbk01/story01.html.
Copyright © 2001 by **Anne Frank Center USA Inc.** Reprinted by permission of the publisher.

An Anne Frank Scrapbook   **169**

DECODING TIP

This selection contains many European names. Languages such as German and Dutch pronounce many letters differently from English. For example, in *Aachen* (line 7), the *ch* is not pronounced as in *church*. It is pronounced as in *Bach*.

VOCABULARY DEVELOPMENT

tolerance (täl'ər·əns) *n.:* respect for views different from your own.

INTERPRET

What is ironic about Otto Frank's having served in the German army?

_____

_____

_____

_____

_____

_____

_____

_____

_____

_____

_____

Otto Frank could trace his family heritage in Frankfurt back to the seventeenth century, and Edith Hollander Frank came from a prominent Aachen family.

Anne and her older sister, Margot, were raised in Germany in an atmosphere of **tolerance;** the Franks had friends
10 of many faiths and nationalities. Otto Frank served honorably as an officer in the German army during World War I.

Anne and her sister, Margot, with their father before their move to Amsterdam.

The Move to Amsterdam ■ 1933–1940

However, the circumstances of the early 1930s dramatically altered the situation for the Frank family. In the summer of 1933, Otto Frank left Frankfurt for Amsterdam to set up a branch of his brother's company called the Dutch Opekta Company.

Anne, her mother, and Margot hold hands in Frankfurt before their move.

Less than a year later, Edith, Margot, and Anne (four
20   years old) joined Otto in Amsterdam.

A portrait (right) of Anne taken in a photo booth. The date and her weight are printed on the border.

By the mid-1930s, the Franks were settling into a normal routine in their apartment at 37 Merwedeplein: The girls were attending school, the family took vacations at the beach, and their circle of Jewish and non-Jewish friends grew.

A page from Anne's photo album, with portraits and beach scenes.

In 1938, Otto expanded his business, going into partnership with a merchant, Hermann van Pels, also a Jewish refugee from Nazi Germany.

Living Under Nazi Rule ■ 1940–1942

30 Unfortunately, the Frank's belief that Amsterdam offered them a safe **haven** from Nazism was shattered when, in May 1940, Germany invaded the Netherlands and the Franks were once again forced to live under Nazi rule.

Anne Frank attended the local Montessori school, but after summer recess in 1941, the Nazi authorities forbade Jews to attend school with non-Jews.

In the first few years of the occupation, Anne and Margot continued to socialize with their friends and attend school.

But the Nazi administration, **in conjunction with** the Dutch Nazi Party and civil service, began issuing anti-Jewish decrees.

VOCABULARY DEVELOPMENT

haven (hā′vən) *n.:* safe place, refuge.

What clue word helps you with the meaning of *haven*? Circle it.

in conjunction (kən·juŋk′ shən) **with:** in cooperation with.

· · · · · · **Notes** · · · · · ·

_____

_____

_____

_____

_____

_____

_____

_____

_____

_____

_____

WORD KNOWLEDGE

The word *mandatory*, in the first line under the heading, means "forced." It means that the Jews were handed over to authorities and forced to work in the camps.

The word is based on *manus,* Latin for "hand." How is *manus* used in *manufacture, manual,* and *mandate*?

_____

_____

_____

_____

_____

_____

In May 1942, all Jews aged six and older were required to wear a yellow Star of David on their clothes. This was to set them apart from non-Jews.

40   All Jews had to register their businesses and, later, surrender them to non-Jews. Fortunately, Otto Frank, in anticipation of this decree, had already turned his business over to his non-Jewish colleagues Victor Kugler and Johannes Kleiman.

The Franks Plan to Go into Hiding ■ 1942

By 1942, mass arrests of Jews and mandatory service in German "work camps" were becoming routine. Fearful for their lives, the Frank family began to prepare to go into hiding.

50   They already had a place in mind—an annex of rooms above Otto Frank's office at 263 Prinsengracht in Amsterdam.

In addition, people on the office staff in the Dutch Opekta Company had agreed to help them. Besides Kugler and Kleiman, there were Miep and Jan Gies, Bep Voskuijl, and Bep's father—all considered to be trustworthy.

The Frank family in Amsterdam.

These friends and employees not only agreed to keep the business operating in their employer's absence; they agreed to risk their lives to help the Frank family survive.

60 Mr. Frank also made arrangements for his business partner, Hermann van Pels, along with his wife, Auguste, and their son, Peter, to share the Prinsengracht hideaway.

The Secret Annex ■ 1942–1944

While these preparations were secretly under way, Anne celebrated her thirteenth birthday on June 12, 1942. On July 5, 1942, her sister, Margot, received a call-up notice to be deported to a Nazi "work camp."

Even though the hiding place was not yet ready, the Frank family realized that they had to move right away. They hurriedly packed their belongings and left notes implying
70 that they had left the country. On the evening of July 6, they moved into their hiding place.

WORD KNOWLEDGE

The word *implying* (line 69) means "suggesting." *Imply* and *infer* are closely linked. Speakers or writers imply; listeners and readers infer.

The people reading the notes would *infer*, or guess, that the Franks had left the country.

IDENTIFY

What caused the Frank family to flee to a hiding place?

Less than two months after this photo was taken, Anne and her family went into hiding.

A week later, on July 13, the van Pels family joined the Franks. On November 16, 1942, the seven residents of the Secret Annex were joined by its eighth and final resident, Fritz Pfeffer.

For two years the Franks were part of an extended family in the Annex, sharing a confined space and living under constant dread of detection and arrest by the Nazis and their Dutch sympathizers.

80

Arrest and Deportation ■ 1944

At approximately 10 A.M., August 4, 1944, the Frank family's greatest fear came true. A Nazi policeman and several Dutch collaborators appeared at 263 Prinsengracht, having received an anonymous phone call about Jews hiding there. They charged straight for the bookcase leading to the Secret Annex.

WORD KNOWLEDGE

A *collaborator* (kə·lab′ə·rā·tər) in this context (line 83) is someone who works with the enemy. Collaborators can also be people who work together on projects.

Karl Joseph Silberbauer, an Austrian Nazi, forced the
residents to turn over all valuables. When he found out
that Otto Frank had been a lieutenant in the German
90 army during World War I, he was a little less hostile. The
residents were taken from the house, forced into a covered
truck, taken to the Central Office for Jewish Emigration,
and then to Weteringschans Prison.

Two of the helpers, Victor Kugler and Johannes Kleiman,
were also imprisoned for their role in hiding the family.
Miep Gies and Bep Voskuijl were not arrested, although
Miep was brought in for questioning by the police.

*A hinged bookcase
at the rear of the
office wall was all
that separated the
Secret Annex from
the outside world.*

On August 8, 1944, after a brief stay in Weteringschans
Prison, the residents of the Secret Annex were moved to
100 Westerbork transit camp. They remained there for nearly a
month, until September 3, when they were transported to
the Auschwitz death camp in Poland. It was the last
Auschwitz-bound transport ever to leave Westerbork.

INTERPRET

Re-read the last sentence on
this page. What powerful
irony does this sentence
convey—that is, a sense that
we know something that the
people involved do not
know?

In October 1944, Anne and Margot were transported from Auschwitz to the Bergen-Belsen concentration camp in Germany. Thousands died from planned starvation and epidemics at Bergen-Belsen, which was without food, heat, medicine, or elementary sanitary conditions.

Hundreds of women and children were packed into one room at the Bergen-Belsen concentration camp. Bergen-Belsen became overcrowded with prisoners as the Nazis retreated from the Eastern Front.

110   Anne and Margot, already **debilitated,** contracted typhus and grew even sicker. Margot, nineteen years old, and Anne, fifteen years old, died in February and March, 1945.

After the War

Otto Frank was the only resident of the Annex to survive the Holocaust. He found it difficult to settle permanently in Amsterdam with its constant reminders of his lost family.

He and his second wife, Elfried Geiringer, also an Auschwitz survivor, moved to Basel, Switzerland, in 1953. Otto Frank died on August 19, 1980; he was ninety-one.

VOCABULARY DEVELOPMENT

debilitated (dē·bil′ə·tāt′əd) *adj.:* weakened; made feeble.

Circle the words that help you figure out the meaning of *debilitated.*

CONNECT

This Web site reveals what one family—the Franks—experienced during World War II. Where might you look to find other sources on the topic of World War II?

OWN THE TEXT

Main Ideas   What ideas about the human condition can you draw from this collection of photographs and text?

Work with a partner to write a paragraph about the main ideas you can infer from "An Anne Frank Scrapbook" and from Gerda Weissmann Klein's account of her experiences.

_____

_____

_____

_____

A Poem from a Photograph   Take one of the photographs in this scrapbook that you find especially interesting. Write a poem about the picture and the people in it. You do not have to find rhymes; you should find strong images to describe what you see in the picture and how it makes you feel. Give your poem a title.

_____

_____

_____

_____

KEEPING TRACK

Personal Word List   Add the new words you encountered to your Personal Word List. Look and listen for new words about history in newspapers, in magazines, and on television.

Personal Reading Log   As you add this selection to your Personal Reading Log, write about the part that most interested you. Give yourself 2 points on the Reading Meter.

Checklist for Standards Mastery   Use the Checklist for Standards Mastery to see how far you have come in mastering the standards.

An Anne Frank Scrapbook ■ *Interactive Reading,* page 169

Go Beyond an Informational Text

Web Page   Suppose you were to create a Web page that contains a scrapbook of photographs of you and your family from different stages in your lives. What would you select to include in it?

Write a list of six possible kinds of photos you would include. (You don't have to be thinking of specific photographs.) Write a heading and a caption for each photo.

Photo/Description	Heading/Caption for Photo
#1	
#2	
#3	
#4	
#5	
#6	

Literature

BEFORE YOU READ

The Diary of Anne Frank would never have been published if it weren't for Miep Gies (mēp gēs). Miep saved Anne's diaries and the family photographs that she found in the attic after the family had been taken by the SS.

The next selection is from Miep Gies's book *Anne Frank Remembered,* which she published in 1987. Here she describes a night in the Secret Annex.

Before reading the selection, here is what you should know:
- Henk is Miep's husband.
- Jo Koophius is managing the factory that once belonged to Otto Frank.

Reading Standard 3.5
Identify and analyze recurring themes (e.g., good versus evil) across traditional and contemporary works.

A Family in Hiding

Miep Gies with Alison Leslie Gold

Anne and the others had been after us to come and sleep upstairs in the hiding place. There was something always imploring about the way they asked, so one day I took some things from home with me to work, some night-clothes for Henk and myself.

When I announced to Anne and Mrs. Frank that we would finally come to spend the night, the **enthusiasm** was extraordinary. You'd have thought that Queen Wilhelmina herself was about to make a visit. Rubbing her hands together, Anne was filled with excitement. "Miep and Henk will be sleeping over tonight," she ran to tell the others upstairs.

10

INFER

Implore (line 3) means "beg." It comes from a Latin word meaning "cry out, weep." What does this word suggest about the family?

_____

_____

_____

From *Anne Frank Remembered: The Story of the Woman Who Helped to Hide the Frank Family* by Miep with Alison Leslie Gold. Copyright © 1987 by Miep Gies and Alison Leslie Gold. Reprinted by permission **Simon & Schuster, Inc.**

Backyards

Private Office

Kitchen

Rear Office

Small Storeroom

Front Office

1st Floor

Swinging Cupboard

Landing

Bed

Bed

Bed

Sofa

Storeroom

Storeroom

Storeroom

2nd Floor

Folding Bed

Bed

Table

Kitchen Dresser

Bed

Cupboard

Flat Roof

Attic

3rd Floor

Prinsengracht Street

Hoping to moderate her mood, I told Mrs. Frank, "We don't want any fuss."

Mrs. Frank smiled, put her hand on my shoulder, and squeezed. On my way out, I repeated my request to Mr. Frank, who was climbing downstairs: "Now, no fuss, please."

With a smile on his face, he shook his head. "No, no, of ...e not."

Chapter 4

We Still Bel...

During the day I told Jo Koophuis of our plan. After work Henk came, and when the last worker had gone home at five-thirty, the end of the workday, Mr. Koophuis bade us good night. He locked the door of the building behind him. The office was quite silent with everyone gone. We made sure that the lights had been turned off; then we went up the stairway, pulled open the bookcase, and went in. I closed it behind us.

30   Each of our friends greeted us happily as we made our way upstairs. "The last worker has gone," I informed them. Right away, there were voices, footsteps, the toilet flushing, a cabinet shutting. Already, it was noisy upstairs; the place had come alive.

    Anne directed us toward the bedroom she shared with Margot. At Anne's insistence, Henk and I had been **allotted** their room. Anne and Margot were going into the room with their parents for the night. Anne pulled me to her bed, neatly made up, and told me she wanted me to put my things there. Amused, I told her that I'd be honored, and
40   put my night things on her bed, and Henk's on Margot's bed.

    Shortly, it was time for the radio broadcasts, and the entire group trooped down to Mr. Frank's office below to pull up chairs and gather around the Phillips radio on the table. The whole room bristled with excitement when the near-and-yet-so-far voice of Radio Orange came through the radio. "Here is Radio Orange. All things went well today. The English . . ." and on it went, filling us with hope and with information, our only real connection to the
50   still-free outside world.

When it was time to sit down to eat, Henk and I were given seats of honor, as we had been at our anniversary dinner. All nine of us squeezed in around the table.

This time, Mrs. Frank and Margot had supervised the cooking. The food was tasty and filling.

With the blackout frames up and the electric light on, along with the heat from the cooking, the room became toasty-warm, cozy. We sat long over coffee and dessert, talking, our friends devouring the novelty of our presence.

60　They seemed to be **insatiable** for our company.

As I sat, I became aware of what it meant to be imprisoned in these small rooms. As this feeling registered, I felt a taste of the helpless fear that these people were filled with, day and night. Yes, for all of us it was wartime, but Henk and I had the freedom to come and go as we pleased, to stay in or go out. These people were in a prison, a prison with locks inside the doors.

Reluctantly, we said good-nights, remembering that Mr. and Mrs. Van Daan could not go to bed until we'd

70　gone. Henk and I and the Frank family trooped down the stairway to the floor below. Here we said a second round of good-nights, and Henk and I got ready for bed in our little room, surrounded by Anne's movie-star faces on the wall.

I climbed into Anne's hard little bed, which was very toasty with blanket upon blanket, so many blankets that I couldn't imagine how Anne could ever be taken with a chill. The room was cool otherwise, and as I settled in as cozily as I could, I could hear every sound being made in the other rooms: Mr. Van Daan coughing, the squeak of

80　springs, the sound of a slipper dropping beside a bed, the toilet flushing, Mouschi [the cat] landing on his padded feet somewhere above me.

The Westertoren clock struck at fifteen-minute intervals. I'd never heard it so loud; it echoed and **reverberated** through the rooms. The church was right across the back gardens from the Annex. In the office, the building blocked the sound. During the day, by the time I heard the ringing in my front office, the sound had been muted and cushioned by the entire building. It was soothing and distant.

90

All through the night I heard each ringing of the Westertoren clock. I never slept; I couldn't close my eyes. I heard the sound of a rainstorm begin, the wind come up. The quietness of the place was overwhelming. The fright of these people who were locked up here was so thick I could feel it pressing down on me. It was like a thread of terror pulled taut. It was so terrible it never let me close my eyes.

For the first time I knew what it was like to be a Jew in hiding.

reverberated
(ri·vur′bə·rāt·əd) *v.*: echoed.

Underline the context clue that helps you guess that *muted* (line 89) means "muffled" or "softened."

What do we mean when we say that someone is mute?

_____

_____

_____

_____

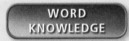

What **figures of speech,** or imaginative comparisons, does Miep use to help us feel her terror? Underline them.

SAVE THE LAST WORD FOR ME

Read through the story again, and identify the most important passage. Then, give two reasons for your choice.

_____

_____

_____

_____

_____

_____

OWN THE STORY

Main Idea   What is the main idea in this part of Miep's story? What passage in the text best supports this idea? Discuss your answers with a partner.

_____

_____

_____

_____

Comparing Ideas   In "A Family in Hiding," Miep sends a strong message to readers about learning to identify with people who are suffering. With a partner, discuss other works you've read or movies you've seen that convey a similar message.

KEEPING TRACK

Personal Word List   As you add the new words you learned in this selection to your Personal Word List, describe how context clues helped you clarify their definitions.

Personal Reading Log   Add this memoir to your Personal Reading Log. Include a note telling which of the stories about Anne Frank in this chapter made the strongest impression on you. You get 2 points on the Reading Meter for completing this selection.

Checklist for Standards Mastery   Assess how well you have mastered the standards for this chapter using the Checklist for Standards Mastery. Where did you make the most progress? Where can you improve?

A Family in Hiding ■ *Interactive Reading,* page 181

Go Beyond a Literary Text

Dramatic Scene   Anne Frank's diary has, of course, been made into a play that has touched the hearts of millions. Now try turning Miep Gies's memoir into a dramatic scene, focusing on the night that Miep and Henk were invited to dine and sleep in the Annex. Outline, write, and perform the scene with a group of classmates.

To help you outline, write a brief description of each character in the list below. Then describe the sets, the lighting and sound effects, and the props the actors will need to use as they re-create Miep Gies's night in hiding.

Cast of Characters: _____
_____
_____
_____
_____
_____

Setting: _____
_____
_____
_____
_____

Light and Sound Effects: _____
_____
_____
_____
_____

Props: _____
_____
_____
_____
_____

Chapter 5

Imagine That!
Literary Devices

Strategy Launch:
"Charting Literary Devices"

LITERARY FOCUS: LITERARY DEVICES

When you interpret a work of literature, you look for **literary devices.** Writers use many literary devices to tell a story or write a poem. Some writers use a great deal of description. They use **similes** to compare unlike things, using a word such as *like* or *as.* They use **metaphors** to compare unlike things without a specific word of comparison. They use **personification** to make a nonhuman thing come alive. They use **irony** to make us sense the gap between what seems appropriate and what actually happens in life. They use **dialect** to help us hear how people talk. Writers also experiment with **sentence length.** Some use long complex sentences. Others prefer short punchy sentences. All of these devices make up a writer's special **style.**

A STRATEGY THAT WORKS: "CHARTING LITERARY DEVICES"

The following strategy will help you examine a text for certain literary devices. Once you have combed the text for these devices, ask yourself: "How do these devices help me interpret a plot, a character, or a theme?"

POINTERS FOR "CHARTING LITERARY DEVICES"

)))➡ First, read the text for enjoyment. Put sticky notes on passages that stand out for you. You'll return to them later. (In this book you can mark up the story, so you might put a star next to passages you think are significant.)

)))➡ Next, re-read the passages you marked up. Mark passages that use devices such as repetition, figures of speech, irony, or dialect.

)))➡ Finally, ask yourself: "What do those passages contribute to the text's plot, characterization, or theme?"

Reading Standard 1.1 Analyze idioms, analogies, metaphors, and similes to infer the literal and figurative meanings of phrases.

Reading Standard 2.8 (Grade 6 Review) Note instances of fallacious reasoning in text.

Reading Standard 3.6 Identify significant literary devices (e.g., metaphor, symbolism, dialect, irony) that define a writer's style, and use those elements to interpret the work.

BEFORE YOU READ

Your roof leaks. You hire someone to fix it, and he turns out to be very strange and a little scary. Not only does he fail to fix the roof, but he keeps asking for more money and threatens you for not paying. You begin to hate him. Hate is a powerful feeling, but can it actually make things happen?

The Overhead Man

Dan Greenberg

CHARTING LITERARY DEVICES

Pause at line 11. Underline words that are repeated so far. What effect does the **repetition** have on you?

_____

_____

WORD KNOWLEDGE

An **idiom** is an expression peculiar to a particular language. An idiom does not mean what it literally says. Underline the idiom in line 15. What does it say literally? What does it mean figuratively?

_____

_____

_____

Drip, drip, drip.

That was how it started. With drips. The roof in my parlor was leaking.

Drip, drip, drip.

The drips were constant, never-ending. Morning, noon, night.

Drip, drip, drip.

What could I do? I thought of trying to fix it, but I couldn't climb up there. When it was built back a hundred

10 years ago, my house had been a barn. Now it's a house with ceilings almost forty feet high.

"You'll need to wait until the rainy season ends," Felton, my next-door neighbor, told me.

Wonderful, I thought. The previous year, 1905, it rained cats and dogs for two and a half months straight here in San Francisco.

Drip, drip, drip.

I didn't know what I was going to do. Then, by pure chance, a notice on a wall jumped at me out of the blue.

20 "MAGGS & SON," it read. "Will fix anything. Chimneys, coal stoves, roofs, leaks. Satisfaction Guaranteed."

Perfect, I thought.

Maggs & Son turned out to be Maggs only. The first of Maggs's lies.

Maggs spat tobacco juice, missing my shoe by a mere inch and a half.

Maggs was a rough and raw sort with wild red-gray hair, a big red mustache, and bulging eyes. His teeth were stained brown with tobacco juice. His face was so red and

30 sore it looked as if he'd scrubbed it with a metal brush.

"What can I do for ye, Mizz—"

"Derby," I said. "Lucy Derby. I have a leak, Mr. Maggs, in my roof."

I showed him the leak. He told me he'd fix it for five dollars. That sounded fine to me, so we shook hands on it. Maggs went about his business, and I went about mine.

Maggs brought over his tools and ladders. Then he climbed up on the roof, tying himself in with ropes for safety. For about an hour, I heard him banging around up

40 there. When he came down, he was even redder in the face, if that were possible.

"She's all done," he told me.

"*She?*" I said.

"Your roof," he said. "Won't be givin' ye problems no more."

I paid him the five dollars, relieved to have the roof fixed. Or so I thought. The leak did stop, at least until midnight that night. Then it started again.

Drip, drip, drip.

WORD KNOWLEDGE

Underline "out of the blue" in line 19. What does this **idiom** mean literally? What does it mean figuratively?

_____

_____

_____

_____

_____

_____

PREDICT

What do you expect to happen later in the story, based on lines 23–24?

_____

_____

PREDICT

Why do you suppose the writer mentions these ropes (line 38)?

_____

_____

CHARTING LITERARY DEVICES

Circle the words that describe Maggs on this page. What kind of character do you think he is?

_____

_____

Pause at line 59. Do you believe Maggs's explanation? Explain.

_____

_____

_____

_____

_____

Pause at line 74. What do you think is going to happen to the red brick house?

_____

_____

_____

_____

Underline the **idiom** "hit the road" in line 76. What does it mean literally? What does it mean figuratively?

_____

_____

_____

_____

50   I went and got Maggs the next morning. He went through the same routine. He climbed up on the roof, banged around awhile, then came down and told me it was all fixed. Only this time, the fee was ten dollars.

"Ten dollars!" I cried.

He explained. It was a new leak, a bigger one this time. Sometimes, he said, fixing one leak caused a new leak to **erupt.** This explanation didn't make much sense to me, but I let it go. I had work to do. I paid him the money, and all was fine—for two days.

60   Drip, drip, drip.

The leak came back. Maggs came back, too, and he did pretty much the same thing. Only this time he asked for fifty dollars.

"Fifty dollars!" I protested. I told I would not pay him fifty dollars, not for fixing the same leak he was supposed to have "fixed" earlier. In fact, I told him that I wasn't going to pay him anything at all.

"Well that's a shame," he said, wiping his grizzled chin.

"Why is that a shame?" I asked.

70   "Because things seem to happen to people who don't pay me my money."

I blinked. "Things?"

"There's a red brick house on Nob Hill, near the hotel," he said. "You watch that house."

Watch that house? Whatever did he mean by that? Maggs wouldn't explain. He hit the road without his money. Two days later, on page 4 of the *Chronicle,* I saw it. A red brick house on Nob Hill had burned to the ground.

A chill went down my spine.

80   Had Maggs been threatening me? Fortunately, my roof was holding up fine. There were no more leaks. I hoped

that was the end of my dealings with Maggs, but I was not so lucky.

Two days after I read about the fire, he showed up.

"Mizz Derby," he said with an oily smile.

"Mr. Maggs," I said. "My roof is fine. The drips haven't returned. I don't believe I called for your services."

He spat some tobacco juice which again nearly hit my feet. "I come for me money," he said.

90　　I explained that I didn't intend to pay him any more money.

"Well," he said. "Ain't that a shame. Did ye hear about the red brick house, Mizz Derby?"

"Are you threatening me?" I asked.

He smiled an evil, tobacco-brown smile. It was clear: In not so many words he *was* threatening me. The price had gone up, too, to one hundred dollars.

"This is outrageous!" I said.

Maggs flashed another evil smile, then spat. "Ye do
100　what ye like, Mizz Derby," he said.

The rest is a blur to me. I remember going inside and trying to forget the whole situation. Then the dripping started again.

Drip, drip, drip.

No, it was not my imagination. But how was it possible? Had Maggs climbed up there and poked a new hole in the roof? How could he have? I would have heard him.

I couldn't sleep that night. The dripping had gotten to me. In the morning I was going to pieces. I had to do
110　something, so I spoke to Felton, my neighbor.

He said he could help. His brother-in-law knew someone. He'd get the word out.

CHARTING LITERARY DEVICES

Circle the words on this page that describe Maggs's appearance and actions. What do these descriptions tell you about the character of Maggs?

_____
_____
_____
_____
_____
_____
_____

WORD KNOWLEDGE

Underline the **idiom** "going to pieces" in line 109. What does it mean literally? What does it mean figuratively?

_____
_____
_____
_____
_____
_____
_____
_____

Circle the **simile** that compares Maggs to a jackal. A *jackal* is a wild dog known for its trickery. Jackals will eat anything, even rotten meat. How is Maggs like a jackal?

_____

_____

_____

_____

VOCABULARY DEVELOPMENT

fuming (fyōōm'iŋ) *v.* used as *adj.*: very angry. Literally, *fuming* means "giving off smoke or gas."

consequences (kän'si·kwen'səz) *n.*: results of an action.

· · · · · · Notes · · · · · ·

_____

_____

_____

_____

_____

_____

_____

_____

_____

At dusk that same day, there was a knock at my door. Oh good, I thought. Felton's fix-it man is here. When I opened the door, I found Maggs grinning at me like a jackal.

"Mr. Maggs," I said. "I did *not* call you here."

"Oh yes ye did," Maggs said.

120 It appeared that the brother-in-law's "friend" was none other than Maggs himself. He was here to fix the leak, and now the price had gone up to two hundred dollars.

"I won't pay it," I said.

"Yes you will," he said, his dim little eyes glittering at me.

And with that, Maggs went up on the roof. He set up his ladders and his ropes.

I went back into the house, **fuming.** I would *not* pay the two hundred dollars. I just wouldn't do it. For that matter, I didn't even *have* two hundred dollars to pay, even if I'd wanted to.

130 Then a strange thing happened. A feeling of hatred passed over me that was so dark and pure that it shook me to the bottoms of my shoes. I hated Maggs. I wanted to hurt Maggs. I wanted to make him suffer. I didn't care about the **consequences.** I didn't care about anything.

The feeling was like a fever. And, like a fever, it suddenly vanished, at just about the time I heard the screaming.

"Mizz Derby!" cried the choking voice. "HALP ME!"

I ran outside, and there was Maggs dangling off the edge of the roof.

140 "The rope!" he gasped, his voice failing.

I was frozen for a moment, trying to take it all in. Apparently, Maggs had fallen off his ladder and the rope from his waist had slipped around his neck.

"C-a-a-an-n-n't breathe!" he croaked.

I grabbed a long broomstick and started climbing the ladder. Only moments ago, I'd wanted to harm this man. Now, his life was in my hands. Should I save him? Suppose I just left him up there? Would the world be any poorer for the loss of a fellow like Maggs?

150 "The knife!" he sputtered. There was a knife on his belt.

I was up to him now. I reached out with the broomstick. He took it in his hand, and I pulled him toward me. Then I took the knife from his belt.

We were nose to nose now. His face had turned a shade of deep purple, shot through with broken blood vessels. His yellow eyes bulged at me.

It was my last chance. I could push him back now and leave him dangling. Or I could cut the rope and save him.

160 I cut the rope. Maggs swung himself onto the ladder. For a moment there, we were holding each other awkwardly. I could feel his fear.

Then we climbed down.

Maggs couldn't look me in the face. He took his gear and left. He turned before he got into his heap of a truck and gave me a look full of daggers.

I never saw Maggs again. I never paid him the two hundred dollars either, nor did I get my roof fixed. Several days later, San Francisco was hit with a **massive** earthquake.

170 Most of the houses in my area were destroyed by fire, including my own. That took care of the drip.

In the time since then, I've often thought about that night. Not the moment when Maggs was dangling there, but earlier, when I'd felt such hatred for the jackal. Had I actually *caused* Maggs's accident? Had Maggs willed that

PREDICT

Pause at line 149. Do you think Lucy will save Maggs? Why or why not?

_____

_____

_____

_____

_____

_____

WORD KNOWLEDGE

Underline the idiom "look full of daggers" in line 166. What does it mean literally? What does it mean figuratively?

_____

_____

_____

_____

_____

_____

_____

VOCABULARY DEVELOPMENT

massive (mas'iv) *adj.:* enormous; large-scale.

house on Nob Hill to catch fire? And my own house—it *did* burn down, though I tended to blame the earthquake and not the nasty Maggs. But still. . . .

OWN THE STORY

PRACTICING THE STANDARDS

Interpretation How would you interpret the story? Is this a story about sinister events that can't be explained, or is Maggs simply an old con man? Write a few sentences in which you interpret what happens in this story. Before you write, fill in the literary-devices chart on the next page. Do any details from the chart help you interpret the story? Explain.

_____

_____

_____

_____

_____

_____

KEEPING TRACK

Personal Word List Record the words you learned from this story in your Personal Word List. Put a star next to words you would like to use in your everyday conversation.

Personal Reading Log As you record this story in your Personal Reading Log, indicate whether or not you think it would make an effective movie. Give yourself 4 points on the Reading Meter.

Checklist for Standards Mastery Keep checking your progress in mastering the standards on the Checklist for Standards Mastery.

The Overhead Man ▪ *Interactive Reading,* page 190

Interact with a Literary Text

Literary Devices Chart   Fill out the following chart with examples from "The Overhead Man." When you are finished, see if your chart helps you interpret the story. Write your interpretation below.

Repetition	Figurative Language	Imagery	Dialect	Irony

My Interpretation: _____

_____

The Tell-Tale Heart

Interact with a Literary Text

Irony Chart   In **verbal irony** a person says one thing but means the opposite. In **situational irony** something happens that is the opposite of what we thought would happen or of what we think is the appropriate thing to happen. In **dramatic irony** the reader (or audience, in drama) knows something that a character in a story or play does not know.

Fill in this irony chart with examples of irony from "The Tell-Tale Heart." Be sure to compare your charts in class.

Verbal Irony	Situational Irony	Dramatic Irony

Edgar Allan Poe: His Life Revealed in His Work

for use with
Holt Literature and Language Arts,
page 364

FALLACIES

Interact with an Informational Text

Fallacy Wheel   Re-read the selection, and find six or more examples of faulty reasoning. Try to find at least one example of each type of fallacy. (To review types of faulty reasoning, see page 363 of *Holt Literature and Language Arts.*) Write each example in the circle with the appropriate label.

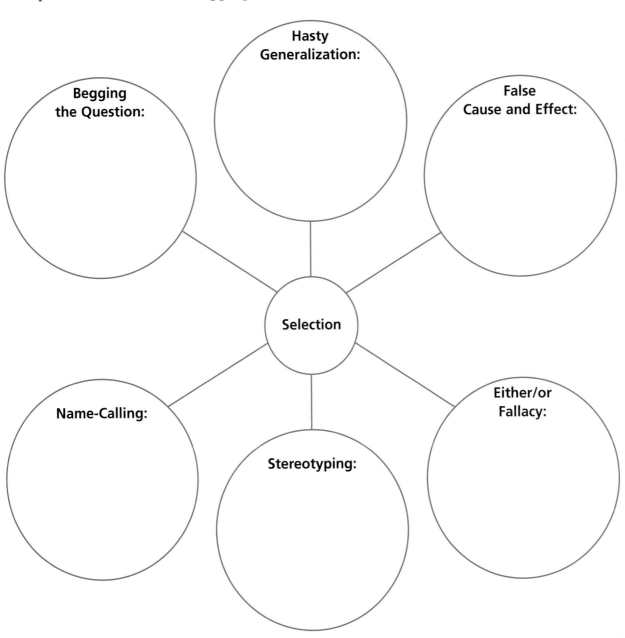

LITERARY
DEVICES

Raymond's Run

Interact with a Literary Text

Literary Device Pie Chart   In "Raymond's Run," Toni Cade
Bambara gives readers a rich feast of literary devices. **Literary devices**
include allusion, dialect, and figures of speech such as similes,
metaphors, and analogies. Find examples in the story of each type of
device, and write them in the chart below.

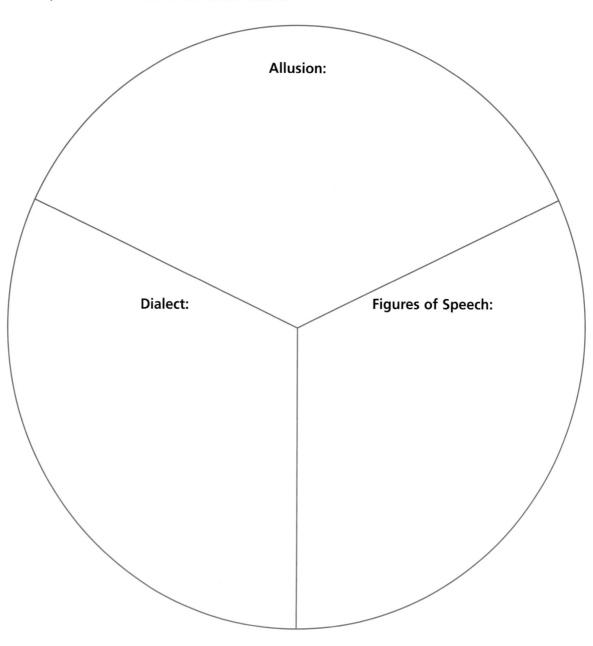

Allusion:

Dialect:

Figures of Speech:

Olympic Games *and* The Old Olympic Games: A Report

Interact with Informational Texts

Inference Chart In the chart below, factual statements from the encyclopedia article "Olympic Games" are listed in the left column. In the middle column, next to each fact, is an unsupported inference made by the writer of "The Old Olympic Games: A Report" using that fact. The right column has been left blank for you to fill in with a supported inference based on each factual statement.

The Olympics

Factual Statement from "Olympic Games"	Unsupported Inference from "The Old Olympic Games: A Report"	Supported Inference
The first recorded Olympic contest took place in 776 B.C.	The Olympic games began a long time ago, before anyone knew how to write.	
The only event in the first thirteen games was a running race of 210 yards.	The only thing the old Greeks could do was race. They weren't very strong, so they could run only 210 yards.	
In 708 B.C., wrestling and pentathlon (jumping, running, discus throw, javelin throw, and wrestling) were added.	Then they learned how to wrestle, jump, and throw things.	
In 648 B.C., the pancratium was added, a combination of boxing, wrestling, and kicking.	They didn't play fair, though, and kicked each other when they were boxing and wrestling.	
The Romans conquered Greece during the 140s B.C. . . . In A.D. 393, Emperor Theodosius I banned the games.	Some of them raced chariots using mules! If they were that silly, it's no wonder the Romans conquered them.	

My Mother Pieced Quilts

for use with
Holt Literature and Language Arts,
page 383

Interact with a Literary Text

Quilt of Literary Devices   In a poem, meaning is created by many
literary devices. Use this quilt of literary devices to sort out three
types of devices used in "My Mother Pieced Quilts."

Metaphor	Personification

Imagery

A word is dead;
The Word/La palabra

for use with
Holt Literature and Language Arts,
page 390

Interact with Literary Texts

Figurative Spokes   In the graphic organizer below, give examples
of the literary devices used in the poems by Emily Dickinson and
Manuel Ulacia. Write each example in the spoke that shows the type
of device and the poet who wrote it.

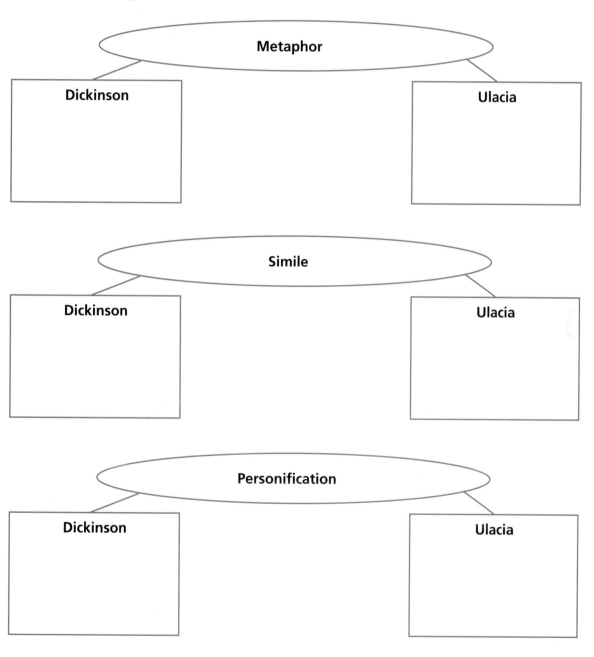

Literature

AUTHOR STUDY

During his lifetime, **Edgar Allan Poe** had some modest success as a writer and critic. It was only after his death, at the age of forty, that Poe achieved lasting fame and admiration. In addition to his stories that explore the dark side of the imagination (like "The Tell-Tale Heart"), Poe wrote detective stories. These tales (one of the most famous is "The Murders on the Rue Morgue") established him as the father of the modern detective story. What is "modern" about Poe's detective is that he uses intuition to solve crimes.

Poe's haunting, musical poetry had a major influence on the great French poets of the nineteenth century. In fact, it was the French poets who reintroduced Poe's poetry to his native land.

BEFORE YOU READ

Almost nothing about Edgar Allan Poe's life remains clear; there are points of confusion and disagreement over almost every aspect of his life and work. The following poem, "The Bells," was published in 1849. According to some scholars, Poe was living in the Bronx in New York City, near Fordham University, when he wrote the poem. He was supposed to have been inspired by the sound of the church bells ringing on the college campus. Other critics say it was the bells of Grace Church that he heard, from his house on Sixth Street in Manhattan.

Reading Standard 3.6 Identify significant literary devices (e.g., metaphor, symbolism, dialect, irony) that define a writer's style, and use those elements to interpret the work.

The Bells

Edgar Allan Poe

I

Hear the sledges[1] with the bells—

Silver bells!

What a world of merriment their melody foretells!

How they tinkle, tinkle, tinkle,

5   In the icy air of night!

While the stars that oversprinkle

All the heavens, seem to twinkle

        With a crystalline delight;

Keeping time, time, time,

10   In a sort of Runic[2] rhyme,

To the tintinnabulation[3] that so musically wells

From the bells, bells, bells, bells,

        Bells, bells, bells—

From the jingling and the tinkling of the bells.

II

15   Hear the mellow wedding bells

        Golden bells!

What a world of happiness their harmony foretells!

        Through the balmy air of night

        How they ring out their delight!—

20   From the molten-golden notes,

        And all in tune,

---

1. **sledges** *n.:* sleds.
2. **Runic** *adj.:* mystical. Runes are old sayings or poems that are very obscure.
3. **tintinnabulation** *n.:* ringing sound of bells. (Sound out the word syllable by syllable.)

IDENTIFY

Circle examples of **repetition** in stanza 1.

COMPARE & CONTRAST

What type of bell is described in stanza 1? What kind of bell is described in stanza 2? Briefly describe the difference in the types of bells.

_____

_____

_____

_____

_____

_____

_____

_____

_____

_____

_____

_____

_____

_____

_____

What a liquid ditty floats

To the turtle-dove that listens, while she gloats

On the moon!

25   Oh, from out the sounding cells,

What a gush of euphony[4] voluminously wells!

How it swells!

How it dwells

On the Future!—how it tells

30   Of the rapture that impels

To the swinging and the ringing

Of the bells, bells, bells—

Of the bells, bells, bells, bells,

Bells, bells, bells—

35   To the rhyming and the chiming of the bells!

III

Hear the loud alarum bells—

Brazen bells!

What a tale of terror, now their turbulency tells!

In the startled ear of night

40   How they scream out their affright!

Too much horrified to speak,

They can only shriek, shriek,

Out of tune,

In a clamorous appealing to the mercy of the fire,

45   In a mad expostulation with[5] the deaf and frantic fire,

Leaping higher, higher, higher,

With a desperate desire,

And a resolute endeavour

Now—now to sit, or never,

---

4. euphony (yōo′fə·nē) *n.:* pleasing sounds.
5. expostulation (ek·späs′chə·lā·shən) **with:** reasoning with; objecting to.

50   By the side of the pale-faced moon.

            Oh, the bells, bells, bells!

            What a tale their terror tells

               Of Despair!

            How they clang, and clash, and roar!

55   What a horror they outpour

       On the bosom of the palpitating air!

            Yet the ear, it fully knows,

              By the twanging,

              And the clanging,

60   How the danger ebbs and flows;

        Yet the ear distinctly tells,

             In the jangling,

             And the wrangling,

       How the danger sinks and swells,

65 By the sinking or the swelling in the anger of the bells—

             Of the bells—

       Of the bells, bells, bells, bells,

          Bells, bells, bells—

    In the clamor and the clanging of the bells!

IV

70   Hear the tolling of the bells—

           Iron bells!

What a world of solemn thought their monody[6] compels!

         In the silence of the night,

        How we shiver with affright

75   At the melancholy menace of their tone!

         For every sound that floats

       From the rust within their throats

---

6. **monody** (män′ə·dē) n.: solo that mourns the death of someone.

Edgar Allan Poe   **207**

Twanging (line 58) is an example of **onomatopoeia**, the use of words that sound like what they mean. Find and circle three other examples of onomatopoeia in stanza III.

DECODING TIP

What word within *affright* in line 74 helps you to figure out its meaning? Circle it.

INTERPRET

What kind of bells do you hear in stanza IV?

_____

_____

_____

_____

_____

_____

_____

_____

FLUENCY

Read aloud the boxed passage twice. As you read, pay careful attention to the dashes, commas, and exclamation marks. Work to capture the poem's rhythm in your delivery.

INTERPRET

In Muslim folklore a *ghoul* is a spirit who robs graves and feeds on the dead. Who are the *Ghouls* Poe refers to in line 88? Why might Poe have chosen to refer to them that way?

_____

_____

_____

_____

_____

_____

_____

_____

IDENTIFY

Whose "merry bosom swells" as "he dances, and he yells" (lines 93 and 95)?

_____

_____

_____

_____

_____

_____

_____

Is a groan.
And the people—ah, the people—
80   They that dwell up in the steeple,
         All alone,
And who, tolling, tolling, tolling,
     In that muffled monotone,
Feel a glory in so rolling
85   On the human heart a stone—
They are neither man nor woman—
They are neither brute nor human—
         They are Ghouls:—

     And their king is who tolls:—
90   And he rolls, rolls, rolls,
         Rolls
     A pæan[7] from the bells!
     And his merry bosom swells
         With the pæan of the bells!
95   And he dances, and he yells;
     Keeping time, time, time,
     In a sort of Runic rhyme,
         To the pæan of the bells:—
         Of the bells:
100   Keeping time, time, time
     In a sort of Runic rhyme,
         To the throbbing of the bells—
     Of the bells, bells, bells—
         To the sobbing of the bells:—
105   Keeping time, time, time,
         As he knells, knells, knells,
     In a happy Runic rhyme,

---

7. **pæan** (pē'ən) *n.:* song of triumph.

To the rolling of the bells—
Of the bells, bells, bells:—
110   To the tolling of the bells—
Of the bells, bells, bells, bells,
Bells, bells, bells—
To the moaning and the groaning of the bells.

STYLE INDICATOR

Re-read the poem. Mark the passages that you find effective. Then, identify the literary devices Poe uses to create those effects.

_____

_____

_____

OWN THE POEM

PRACTICING THE STANDARDS

Analyzing a Poem   What literary devices does Edgar Allan Poe use to create meaning? How would the poem be different if the poet had chosen a different style? Briefly analyze Poe's use of literary devices on the lines below.

_____

_____

_____

_____

_____

KEEPING TRACK

Personal Word List   "The Bells" is packed with interesting words. Record the words you find most interesting or challenging in your Personal Word List.

Personal Reading Log   Note "The Bells" in your Personal Reading Log, and give yourself 1 point on the Reading Meter.

Checklist for Standards Mastery   Use the Checklist for Standards Mastery to keep track of your progress.

The Bells ■ *Interactive Reading, page 204*

Go Beyond a Literary Text

Annotated List of Works   Find out more about Edgar Allan Poe's works by researching and naming at least three of his most famous stories and three of his most famous poems. Provide a one-sentence description of what each is about. Ask a librarian to help you find Poe's works and identify their subjects.

Story Title	Is About . . .

Poem Title	Is About . . .

Information

BEFORE YOU READ

Just about everything about Edgar Allan Poe's life is a mystery. Scholars often disagree about when and where he wrote his great works. Even more people disagree about what caused Poe's death in Baltimore, Maryland, in 1849. Was it drink? murder? rabies? Read on to find out about a modern mystery connected with Poe's death.

Reading Standard 2.8 **(Grade 6 Review)** Note instances of fallacious reasoning in text.

from Beyond the Grave

Troy Taylor

One of the most **compelling** cemeteries on the east coast is located in Baltimore, although many people are unaware that a portion of it even exists. It is called the Old Western Burial Ground, and it holds the remains of people such as Edgar Allan Poe, the son of Francis Scott Key, the grandfather of President James Buchanan, five former mayors of Baltimore, and fifteen generals from the Revolutionary War and the War of 1812.

Not all of the cemetery is easy to find, for the
10 Westminster Presbyterian Church (now Westminster Hall) was built over a large portion of the cemetery. These graves and tombs date back to a century before the church was built. Much of the cemetery, where Poe is buried, is still accessible above ground in the churchyard, but a large portion of the graveyard can only be reached by way of the catacombs underneath the building. It is here where the ghosts of this eerie graveyard are said to walk. Strangely

VOCABULARY DEVELOPMENT

compelling (kəm·pel'iŋ) *adj.*: irresistibly interesting; captivating.

WORD KNOWLEDGE

Catacombs (line 16) are a series of vaults or galleries in an underground burial place.

· · · · · · Notes · · · · · ·

_____

_____

_____

_____

_____

_____

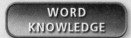

A *fedora* (line 24) is a type of hat.

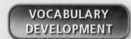

Pause at line 26. How is the mysterious visitor described? Circle the words that people use to describe him.

_____

_____

_____

VOCABULARY DEVELOPMENT

tangible (tan′jə·bəl) *adj.:* able to be touched; actual or real.

ritual (rich′o͞o·əl) *n.:* ceremony.

· · · · · · **Notes** · · · · · ·

_____

_____

_____

_____

_____

_____

_____

_____

though, these restless spirits are not the most enduring mystery of the Western Burial Ground.

20   This famous and unsolved mystery involves a man who has been seen in the graveyard for more than fifty years. Whoever this strange figure may be, he is always described in the same way. Dressed completely in black, including a black fedora and a black scarf to hide his face, he carries a walking stick and strolls into the cemetery every year on January 19, the birth date of Edgar Allan Poe. On every occasion, he has left behind a bottle of cognac and three red roses on the gravesite of the late author. After placing these items with care, he then stands, tips his hat,

30 and walks away. The offerings always remain on the grave. One year, they were accompanied by a note, bearing no signature, which read: "Edgar, I haven't forgotten you."

    There have been many stories that claim the ghost of Edgar Allan Poe haunts his gravesite, but the man in black seems to be quite **tangible,** although who he is remains a riddle. In addition, scholars and curiosity seekers remain puzzled by the odd **ritual** he carries out and the significance of the items he leaves behind. The roses and cognac have been brought to the cemetery every January

40 since 1949, and yet no clue has been offered as to the origin or true meaning of the offerings.

    The identity of the man has been an intriguing mystery for years. Many people, including Jeff Jerome, the curator of the nearby Edgar Allan Poe house, believe that there may be more than one person leaving the tributes. Jerome himself has seen a white-haired man while other observers have reported a man with black hair. Possibly, the second person may be the son of the man who originated the ritual. Regardless, Jerome has been quoted as saying

50   that if he has his way, the man's identity will never be known. This is something that most Baltimore residents agree with. Jerome has received numerous telephone calls from people requesting that no attempt ever be made to approach the man.

For some time, rumors persisted that Jerome was the mysterious man in black, so in 1983, he invited 70 people to gather at the graveyard at midnight on January 19. They had a celebration in honor of the author's birthday with a glass of amontillado, a Spanish sherry featured in one of

60   Poe's horror tales, and readings from the author's works. At about an hour past midnight, the celebrants were startled to see a man run through the cemetery in a black frock coat. He was fair-haired and carrying a walking stick and quickly disappeared around the cemetery's east wall. The roses and cognac were found on Poe's grave as usual.

Not in an effort to solve the mystery, but merely to enhance it, Jerome allowed a photographer to try and capture the **elusive** man on film. The photographer was backed by *Life* magazine and was equipped with rented

70   infrared night-vision photo equipment. A radio signal triggered the camera so that the photographer could remain out of sight. The picture appeared in the July 1990 issue of *Life* and showed the back of a heavyset man kneeling at Poe's grave. His face cannot really be seen because it was shadowed by his black hat. No one else has ever been able to photograph the mysterious man again.

INFER

Why might Jerome wish the visitor's identity to remain a secret?

VOCABULARY DEVELOPMENT

elusive (ē·loo'siv) *adj.:* hard to capture or get hold of.

· · · · · · Notes · · · · · ·

PRACTICING THE STANDARDS

Fallacious Reasoning   This excerpt from *Beyond the Grave* contains examples of the writer's reasoning about the mystery. On the chart below, enter examples of the writer's reasoning about the mystery. Then, decide whether each example of reasoning is valid or fallacious. Compare your charts in class.

Writer's Reasoning	Valid or Fallacious?

KEEPING TRACK

Personal Word List   Record this selection's vocabulary words in your Personal Word List. Use each word in a sentence to make sure you understand its meaning.

Personal Reading Log   Give yourself 2 points on the Reading Meter for this selection. What fact about the mystery did you find most interesting? Enter your ideas in your Personal Reading Log.

Checklist for Standards Mastery   Use the Checklist for Standards Mastery to keep track of your progress.

from **Beyond the Grave** ▪ *Interactive Reading,* page 211

Go Beyond an Informational Text

Baltimore Brochure   Baltimore, Maryland, is a very old city with a rich history. Find out more about Baltimore—its famous foods, its sports teams, its famous residents, and so on. Then, create a travel brochure in which you list Baltimore's highlights. Share your completed brochure with the class.

Use the following chart to help you organize your research.

Baltimore

Historic dates in city's history	
Location and how to get there	
Places to stay/ Places to eat	
Historic buildings and locations	
Museums/ Visitor's bureau	
Sports/Theater/Dance events	

Literature

BEFORE YOU READ

Writers use the same basic tools to communicate—words. What makes some writing memorable and effective is the writer's *use* of the words. The following poems are about life. Each poet has something different to say about life, and each poet uses language differently, in his or her own style. Read on to see how each poet's style affects you, the reader.

Reading Standard 3.6 Identify significant literary devices (e.g., metaphor, symbolism, dialect, irony) that define a writer's style, and use those elements to interpret the work.

A Dream Within a Dream

Edgar Allan Poe

IDENTIFY

What is the poem's speaker doing in lines 1 and 2?

_____

_____

INTERPRET

What might the speaker refer to when he says "my days" (line 5)?

_____

_____

INTERPRET

What might the grains of sand symbolize (line 15)?

_____

_____

Take this kiss upon the brow!
And, in parting from you now,
Thus much let me avow—
You are not wrong, who deem

5   That my days have been a dream;
Yet if hope has flown away
In a night, or in a day,
In a vision, or in none,
Is it therefore the less *gone?*

10   *All* that we see or seem
Is but a dream within a dream.

I stand amid the roar
Of a surf-tormented shore,
And I hold within my hand

15   Grains of the golden sand—

How few! yet how they creep

Through my fingers to the deep,

While I weep—while I weep!

O God! can I not grasp

20   Them with a tighter clasp?

O God! can I not save

One from the pitiless wave?

Is *all* that we see or seem

But a dream within a dream?

Life

Naomi Long Madgett

Life is but a toy that swings on a bright gold chain

Ticking for a little while

To amuse a fascinated infant,

Until the keeper, a very old man,

5   Becomes tired of the game

And lets the watch run down.

CHARTING LITERARY DEVICES

Re-read "A Dream Within a Dream." Circle words that rhyme, underline repetition, and put a star next to examples of imagery and metaphor.

IDENTIFY

To what is life compared in "Life"? To what is death compared? Circle your answers.

INTERPRET

Who is the keeper? What might the "game" be (lines 4–5)?

_____

_____

_____

FLUENCY

Read aloud "A Dream Within a Dream." Then, read aloud "Life." In which poem is sound more important? Why?

_____

_____

_____

CHARTING LITERARY DEVICES

Re-read "Life," identifying passages you find particularly effective. Then, identify the literary devices the poet uses in those passages.

OWN THE POEMS

Compare Literary Devices   One of these poems is fairly recent. The other poem is over a hundred years old. Compare and contrast the way each speaker sees life. What **metaphor** or metaphors does each speaker use to describe what life is like? What is the **tone** of each poem—that is, what attitude toward life does each speaker express? In your answer, be sure to quote lines from the poems.

_____

_____

_____

_____

Compare Style   Write a brief description of the sounds you hear in Edgar Allan Poe's poem and in Naomi Long Madgett's poem. Use examples from the poems to support your analysis.

_____

_____

_____

_____

Personal Word List   Write the words you learned from these poems in your Personal Word List. Practice at least two of the words in everyday conversation.

Personal Reading Log   Enter your ideas about author's style in your Personal Reading Log. Then, give yourself 1 point on the Reading Meter.

Checklist for Standards Mastery   Update the Checklist for Standards Mastery to indicate your understanding of author's style.

A Dream Within a Dream; Life
■ *Interactive Reading*, page 216

Go Beyond Literary Texts

Imitation of Style   The style of most famous writers is immediately recognizable. Think, for example, of William Shakespeare, Emily Dickinson, and Dr. Seuss. Choose a writer you admire, and write a brief story or poem in which you imitate that writer's style. Use the following style worksheet to help you identify the style of the writer of your choice.

Writer's Use of . . .	Examples
Repetition, Rhyme, Rhythm	
Figurative Language	
Imagery or Symbolism	
Dialect	
Irony	
Sentence Length and Structure	

Chapter 6

Sound and Sense
Forms of Poetry

Chapter Preview In this chapter you will—

Strategy Launch: "Text Reformulation"

LITERARY FOCUS: POETRY

Poems take many different forms and have many purposes. Some poems, like **sonnets,** follow strict patterns of rhyme and meter. Other poems are written in **free verse.** Some, like **lyric poems,** express a feeling or an idea; others, like **narrative poems, ballads,** and **epic poems** tell stories. Ballads sing simple stories about love, betrayal, or death, and epics tell complex stories of heroic quests. **Odes** are written in praise of a person, place, or thing; **elegies** usually praise someone who has died. Emily Dickinson, a very great poet, said that she knew she was reading poetry when she felt the top of her head lift off. Not every poem makes readers feel that way. But every serious poem tries to.

A STRATEGY THAT WORKS: "TEXT REFORMULATION"

Sometimes poems can be hard to understand. To help make a poem's meaning clear, you can use a strategy called "Text Reformulation," in which you put the content of the poem into a different form.

POINTERS FOR USING "TEXT REFORMULATION"

⟫➤ Rewrite a **lyric poem** as a journal entry or a letter.

⟫➤ Rewrite a **narrative poem** as a news story.

⟫➤ Rewrite a **ballad** as a hip-hop song.

⟫➤ Rewrite an **epic poem** as a script for a feature film.

Reading Standard 2.4
Compare the original text to a summary to determine whether the summary accurately captures the main ideas, includes critical details, and conveys the underlying meaning.

Reading Standard 3.1
Determine and articulate the relationship between the purposes and characteristics of different forms of poetry (for example, ballad, lyric, couplet, epic, elegy, ode, sonnet).

BEFORE YOU READ

Suppose you could build your own rocket ship—a tiny rocket ship, actually, because it would have to fit in a small basement. In this lyric poem, written in free verse, one poet imagines building such a rocket ship. Then he turns the rocket ship into a poem.

Reading Standard 3.1 Determine and articulate the relationship between the purposes and characteristics of different forms of poetry.

SKYWRITING

Michael Ellis

IDENTIFY

To whom is the poet speaking?

_____

WORD KNOWLEDGE

Infinite (in′fə·nit) is an adjective meaning "without end."

There are three *i*'s in *infinite,* and all three are short. The final *e* is silent. A closely related word that has a long *e* sound at the end is *infinity.* Another closely related word, *finite,* has two long *i* sounds.

INTERPRET

How can words "carry lots of weight," even though they "don't weigh much" (lines 12–13)?

_____

Just suppose you could build your own
rocket ship. A little one, most likely,
unless your basement is a whole lot bigger
than mine.

5   You won't be going into space yourself. I guess
you could send a cat in your place. But what
would a cat find
to do way up there, in the infinite twinkling dark?
Chase space mice? Don't kid yourself. That rocket
10   isn't even big enough for a cat.
All it can lift is a piece of paper. You could write a poem
on the paper. Words don't weigh much.

But words can carry lots of weight. A friend of mine
once wrote a short poem to the world. He published it
15   in massive type, on billboards over streets
in towns where thousands could read it:
"War is over if you want it."

He understood what words are for. They are
thoughts made visible.

20   The sky is vast and fills our eyes, a giant
billboard everyone can see. Maybe the stars
spell out a poem written in a voice
we all forgot a long time past. Maybe the sky
whispers the lines, so quietly we can't quite hear.
25   There's room up there for your words too.
Write something that explains just who you are and
where you've been, or what you want and
how you see it. Write what you like—it's your rocket.

Launch a poem, and watch it make its way
30   across the universe.

INTERPRET

How would you state lines 17–19 in your own words?

_____

_____

_____

_____

INTERPRET

What is the speaker comparing a poem to in lines 29–30?

_____

_____

_____

OWN THE POEM

PRACTICING THE STANDARDS

Text Reformulation   Reformulate this poem as a letter to a young poet. Use the graphic organizer on the next page for help with the personal letter format.

KEEPING TRACK

Personal Word List   Record the new words you learned from this poem in your Personal Word List.

Personal Reading Log   Record this poem in your Personal Reading Log, and give yourself 1 point on the Reading Meter.

Checklist for Standards Mastery   Check your progress in mastering the standards on the Checklist for Standards Mastery.

Skywriting ▪ *Interactive Reading, page 222*

Interact with a Literary Text

Text Reformulation: Personal Letter   Here is a personal-letter format. You can use this format to reformulate another kind of text as a personal letter. Try reformulating "Skywriting," a lyric poem, in the format of a personal letter.

_____

_____

_____

_____

Dear _____

_____

_____

_____

_____

_____

_____

_____

_____

_____

_____

_____

_____

_____

_____

_____

Reading Standard 3.1 Determine and articulate the relationship between the purposes and characteristics of different forms of poetry.

BEFORE YOU READ

"The Midnight Ride of Billy Dawes" is a narrative poem based on historical fact. There really was a Billy Dawes. He was sent on a southern route to warn colonists that the British were coming. Paul Revere went to the north. Dawes ended the night a free man. Paul Revere was captured. There was actually a third rider, Dr. Samuel Prescott, who was the only one to make it all the way to Concord.

The Midnight Ride of Billy Dawes

Dan Greenberg

Gather round, readers
And hear my just cause:
I tell of a hero
Named young William Dawes.
5 Of Paul Revere's ride
This much is now known:
Revere did not travel
Completely alone.
A second brave rider
10 That night rode to glory.
His name was Bill Dawes
And this is his story.
It starts out in April
Of that fateful year.
15 The folks then in Boston

TEXT REFORMULATION

Reformulate lines 1–12 as a newspaper headline.

_____

_____

_____

_____

_____

FLUENCY

Read lines 1–20 aloud. Pay attention to the punctuation, and pause only when you see a comma, a colon, or a period. Re-read the stanza aloud until you can read it quickly and smoothly.

_____

_____

_____

_____

_____

_____

_____

_____

_____

_____

_____

_____

_____

Felt conflict and fear

The British controlled things—

And that was not right!

Sooner or later

20   It would come to a fight.

Then the word leaked out

That the British, in fact,

Were already marching—

They planned to attack!

25   There was no time to waste—

That much was clear—

So they called Billy Dawes

And his friend Paul Revere.

They said: Ride through the country

30   Make yourself heard:

"The British are coming!"

Shout out every word.

So out went Bill Dawes

And out went Revere

35   They flew down the road

On a night cool and clear.

For miles Billy raced,

Then came his big test:

"Stop!" cried the soldiers,

40   "You're under arrest!"

"*Oh no!*" thought young Billy,

"*Is it over? Am I done?*"

He looked down the barrel

Of the soldier's loaded gun.

VISUALIZE

How do you visualize the
scene in lines 37–44?

_____

_____

_____

_____

_____

_____

45   "You're not allowed,"
    Said the soldier, "Get back!"
    Now how would folks learn
    Of the British attack?

    "I'm only a farmer,"
50   sly William Dawes said,
    "Trying to make it home
    To sleep in my bed."
    The soldiers agreed
    To give Bill the okay.
55   By the time they looked up
    He'd galloped away.

    Billy shouted, "To arms!
    The lobsterbacks are near!
    Get yourself ready!
60   Gather your gear!"
    And gather they did—
    The rest is no mystery:
    A shot fired in Lexington
    Rings throughout history.

65   But as for William Dawes
    The question's still clear:
    Why wasn't his name remembered
    Like the name Paul Revere?
    Both men were brave,
70   Each was a hero.
    Why did one get a prize
    And the other get zero?

IDENTIFY

How is Billy's problem resolved in lines 49–56?

_____

_____

_____

_____

_____

_____

_____

_____

INFER

Why do you think Billy called the British "lobsterbacks" (line 58)?

_____

_____

_____

_____

_____

_____

_____

_____

_____

_____

According to the narrator (lines 65–84), why is Paul Revere remembered but Billy Dawes is not?

_____

_____

_____

_____

_____

_____

_____

_____

_____

_____

_____

_____

_____

_____

_____

_____

_____

_____

_____

_____

_____

The answer, perhaps
(And I know this sounds suspicious),
75 Lies in Paul Revere's fame
For his shiny silver dishes!
You see, Paul Revere
Was a silversmith by trade.
Everyone knew his name
80 From the silverware he made.

Billy Dawes, on the other hand,
Had a less famous appellation°
He made shoes for a living
But had no widespread reputation.
85 So when Henry Wadsworth Longfellow
Sat down to write his poem,
He naturally wrote of Paul Revere
As if to say, "I know him!"

The lesson one learns
90 From the poem is quite plain:
If you're going to do something brave
Make sure they know your name!

° **appellation** (ap'ə·lā'shən) *n.:* name or title.

OWN THE POEM

Purpose of Poetry   In the second line of the poem, the narrator tells the reader to "hear my just cause." What is the narrator's cause? Write out your answer in a few sentences.

_____

_____

_____

_____

_____

_____

_____

Text Reformulation   The story in this poem is perfect for reformulation. Reformulate it as a series of cartoon panels. Use the graphic organizer on the next page. Be sure to supply captions and to write the characters' dialogue in bubbles above their heads.

KEEPING TRACK

Personal Word List   In your Personal Word List, write down any words from this poem that gave you trouble.

Personal Reading Log   Take out your Personal Reading Log, and indicate whether or not you would recommend this poem to a friend. Give yourself 1 point on the Reading Meter.

Checklist for Standards Mastery   On the Checklist for Standards Mastery, check your progress mastering the standards. Where did you do well? Where can you improve?

The Midnight Ride of Billy Dawes
Interactive Reading, **page 225**

Interact with a Literary Text

Text Reformulation: Comic Book   Retell the story of Billy Dawes in a series of cartoon panels. Use as many boxes as you need to show all the key events in the poem. Don't worry if you can't draw. Stick figures will do.

"The Midnight Ride of Billy Dawes"   **Retold by** _____

Valentine for Ernest Mann

Interact with a Literary Text

"Most Important Word" Graph   "Most Important Word" is a
strategy that is especially useful in analyzing poems. Here is how it
works. Read the poem you are studying at least twice. After your
second reading, get together with a partner or in a small group. Read
the poem a third time, perhaps aloud together. Then, write down
what you think is the most important word in the poem. (It could
be a word in the title.) Write the word in the space provided in the
graphic. Quote the line the word is found in. Then, list the reasons
you chose this word.

When you have finished, compare your words with those chosen by
other people in your group. Be ready to defend your choice. After
your discussion, return to your graphic. Do you wish to make any
changes, based on your discussions? If so, make the changes now.
Finally, write at the bottom what you think the main idea or message
of the poem is. Use your most important word in explaining the
main idea or message.

1. Most important word: _____

2. Line from poem where word appears: _____

_____

_____

_____

3. Reasons for my choice: _____

_____

_____

_____

4. Main idea or message of poem: _____

_____

_____

_____

Paul Revere's Ride

Interact with a Literary Text

Cause-and-Effect Chart   **Narrative poems,** like "Paul Revere's Ride," tell stories, and stories have characters and plots. Most plots develop according to a cause-and-effect pattern. One event causes another event, which causes yet another event. To put it another way, the effect of one cause becomes the cause of another effect. Sound complicated? Not really. The cause-and-effect chart below will make it all clear.

Fill out the chart with causes and effects that you find in "Paul Revere's Ride." The first cause statement is already done to get you started.

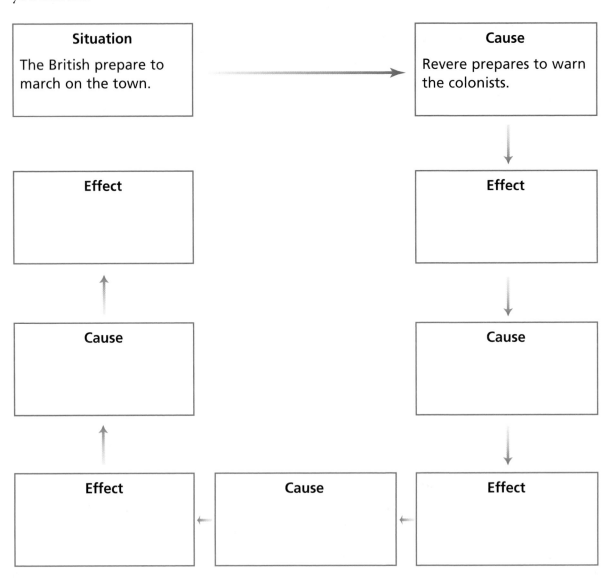

Situation
The British prepare to march on the town.

Cause
Revere prepares to warn the colonists.

Effect

Effect

Cause

Cause

Effect

Cause

Effect

The Cremation of Sam McGee; The Dying Cowboy; Maiden-Savin' Sam

Interact with Literary Texts

Story Map   Like most stories, **ballads** have a plot. A story map shows how one plot element leads to another. Make a story map for any one of the three ballads. For extra practice, try it with all three. You may want to work with a partner.

Characters	Setting (if important)	Problem or Conflict

Event 1

↓

Event 2

↓

Event 3

↓

Climax

↓

Resolution

from Beowulf;
Casey at the Bat

Interact with Literary Texts

Comparison Chart   **Epic poems,** like ballads and narrative poems, tell stories. A traditional epic poem tells the story of a great hero who represents the values of his or her culture. A **mock epic,** on the other hand, uses the epic form to make fun of its subject. Fill in the epic comparison chart below to see how the ballplayer Casey is like and unlike the hero Beowulf.

Casey

Differences

_____
_____
_____
_____
_____
_____
_____

Beowulf

Differences

_____
_____
_____
_____
_____
_____
_____

Casey and Beowulf

Similarities

_____
_____
_____
_____
_____
_____
_____

Summaries of "Casey at the Bat"

Interact with Informational Texts

Summary-Event List   A good summary includes all the important events or details of a text and leaves out unnecessary details. In the chart below, list all the important events in "Casey at the Bat." Then, compare your list with a partner's. If one of you has listed any events the other left out, try to decide together whether they are important events or unnecessary details. (You don't have to fill in all the lines.)

"Casey at the Bat" Event List

1. _____
   _____
2. _____
   _____
3. _____
   _____
4. _____
   _____
5. _____
   _____
6. _____
   _____
7. _____
   _____
8. _____
   _____
9. _____
   _____
10. _____
    _____

ODES

Oda a las gracias/ Ode to Thanks; Birdfoot's Grampa; Ode to a Toad

for use with
Holt Literature and Language Arts,
page 437

Interact with Literary Texts

Cluster Map   An **ode** is a poem written in praise of someone or something. "Oda a las gracias/Ode to Thanks" praises the simple word *thanks*. Fill in the cluster diagram below with details that tell what the poet says *thanks* is or does.

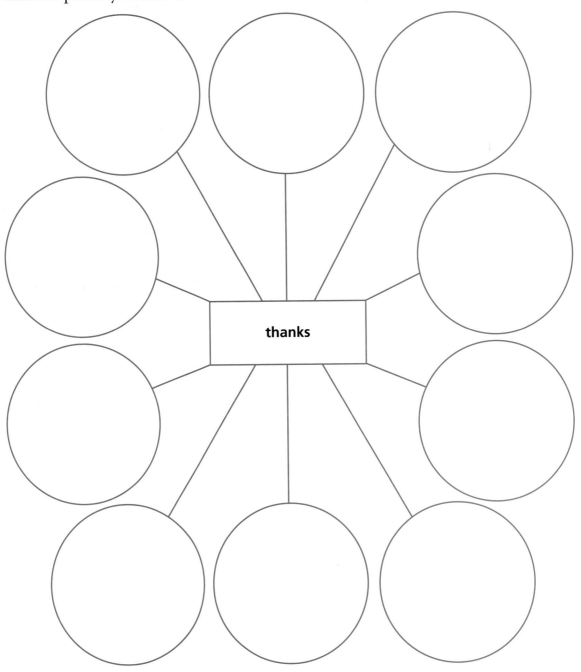

thanks

Graphic Organizer Graphic Organizer

236   Chapter 6   **Sound and Sense: Forms of Poetry**

On the Grasshopper and the Cricket

Interact with a Literary Text

Line-by-Line Paraphrase   "On the Grasshopper and the Cricket" is a **sonnet,** and like all sonnets it has fourteen lines. This sonnet is in the Italian form. That means that the first eight lines ask a question or make a point, and the last six lines answer or expand on the point. Since "On the Grasshopper and the Cricket" was written over a hundred years ago, you might find it a bit hard to understand. Paraphrasing the poem (restating it in your own words) can help. Using your own words, paraphrase each line of "On the Grasshopper and the Cricket" on the corresponding line of the graphic organizer below. The first four lines are done to get you started.

When you paraphrase a poem, it is important that you explain the figures of speech in your own words.

"On the Grasshopper and the Cricket"

1. Earth has a poetry of its own, which never dies.
2. In summer, when it's so hot the birds are fainting,
3. And they are hiding in the shade to get cool, you can hear a voice
4. In the hedges bordering the freshly mowed meadow;
5. _____
6. _____
7. _____
8. _____
9. _____
10. _____
11. _____
12. _____
13. _____
14. _____

ELEGY

O Captain! My Captain!

for use with
Holt Literature and Language Arts,
page 447

Interact with a Literary Text

Extended-Metaphor Chart   "O Captain! My Captain!" is an **elegy,** or a poem in praise of someone who has died. It uses an extended metaphor. This means that throughout the poem, the captain of the ship represents President Abraham Lincoln. The ship itself represents the United States. Filling out an extended-metaphor chart can help you track the extension of the metaphor throughout the entire poem. In the chart below, the first stanza is done for you.

"O Captain! My Captain!"

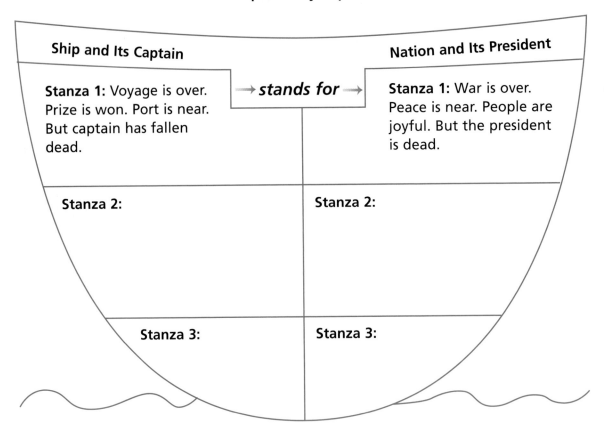

Ship and Its Captain		Nation and Its President
Stanza 1: Voyage is over. Prize is won. Port is near. But captain has fallen dead.	→ *stands for* →	**Stanza 1:** War is over. Peace is near. People are joyful. But the president is dead.
Stanza 2:		**Stanza 2:**
Stanza 3:		**Stanza 3:**

238   Chapter 6   **Sound and Sense: Forms of Poetry**

I Hear America Singing;
I, Too

for use with
Holt Literature and Language Arts,
page 451

**FREE
VERSE**

Interact with Literary Texts

Venn Diagram   "I Hear America Singing" and "I, Too" are both
free-verse poems. That means they do not follow a regular meter or
rhyme scheme, though they do use strong rhythms and repetition.
The two poems have other things in common. In fact, "I, Too" was
written as a response to "I Hear America Singing."

The Venn diagram is useful for comparing two texts. On the diagram
below, show what "I Hear America Singing" and "I, Too" have in
common—and what they don't.

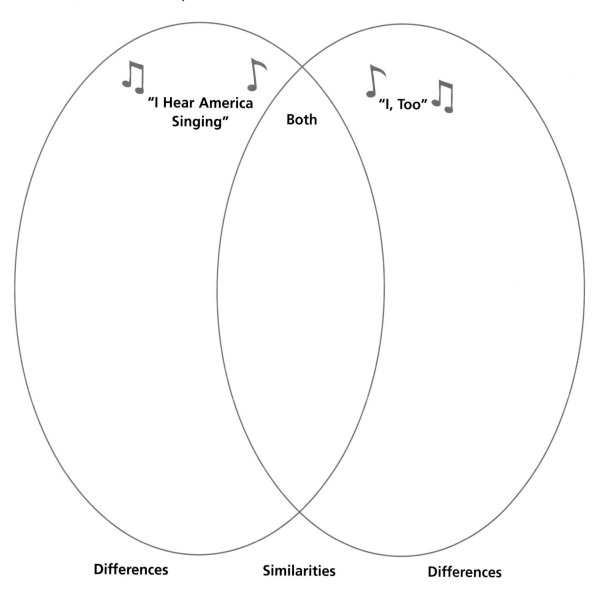

**"I Hear America
Singing"**   **Both**   **"I, Too"**

Differences   **Similarities**   **Differences**

Langston Hughes: A Biography; "Langston Hughes": A Summary

for use with
Holt Literature and Language Arts,
page 455

Interact with Informational Texts

Summary-Notes Chart   When you write a **summary** of an informational text, you must include all the main ideas along with their important supporting details. Minor details should be left out. Prepare to write a summary of "Langston Hughes: A Biography" by filling in the main idea and the supporting details for each paragraph.

Title: "Langston Hughes: A Biography"
Author: unknown
Topic:

	Main Idea	Supporting Details
1		
2		
3		
4		
5		

Literature

AUTHOR STUDY

Henry Wadsworth Longfellow has been one of the most popular American poets for over a century. In his lifetime, people eagerly awaited his next poem just as music fans today eagerly await the latest CD from a favorite singer. One poem, "The Courtship of Miles Standish," sold ten thousand copies in one day.

BEFORE YOU READ

Suppose it's the 1850s and you're sitting around at home wondering what to do for entertainment. Where's the remote control? Where's the VCR? Where's the cable-channel guide? Well, you're out of luck. None of those things have been invented yet. But you have something better. You have your imagination. Go sit by the fireplace, stare into the flames, and listen as someone reads a chilling poem about a shipwreck. Before you know it, you're seeing a private video inside your head. This particular video is called "The Wreck of the Hesperus," by Henry Wadsworth Longfellow.

Here's what you'll need to know before reading the poem:

- A schooner is a kind of sailing ship that has two or more masts.
- A mast is a tall pole rising from the deck of a ship.
- Sails are hung on the mast.
- Schooners once transported goods from one port to another. The *Hesperus* was not on a pleasure cruise.

Reading Standard 3.1 Determine and articulate the relationship between the purposes and characteristics of different forms of poetry (for example, ballad, lyric, couplet, epic, elegy, ode, sonnet).

The Wreck of the Hesperus

Henry Wadsworth Longfellow

WORD KNOWLEDGE

Ope (line 8) is a shortened form of *open,* used here to fit with the poem's rhythmic pattern.

IDENTIFY

Pause at line 20. This is a **narrative poem,** which tells a story. Identify the characters, the setting, and the problem so far.

It was the schooner Hesperus,
    That sailed the wintry sea;
And the skipper had taken his little daughter,
    To bear him company.

5   Blue were her eyes as the fairy-flax,[1]
    Her cheeks like the dawn of day,
And her bosom white as the hawthorn buds
    That ope in the month of May.

The skipper he stood beside the helm,
10   His pipe was in his mouth,
And he watched how the veering flaw[2] did blow
    The smoke now West, now South.

Then up and spake an old Sailor,
    Had sailed to the Spanish Main,[3]
15   "I pray thee, put into yonder port,
    For I fear a hurricane.

"Last night, the moon had a golden ring,
    And tonight no moon we see!"
The skipper, he blew a whiff from his pipe,
20   And a scornful laugh laughed he.

---

1. **fairy-flax:** plant with blue flowers.
2. **veering flaw:** sudden, short gust of wind ("flaw") that changes directions ("veers").
3. **Spanish Main:** Caribbean Sea, especially the part north of South America.

Colder and louder blew the wind,
    A gale from the Northeast,
The snow fell hissing in the brine,
    And the billows frothed like yeast.

25 Down came the storm, and smote amain[4]
    The vessel in its strength;
She shuddered and paused, like a frighted steed,
    Then leaped her cable's length.

"Come hither! come hither! my little daughter,
30   And do not tremble so;
For I can weather the roughest gale
    That ever wind did blow."

He wrapped her warm in his seaman's coat
    Against the stinging blast;
35 He cut a rope from a broken spar,[5]
    And bound her to the mast.

"O father! I hear the church bells ring,
    Oh say, what may it be?"
" 'Tis a fog bell on a rock-bound coast!"—
40   And he steered for the open sea.

"O father! I hear the sound of guns,
    Oh say, what may it be?"
"Some ship in distress, that cannot live
    In such an angry sea!"

WORD KNOWLEDGE

A **simile** compares two different things using a word such as *like, as,* or *resembles.* Underline the simile in line 27. What do you see happening?

_____

_____

_____

INTERPRET

Why does the skipper tie his daughter to the mast (line 36)?

_____

_____

_____

_____

FLUENCY

Generations of students have recited "The Wreck of the Hesperus" and other poems by Longfellow. See how you do by reciting lines 29–48. Perhaps you and some classmates can take roles and read the passage aloud together. How many voices do you need, and whose are they?

_____

_____

_____

_____

4. **smote amain:** struck with full force.
5. **spar:** any pole holding sails on a ship.

Underline the words that
tell what happens to the
father. What do you predict
will happen to the daughter?

45   "O father! I see a gleaming light,
         Oh say, what may it be?"
     But the father answered never a word,
         A frozen corpse was he.

     Lashed to the helm, all stiff and dark,
50   With his face turned to the skies,
     The lantern gleamed through the gleaming snow
         On his fixed and glassy eyes.

     Then the maiden clasped her hands and prayed
         That saved she might be;
55   And she thought of Christ, who stilled the wave,
         On the Lake of Galilee.

     And fast through the midnight dark and drear,
         Through the whistling sleet and snow,
     Like a sheeted ghost, the vessel swept
60   Towards the reef of Norman's Woe.[6]

     And ever the fitful gusts between
         A sound came from the land;
     It was the sound of the trampling surf
         On the rocks and the hard sea sand.

65   The breakers were right beneath her bows,
         She drifted a dreary wreck,
     And a whooping billow swept the crew
         Like icicles from her deck.

6. **reef of Norman's Woe:** ridge of rocks and sand, off Cape Ann,
   Massachusetts.

She struck where the white and fleecy waves

70   Looked soft as carded wool,[7]

But the cruel rocks, they gored her side

        Like the horns of an angry bull.

Her rattling shrouds,[8] all sheathed in ice,

        With the masts, went by the board;

75 Like a vessel of glass, she stove and sank,

        Ho! ho! the breakers roared!

At daybreak, on the bleak sea-beach,

        A fisherman stood aghast,

To see the form of a maiden fair,

80   Lashed close to a drifting mast.

The salt sea was frozen on her breast,

        The salt tears in her eyes;

And he saw her hair, like the brown sea-weed,

        On the billows fall and rise.

85 Such was the wreck of the Hesperus,

        In the midnight and the snow!

Christ save us all from a death like this,

        On the reef of Norman's Woe!

IDENTIFY

Underline the **simile** in lines 71–72. What do you see happening?

_____

_____

_____

_____

_____

_____

_____

VISUALIZE

You're sitting in front of your fireplace one hundred or so years ago, listening to someone recite this poem aloud. Describe the pictures that lines 77–84 create in your mind.

_____

_____

_____

_____

_____

_____

_____

_____

_____

---

7. **carded wool**: wool that has been cleaned and combed with a hand tool called a card.
8. **shrouds** *n.*: ropes that support the mast; also, burial garments.

OWN THE POEM

Text Reformulation   Longfellow's famous poem is a **narrative,** which means it tells a story. Reformulate this story of a tragic shipwreck and a fisherman's horrible discovery as a news article. Use the graphic organizer like the one that follows to organize your details.

A news article is usually described as an inverted pyramid. The most important information about the story is at the top of the inverted pyramid. This is called the *lead* (rhymes with *need*). The lead usually is a paragraph that answers *who? what? when? where?* and *why?* The rest of the article adds details, perhaps direct quotes from eye-witnesses or from police, and so on.

News stories are often structured like this inverted pyramid, with the most important information up front, because it permits editors to cut copy, if necessary, to make way for other late-breaking news.

News Article

Headline _____

_____

Dateline _____

Byline (your name) _____

Lead _____

_____

Rest of article

_____

_____

_____

_____

_____

_____

_____

KEEPING TRACK

Personal Word List   List words from the footnotes that interest you. Also list words you learned as you read.

Personal Reading Log   Give yourself 4 points for reading this narrative poem. Did any aspects of the poem give you trouble in reading? Jot down your answers, along with your responses to the poem itself, in your Personal Reading Log.

Checklist for Standards Mastery   Use the Checklist for Standards Mastery to note your progress in mastering the standards. Identify areas in which you can improve.

The Wreck of the Hesperus ■ *Interactive Reading,* page 242

Go Beyond a Literary Text

Author Profile   Use your library and the Internet to find out more about Henry Wadsworth Longfellow. Then use your research to fill in the author profile below.

Personal Data	**Author's Name:** _____ **Date and Place of Birth:** _____ **Family Members:** _____ _____ _____ **Education:** _____ **Date and Place of Death:** _____
Important Events in Life	_____ _____ _____ _____
Works by Author	_____ _____ _____
Quotation (something the author said or wrote that is meaningful to you)	_____ _____ _____ _____

BEFORE YOU READ

If you wondered what the schooner *Hesperus* in Longfellow's poem looked like, the pictures in this selection will give you an idea.

Here is what you should know about the next selection, which is made up of two excerpts:

- Gloucester is a port in Massachusetts. Grand Banks is the name of the North Atlantic fishing grounds located off the coast of Newfoundland.
- "Letters of marque" gave citizens permission to raid enemy ships.
- The nautical terms you should know are: *fore-and-aft,* "front and back"; *rigged,* "fitted with sails"; *holds,* "cargo areas"; *keel,* "long beam supporting bottom of boat"; *bow,* "front of boat"; and *hull,* "main body of boat."

Reading Standard 2.4
Compare the original text to a summary to determine whether the summary accurately captures the main ideas, includes critical details, and conveys the underlying meaning.

from Oars, Sails, and Steam

Schooners

Edwin Tunis

All schooners have two or more masts and have fore-and-aft sails, though in the old days they could carry a square topsail or two and still be schooners. The Baltimore clippers were usually rigged that way.

Quite different and very fine schooners turned up in New England: the Gloucester Fishermen. These worked on the Grand Banks before the days of refrigeration. When the catch was in the holds, the boats staged a race for home.

SUMMARIZE

What is the main idea of the first paragraph?

_____

_____

_____

_____

_____

Fishing schooner.

The winning skipper, since he was the likeliest to arrive
10   with fresh fish, got the best price.

    As new boats were built, they were made sharper and
sharper. Yacht designers were called in to mold as much
speed into them as possible. Gradually an interest grew in
racing them for the sake of the race, regardless of the price
of fish. This interest came to be shared by the public and
kept the schooners in business long after power-driven,
refrigerated boats had taken over the real work on the
banks. . . .

    The photograph shows one of the older, working
20   schooners, which were fast, but fast for practical purposes
only.

☆ ☆ ☆ ☆ ☆ ☆ ☆ ☆ ☆ ☆

The Baltimore clippers are not to be confused with the
clipper ships which developed later. The Baltimore design
seems to have grown out of a type used in Bermuda and
the West Indies; "very much on the Bermuda mold," says an
old Baltimore newspaper advertisement.

SUMMARIZE

What are the critical details in
this paragraph (lines 11–18)?

The clippers were superbly fast sailers, far faster than anything afloat in their time. For this reason they were much used as privateers[1] in the War of 1812 and later, for the same reason, as slavers.[2]

During that second war against England, the American government issued "letters of marque" to privately owned vessels, which then had the privilege of annoying the British. The clippers did this with great success and with considerable profits to their owners. Profits came from the sale of "prizes," that is, captured ships and their cargoes. The *Rossie,* commanded by doughty[3] Joshua Barney, sank or captured fifteen British ships in forty-five days. Captain Boyle, in the *Chasseur,* declared a one-ship blockade of the British Isles!

These Baltimore clippers were very sharp—long, narrow, and deep—and the keel grew deeper as it ran aft, giving them what is called "drag," but not in the sense of

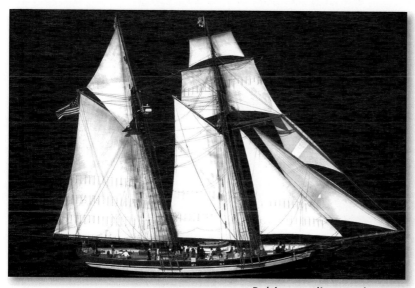

Baltimore clipper schooner.

---

1. **privateers** *n.:* privately owned ships sent by the government to capture enemy ships, especially merchant ships, for their cargo.
2. **slavers** *n.:* ships that carried men, women, and children from Africa to be sold in U.S. markets.
3. **doughty** (dout'ē) *adj.:* brave.

What context clues help you guess at the meaning of "letters of marque" (märk)? Underline the clues.

COMPARE & CONTRAST

How are the Gloucester schooners different from the Baltimore clippers?

_____

_____

_____

_____

_____

_____

_____

_____

_____

_____

_____

_____

_____

_____

_____

_____

_____

_____

_____

slowing them down. The bow was shaped so that it was thin below the waterline and tended to slice through the water.

Most of these boats had two masts and were rigged as topsail schooners, though there were departures from this. Their deep keels made them "stiff" in the water, so they could carry much more sail than an ordinary hull of their
50 size could stand.

OWN THE TEXT

PRACTICING THE STANDARDS

Summary   Meet with a partner, and establish four criteria for a perfect summary. Then, write a summary of "Schooners" on your own. Exchange summaries with your partner. Look for major details that should be included and any minor details that should be omitted. Make any necessary changes in your own summary. Rate each other's summaries. Score between 1 and 4 (4 is the highest).

_____

_____

_____

_____

_____

_____

KEEPING TRACK

Personal Reading Log   Give yourself 1 point for reading this selection. What was the most interesting thing you learned from this selection? What details were you not interested in?

Checklist for Standards Mastery   Track your progress in summarizing using the Checklist for Standards Mastery.

Schooners ▪ *Interactive Reading*, page 249

Interact with an Informational Text

Text Reformulation   Reformulate the information you have read in these two texts as a definition of the word *schooner,* with two subentries, one for the *Gloucester schooner* and one for the *Baltimore clipper schooner.* Here are some tips for writing definitions (it is not as simple as you might imagine):

1. A definition opens with the **entry word** followed, in parentheses, by its **pronunciation.**

2. The **general definition** should cite the characteristics of all schooners. First, tell what larger group of things your term is part of. That is, if you were defining a 747, you would first say that it is a type of jet plane.

3. Define each specific type of schooner, and tell how one type is different from the other type.

A Definition

Word: schooner _____   Pronunciation: (_____)

General Definition: _____

_____

_____

_____

_____

1. Gloucester fishing schooner: _____

_____

_____

_____

_____

2. Baltimore clipper schooner: _____

_____

_____

_____

_____

Langston Hughes and Carl Sandburg are two great American poets of the twentieth century. Both wrote **free verse**—poetry that imitates the rhythms of ordinary conversation.

Here is what you need to know before reading the poems:

- Langston Hughes wrote "Lincoln Monument: Washington" in 1927. The Lincoln Monument was dedicated in 1927.
- Carl Sandburg wrote "Mr. Longfellow and His Boy" in 1941, during World War II, when Franklin Delano Roosevelt was president of the United States and Winston Churchill was prime minister of England.
- Henry Wadsworth Longfellow wrote the poem that Sandburg quotes in 1849, during the Civil War, when Abraham Lincoln was president of the United States.

Reading Standard 3.1 Determine and articulate the relationship between the purposes and characteristics of different forms of poetry (for example, ballad, lyric, couplet, epic, elegy, ode, sonnet).

Lincoln Monument: Washington

Langston Hughes

Abraham Lincoln died in 1865. How, then, would you explain lines 4–5?

_____

_____

_____

_____

_____

_____

Let's go see old Abe
Sitting in the marble and the moonlight,
Sitting lonely in the marble and the moonlight,
Quiet for ten thousand centuries, old Abe.
5 Quiet for a million, million years.

Quiet—

And yet a voice forever
Against the
Timeless walls
10 Of time—
Old Abe.

"Lincoln Monument: Washington" from *The Collected Poems of Langston Hughes*. Copyright © 1994 by the Estate of Langston Hughes. Reprinted by permission of **Alfred A. Knopf, Inc., a division of Random House, Inc.**

Mr. Longfellow and His Boy

An old-fashioned recitation to be read aloud

Carl Sandburg

Mr. Longfellow, Henry Wadsworth Longfellow,
    the Harvard professor,
      the poet whose pieces you see in all the schoolbooks,
"Tell me not in mournful numbers
5   life is but an empty dream . . ."
Mr. Longfellow sits in his Boston library writing,
Mr. Longfellow looks across the room
    and sees his nineteen-year-old boy
propped up in a chair at a window,
10 home from the war,
a rifle ball through right and left shoulders.

In his diary the father writes about his boy:
    "He has a wound through him a foot long.
    He pretends it does not hurt him."
15 And the father if he had known
would have told the boy propped up in a chair
how one of the poems written in that room
    made President Lincoln cry.
And both the father and the boy
20 would have smiled to each other and felt good
about why the President had tears over that poem.

Noah Brooks, the California newspaperman,
could have told the Longfellows how one day
Brooks heard the President saying two lines:

INFER

Longfellow was born in 1807 and died in 1882. What war would his son (see lines 8–11) have been wounded in?

_____

_____

_____

_____

INFER

Why would Longfellow and his son have "felt good" that Longfellow's poem "made President Lincoln cry" (lines 15–21)?

_____

_____

_____

_____

_____

_____

_____

_____

_____

Re-read lines 25–26. These lines of the poem that made Lincoln cry use the metaphor of a sailing ship. What is compared to a sailing ship?

_____

_____

_____

_____

_____

INFER

Lines 28–49 of Sandburg's poem quote Longfellow's poem (which is titled "The Building of the Ship"), which made Lincoln cry. Sandburg wrote this poem during the early years of World War II. Why do you think he includes these lines by Longfellow here?

_____

_____

_____

_____

_____

_____

_____

_____

25   "Thou, too, sail on, O Ship of State!

Sail on, O Union, strong and great!"

Noah Brooks, remembering more of the poem, speaks:

"Thou, too, sail on, O Ship of State!

Sail on, O Union, strong and great!

30   Humanity with all its fears,

With all the hopes of future years,

Is hanging breathless on thy fate!

We know what Master laid thy keel,

What workmen wrought thy ribs of steel,

35   Who made each mast, and sail, and rope,

What anvils rang, what hammers beat,

In what a forge and what a heat

Were shaped the anchors of thy hope!

Fear not each sudden sound and shock,

40   'Tis of the wave and not the rock;

'Tis but the flapping of the sail,

And not a rent made by the gale!

In spite of rock and tempest's roar,

In spite of false lights on the shore,

45   Sail on, nor fear to breast the sea!

Our hearts, our hopes, are all with thee,

Our hearts, our hopes, our prayers, our tears,

Our faith triumphant o'er our fears,

Are all with thee—are all with thee!"

50   Noah Brooks sees Lincoln's eyes filled with tears,

the cheeks wet.

They sit quiet a little while, then Lincoln saying:

"It is a wonderful gift to be able to stir men like that."

Mr. Longfellow—and his boy sitting propped up in a

chair—

55   with a bullet wound a foot long in his shoulders—
would have liked to hear President Lincoln saying
        those words.

Now Mr. Longfellow is gone far away, his boy, too,
        gone far away,
and they never dreamed how seventy-eight years later
the living President of the United States, in the White
        House at Washington,
60   takes a pen, writes with his own hand on a sheet of paper
about the Union Ship of State sailing on and on—
        never going down—
how the President hands that sheet of paper
to a citizen soon riding high in the air, high over salt water,
high in the rain and the sun and the mist over the Atlantic
        Ocean,
65   riding, pounding, flying, everything under control,
crossing the deep, wide Atlantic in a day and a night,
coming to London on the Thames in England,
standing before the First Minister of the United Kingdom
so the whole English-language world
70   from England across North America to Australia and
        New Zealand
can never forget Mr. Longfellow's lines:
        "Thou, too, sail on, O Ship of State!
        Sail on, O Union, strong and great!"
               [*Collier's,* June 14, 1941]

INTERPRET

The date at the bottom of the poem tells us that the poem was published in 1941, when Franklin Delano Roosevelt was president. Where have Longfellow and his boy gone? (Line 57)

_____

_____

_____

_____

_____

INTERPRET

The paper President Roosevelt sent to London was a commitment by the United States to aid England in World War II. Why do you think Roosevelt wanted England to remember Longfellow's lines?

_____

_____

_____

_____

_____

_____

_____

_____

_____

OWN THE POEMS

PRACTICING THE STANDARDS

Fluency   Prepare these two poems for a performance. You will have to work with a group and assign parts. Your first task will be to determine the number of speakers you will need. Then, make scripts of the poems, and block out each speaker's part. (You might want to use a chorus to speak the narrator's part in Sandburg's poem.) Rehearse your reading in front of a group of classmates. Ask them to evaluate your performance. When you are satisfied with your readings, take your show on the road!

KEEPING TRACK

Personal Word List   Record any unfamiliar words from these poems in your Personal Word List.

Personal Reading Log   Rate each poem in terms of your personal enjoyment. Why do you like one more than another? Write down your rating and your analysis of it in your Personal Reading Log. Award yourself 2 points on the Reading Meter.

Checklist for Standards Mastery   Use the Checklist for Standards Mastery to evaluate your mastery of the forms of poetry.

Lincoln Monument: Washington;
Mr. Longfellow and His Boy ■ *Interactive Reading*, page 254

Go Beyond Literary Texts

Poetry Dartboard   Do you sometimes have trouble thinking of
ideas for creative writing? Try this: Close your eyes, and put your
finger on the "Subjects" dartboard. The spot your finger lands on
gives you your **subject.** Next, go to the "Speakers" dartboard. This
will tell you who should be the **speaker** of your poem. Put the
subject and speaker together, and you're on your way.

Now, write a poem *at least* ten lines long. You will have to decide
what form of poetry you'd like to write: **ballad, lyric, epic, elegy,
ode,** or **sonnet.** In other words, do you want to tell a story? express a
feeling or an idea? mourn someone or something that has died, or
sing the praises of someone or something that is living? You will also
have to decide if you want to use rhyme and meter, or if you prefer
the looser form of free verse.

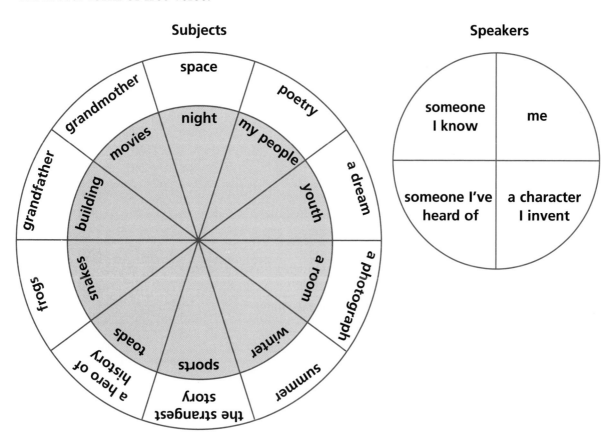

Subjects

Speakers

Chapter 7

Literary Criticism

The Person Behind the Text

Chapter Preview In this chapter you will—

Strategy Launch: "Think-Aloud"

LITERARY FOCUS: LITERARY CRITICISM

Some writers write about their own experiences. They focus on the streets or farms or suburbs that they have lived in and know. Other writers use their imaginations. They write about countries and worlds where they have never set foot. But even a completely made-up story reflects what the writer has observed about the ways people act.

Stories often reflect a writer's attitudes toward the world. If a writer is generally optimistic, his stories are usually positive and end happily. If a writer thinks that the world usually makes a mockery of our dreams, her stories will probably, in some ways, reflect that attitude.

When you evaluate a story (which means you are writing "literary criticism"), you might want to focus on how a text reflects the writer's life experiences.

A STRATEGY THAT WORKS: "THINK-ALOUD"

Before you can evaluate a text, you have to understand it. A strategy called "Think-Aloud" will help you.

POINTERS FOR USING "THINK-ALOUD"

))⇒ As you read, stop to ask questions or comment on the text.

))⇒ Your questions and comments may do any of the following:
- question what you don't understand
- predict what will happen next
- visualize the scene or character
- make comparisons with other texts or with your own experiences
- disagree with something the writer or a character says
- correct misreadings

You don't have to work with a partner to do "Think-Aloud," but it helps to have someone respond to your ideas and questions.

Reading Standard
1.1 Analyze idioms, analogies, metaphors, and similes to infer the literal and figurative meanings of phrases.
1.3 Use words within the appropriate context, and show ability to verify those meanings by definition, restatement, example, comparison, or contrast.

Reading Standard 2.7 Evaluate the unity, coherence, logic, internal consistency, and structural patterns of text.

Reading Standard 3.7 Analyze a work of literature, showing how it reflects the heritage, traditions, attitudes, and beliefs of its author (biographical approach).

Practice Read

Their cultures are very different. Benny is a teenager who loves his hometown of Los Angeles. His grandparents are older people who love their tiny Mexican American village in the mountains of New Mexico. One day Benny sees their lives through new eyes.

Here's what you need to know before you begin the story:
- New Mexico was settled by the Spanish before the state became part of the United States.
- Heidi Schulman, the author of the story, once lived in Los Angeles. She now lives in New Mexico, in a little village where most of the residents are Mexican Americans.

It's About Time

Heidi Schulman

WORD KNOWLEDGE

What words or phrases in the first paragraph give context clues to the meaning of *quirk* (line 4)? Circle them.

· · · · · · **Notes** · · · · · ·

Ever since I've been a little kid, I've had a really strange habit: Every day, while I'm having breakfast, I check the kitchen calendar to make sure I know the date. Don't ask me why. I guess you'd call it a quirk. People at school know about it, too. They say "Hey, Benny, what's the date?" and I always know. Some people think I'm doing it to seem different, but that's not true. If I wanted to be different, don't you think I could find a better way than memorizing the date? It just goes to show that people can be really
10 wrong about each other.

Anyway, this morning, when I turned the calendar from May to June, I rolled my eyes. That's because on this date, every year, my parents start bugging me about visiting my grandparents for my birthday.

My mother started up right on cue. "Benny, dear," she said, in a sweet tone of voice. I tried to slosh down my orange juice and zoom out the door to avoid what was next. I was getting up when my father's voice stopped me.

"Ben, son, your mother and I . . ."

20 Uh oh. My dad was pausing a lot between words. He spoke that way when he wanted me to sit down, be quiet, and listen. Since he was driving me to school, I couldn't leave without him. I was a captive audience.

"We're thinking you should visit . . ."

I didn't have to listen to the rest. Dad was about to say how great it would be to visit my grandparents at their home in Middle-of-Nowhere, New Mexico. That's not really the name of the town, of course, but when you hear descriptions of the place, that's what it sounds like. I'd bet

30 my last dollar there's nothing to do there, not for a kid from L.A. who lives near the beach.

"It'll be fun, Benny," said my mother. "It's a sweet town, and your father grew up there."

"Your mother is right," said Dad, pulling me back into the room with his slow, steady words. "Your *abuelo* and *abuela* want to see you. It's about time."

I knew *abuelo* and *abuela* meant "grandfather" and "grandmother" in Spanish, but I didn't know many other Spanish words. I didn't need Spanish to play computer

40 games or basketball or go to the beach with Tracey, the nicest girl in the whole city of Los Angeles. Come to think of it, I'd be missing all of those things if I got shipped off to Nowheresville for my birthday. I'd be a prisoner in a small mountain village, population 250. I'd been able to wriggle

THINK-ALOUD

Pause at line 14. Who is the narrator of this story? How do you know the "I" in the story is not the writer?

_____

_____

_____

_____

THINK-ALOUD

What details in lines 25–31 seem to link with the writer's experience?

_____

_____

_____

_____

_____

_____

THINK-ALOUD

Without stopping to criticize your ideas, jot down a couple of things you predict might happen in the story.

_____

_____

_____

THINK-ALOUD

What do you think so far about Benny's character?

_____

_____

_____

_____

_____

_____

_____

_____

_____

_____

_____

THINK-ALOUD

Comment on the writer's use of Spanish words in the story. Do you like this technique? Or does it make your reading difficult?

_____

_____

_____

_____

_____

_____

_____

_____

out of the trip every year so far, but sooner or later everybody's luck runs out. My turn had come.

It takes a really long time to get from somewhere to nowhere, and don't let anybody tell you any different.
Somewhere was Los Angeles. Nowhere was Tierra Linda,
50 New Mexico.

Tierra Linda is Spanish for "beautiful earth," but names can fool you. After a three-hour drive from the airport, you turn onto a dirt road and there you are in a rundown little village in the mountains. The main street, if you can call it a street, has maybe ten houses, a post office, and a tiny general store. The houses are all different colors—pink, blue, green, you name it, and they all have tin roofs. The day I arrived, the only things moving on the main street were two beat-up old trucks and some dogs. What a yawn.

60 My cousin Mariano picked me up at the airport. He's twenty and actually pretty cool, except it's weird the way he acted like we'd known each other forever, when we'd never met or talked before.

"Hey, Benito," he said, calling me by my given name—a name I rarely used. "*Bienvenidos, primo.*[1] Everybody's waiting to meet you. *Todo la familia.*"[2]

Mariano spent the whole trip from the airport talking about our relatives and the village.

"This village was built more than two hundred and
70 fifty years ago," he said. "Some of the people came from Mexico, and some from Spain. Our great-great grandparents were from Mexico. They still have customs from the old days. You'll get to see many things. There's lots to do."

---

1. **Bienvenidos, primo:** Welcome, cousin.
2. **Todo la familia:** the whole family.

Mariano was getting to the "lots to do" part of the conversation when we arrived at the village. I looked around and wondered what he was talking about. There weren't even any TV antennas.

"No TV?" I asked Mariano.

80 "No, *primo,*" he said. "The mountains get in the way of the reception. But Uncle Cipriano has a satellite dish, so you won't miss your Lakers games. Don't worry, little cousin. We're happy you're coming home."

We arrived at my grandparents' house as the sun was setting. It was a tiny white house, just off the main street. Mariano told me the house was built out of adobe bricks, made from clay. It had a shiny tin roof, a front porch called a "portal," and a front door painted the brightest shade of turquoise you've ever seen.

90 Mariano told me that Grandfather built the house himself, after he and Grandmother got married. My grandparents had lived in the house for 60 years and raised their four children there. That sounded like a long time to me, but then again, I was only 14 and I'd already lived in four different places.

Inside, the walls of the house were covered with family pictures. I even saw a picture of myself, next to pictures of my parents. Which brings up an interesting point.

Another funny thing about me, aside from liking to
100 know the date, is that I don't look a lot like my parents. They both have light brown, wavy hair. I have dark, straight hair. They're tall, and I'm kind of short, though I'd put odds on the fact that I'll be tall enough to play for the Lakers one day. My nose has kind of a hook, and my parents' noses are straight. I don't think about it much, but

Circle the words that give you clues to the meaning of *adobe* (line 86).

DECODING TIP

Turquoise (line 89) is pronounced "tʉr'kwɔiz." It means "blue-green." Think of words that rhyme with *turquoise*, words that have the *-oise* ending (pronounced "ɔiz").

_____

_____

_____

_____

THINK-ALOUD

Even if your background is different from Benny's, what parts of his experience and feelings, if any, can you identify with?

_____

_____

_____

_____

_____

_____

_____

Circle the context clue
that defines *cumpleaños*
(line 125).

WORD
KNOWLEDGE

Which of the Spanish words
in the story have been
adopted as English words?

looking at those pictures on the wall, I could really see the
differences.

 I was looking at the pictures when my grandfather
came into the living room. I hadn't seen him since I was
110 five, so his looks kind of shook me up. We looked a lot
alike, except that I'm 14 and he's 86. In fact, I felt like I was
seeing what I'd look like as an old man. Grandfather's hair
was gray, but straight and thick like mine. We had the same
almond-shaped eyes, and he was even shorter than I am.
Another funny thing was I looked like my grandmother
too. Same nose.

 My grandparents gave me about a zillion hugs, though
I tried to squirm away. Grandma cried and talked in
Spanish. She only switched into English when she realized
120 I didn't know what she was saying. Grandpa kept his arm
around my shoulder.

 "Welcome home, *hijo*,"[3] he said. "Finally you are
here. Tonight the family is coming for dinner. Tomorrow
morning you and I have something important to do to
prepare for your *cumpleaños*—your birthday."

 The family was about twenty-five people. Over dinner,
everybody talked in English and Spanish and made me
taste everything. Of course I'd eaten enchiladas and tamales
before, but they also served a delicious custard called flan
130 and puffy fried bread called *sopapillas,* which you eat with
honey. Everybody was happy and noisy. You couldn't tell
which people liked better: eating or talking. I was so stuffed
I practically fell asleep at the table.

3. **hijo:** son.

The next morning, Grandfather woke me up at six in the morning. We drank coffee, ate leftover flan, packed a lunch, and went out.

We walked through the village, down into the valley. The sun was shining a pink light over the mountains. Soon, we stopped at a gate. Grandfather put his arm around me.

140   "*Hijo,* today is your birthday. Today, I want you to have something that will last your whole life. Come. Open the gate."

Past the gate was a huge field of sunflowers—at least two acres of land leading to a river. Abuelo walked as he spoke, and I followed him.

"Your life is different from mine, my grandson. You live in a big city filled with excitement. I have lived my whole life in this very small place, and I can tell you do not think too much of it yet. But today, I ask you to look 150   at it through my eyes.

"This land we walk on now is the land your *abuela* and I farmed most of our lives. It gave us our vegetables, and fed the animals we raised for milk and meat.

"The mud and sand we used to make the adobe bricks for our home came from this land. After we made the bricks, we dried them under the same sun that shines on us now.

"The trees gave us firewood, and the river gave us fish.

"Our lives were not easy, but they were happy. We had 160   our family around us, and the closeness filled our hearts.

"We were also happy because the land gave us everything. All it asked was that we take care of it."

By this time we had reached the river. Abuelo sat down on a log.

THINK-ALOUD

This is a good spot to "Think-Aloud" about the scene. What do you visualize in lines 137–144?

_____

_____

_____

_____

_____

_____

THINK-ALOUD

Pause at line 162. How is his grandparents' world different from Benny's? What do you think of Abuelo's speech?

_____

_____

_____

_____

_____

_____

_____

_____

_____

_____

THINK-ALOUD

Pause at line 179. Do you think that remembering where you come from is important? Why or why not?

_____

_____

_____

_____

_____

_____

_____

THINK-ALOUD

Pause at line 187. Do you think heritage is important? Explain.

_____

_____

_____

_____

_____

_____

_____

_____

_____

_____

"Your big world is beautiful, _hijo_. It gives you many opportunities, and this is good. For your birthday, your grandmother and I want to give you another opportunity. We are giving you this land. Your uncles and aunts and cousins have their own land, but they will help us care for

170 your land until you are grown. What you do with it then is your decision.

"We want you to have this land," Abuelo continued, "so you always remember where you came from. This is something you must know. It will give you strength. It will let you take part of your _abuela_ and me with you wherever you go. We have always been with you, of course. See how much we look alike?" Abuelo pinched my cheek. "As you grow up, you will discover many other things that tie us, many other similarities. You will see."

180 We sat for a long time and then ate our lunch in silence. The birds kept us company, waiting for crumbs.

Then, it was time to walk back to the house.

"We must go, _hijo_," said Abuelo, "to get ready for your birthday celebration tonight. But we have already done the most important thing. Tomorrow morning when you wake up, look out at this land and remember that it is yours. It is your heritage."

My birthday celebration was a repeat of the first night's dinner, except there were presents, even more food,

190 and a big cake with candles. Everybody stayed up late and told stories about my parents. They teased me about how I looked like this cousin or that uncle or aunt. My relatives' eyes lit up talking about the old days when they rounded up wild horses and had parties at the local dance hall.

I got more and more comfortable in Tierra Linda, helping with horses, fishing in the river, walking on the land that had been given to me. One morning before breakfast I realized I hadn't looked at the calendar since I'd arrived. In fact, there wasn't even a calendar in the kitchen.

200   Just then I spotted my grandfather through the open bedroom door. I could see him putting on his gold reading glasses, flipping through a calendar.

"What are you doing, Abuelo?" I asked.

"Oh, *m'ijo*,"[4] he answered. "It's a funny thing. Since I have been a little boy, I have begun my day in two ways. First, I look out at the beauty of the morning and am thankful for another day. Then I check the calendar to see the date. I cannot say why I do this but it has always been."

"They call it a quirk, Abuelo," I said to my grandfather.
210 "It's a funny habit you can't explain."

I wanted to tell Abuelo that I have the same quirk, but for some reason, I didn't. But I still think about it now that I'm back home in L.A., just like I think about the land, and the other things I can't explain that make me feel close to my grandparents.

I also think that next year, when my parents suggest I visit my grandparents for my birthday, I might say yes. As they say in Tierra Linda, "*vamos a ver*"—we'll see.

THINK-ALOUD

Pause at line 210. What do you think of this calendar link between Benny and his grandfather? Write your thoughts.

_____

_____

_____

THINK-ALOUD

What do you think Benny's use of Spanish in the story's last line suggests? Will he return to Tierra Linda?

_____

_____

_____

_____

_____

THINK-ALOUD

Now that you've finished the story, look back at the title. What double meanings can you find in it?

_____

_____

_____

_____

_____

_____

4. **m'ijo:** my son.

Analyzing Literature (Biographical Approach)   Discuss with a partner what Benny learned about his Mexican American heritage in "It's About Time." Then, respond to this question: How does the writer feel about the importance of a person's heritage? Support your response with details from the story. Score each other's responses from 1 to 4, with 4 the highest score. The more details from the story you use to support your opinion, the higher your score!

_____

_____

_____

"Think-Aloud" Assessment   Review the "Think-Aloud" comments you made as you re-read this story with a partner, using the graphic on the next page. Notice which comments you made most often and which ones you did not make much at all. Then, write a brief comment on this strategy by completing this statement: *Using "Think-Aloud" with this story helped/didn't help me because—*

_____

_____

_____

KEEPING TRACK

Personal Word List   In your Personal Word List, record the Spanish words in this story that have become common in English. Note any new words you learned.

Personal Reading Log   As you record this story in your Personal Reading Log, state whether or not you would recommend it to a friend. Give yourself 4 points on the Reading Meter.

Checklist for Standards Mastery   Check your progress using the Checklist for Standards Mastery.

It's About Time ■ *Interactive Reading,* page 262

Interact with a Literary Text

"Think-Aloud" Tally Sheet   Re-read this story with a partner. One of you will read half of the story and make "Think-Aloud" comments—out loud. Your partner will place a tally mark to identify each type of comment. For the second half, switch roles.

• Don't copy down the comments themselves! Just put a tally mark so you can count up the number of comments of each type.

• You may sometimes disagree about which category a certain comment belongs in. That's OK.

Listener: _____

"Think-Aloud" Comments	Tally
Predicting what happens next	
Visualizing the text	
Making comparisons	
Questioning what you don't understand	
Disagreeing with what's said	
Making comments	
Correcting misreadings	

Ribbons

Interact with a Literary Text

Story-Events Ladder   Fill in the following "Story-Events Ladder" with details from "Ribbons." When you finish, answer the question about how the main events of the story might reflect the writer's heritage, attitudes, and beliefs.

Title:	Setting:

Main Characters:

Problem:

Main Events:

1.

2.

3.

4.

Climax:

5.

Resolution:

How does the story reflect the writer's heritage, attitudes, or beliefs?

Getting to the *Pointe*

for use with
Holt Literature and Language Arts,
page 485

ANALYZING STRUCTURE

Interact with an Informational Text

Position Chart   In a logically structured piece of writing, well-chosen reasons support the writer's position. On the chart below, sum up the writer's position on the subject of ballet. Then, find reasons in the text that support that position.

Position Statement:

Reason	Reason	Reason	Reason

Conclusion:

The Treasure of Lemon Brown

for use with
Holt Literature and Language Arts,
page 490

Interact with a Literary Text

Story Map   Fill out the story map below for "The Treasure of Lemon Brown." Then, answer the question about how the story might reflect the writer's heritage, attitudes, and beliefs.

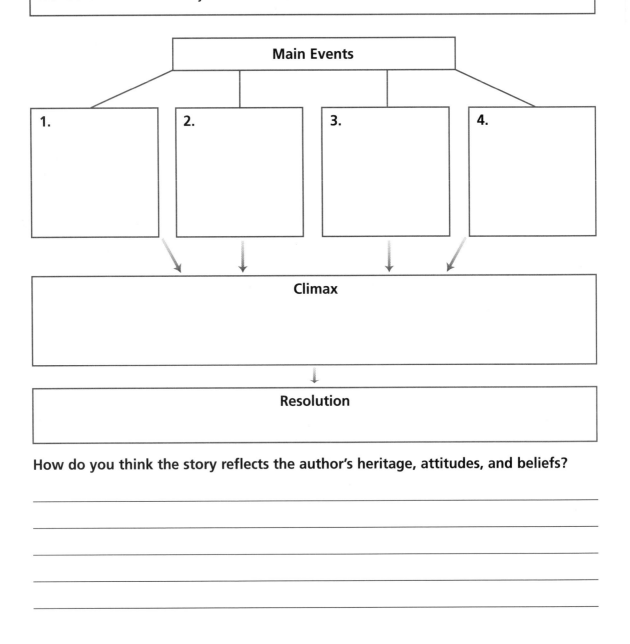

Basic Situation: Greg Ridley, a fourteen-year-old, is at odds with his father because of Greg's disappointing efforts in math. If Greg's next report card doesn't improve, his father won't let him join the basketball team.

Main Events

1.

2.

3.

4.

Climax

Resolution

How do you think the story reflects the author's heritage, attitudes, and beliefs?

_____

_____

_____

_____

_____

Little Walter

Interact with an Informational Text

Idiom Map   An **idiom** is a figurative expression peculiar to a certain language. When you use idioms, you probably don't think about their literal meanings. For example, if you hear your friend say his heart is broken, you know he has probably suffered some emotional pain. You know his heart is not literally broken in pieces.

An idiom map shows the literal and figurative meanings of an expression. It also asks you to use the expression in a sentence. In "Little Walter," the writer uses the idiom "to crash," as in "to crash a party." Explain the idiom by filling out the map. Then, expand your map to explain four common idioms.

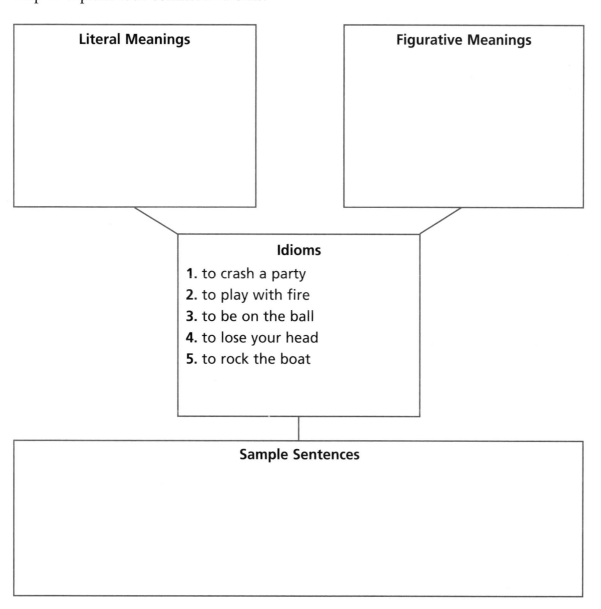

Literal Meanings

Figurative Meanings

Idioms
1. to crash a party
2. to play with fire
3. to be on the ball
4. to lose your head
5. to rock the boat

Sample Sentences

A Smart Cookie/
Bien águila

for use with
Holt Literature and Language Arts,
page 508

Interact with a Literary Text

"Most Important Word" Graph When you analyze a piece of literature, you want to be sure you have grasped its theme. **Theme** is what a story or poem or play reveals to us about our lives. Theme is usually not stated directly. You, the reader, have to read the selection carefully, look for important passages and important words, and then come up with a general statement saying what you think the text tells you about life. Try a strategy called "Most Important Word" to identify the theme of "A Smart Cookie."

Here is how "Most Important Word" works:

- Look for a word that has an impact on you as you read the story. Look for a word that is repeated or a word that is used at the beginning or end of the story and seems important to you.

- Think about how the word relates to the story's characters and to what happens to them. Fill in your ideas on the graphic below.

- Reflect on what you have written. Then, make a generalization about the theme that all of those comments seem to support.

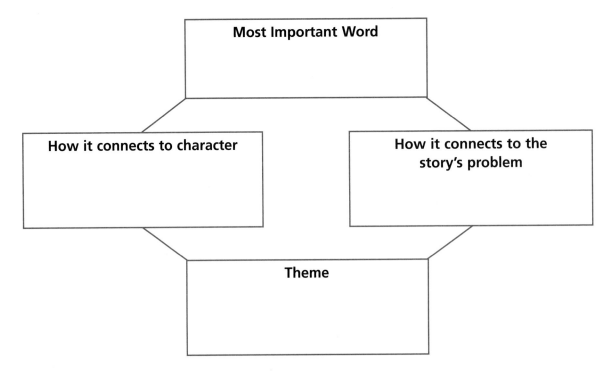

Most Important Word

How it connects to character

How it connects to the story's problem

Theme

Saying Yes

Interact with a Literary Text

Dialogue-Essentials Cartoon   The cartoon below will allow
you to restate the dialogue in "Saying Yes" so that you uncover
its essence, its core of meaning. In each speech balloon, write the
main idea of what that character in "Saying Yes" is saying. In the
thought balloon, write the main idea of what the speaker of the
poem is thinking.

Interviewer

Speaker

Why is there no thought balloon for the interviewer?

_____

_____

**What would you have the writer of this poem think in a thought balloon? How
might this poem reflect the author's heritage, attitudes, and beliefs?**

_____

_____

_____

_____

Literature

FOLK TALE

AUTHOR STUDY

Laurence Yep was born in San Francisco's Chinatown in 1948. At eighteen, he had his first science fiction short story published. Today he is a well-known Asian American writer, having published many novels and short stories. He has written several books about traditional Chinese culture as well as what it is like to be a Chinese immigrant living in America. Laurence Yep has won Newbery Medals for his books *Dragonwings* and *Dragon's Gate.*

BEFORE YOU READ

"The Buried Treasure" is an old Chinese folk tale that has been retold by Laurence Yep. Yep has compiled several collections of stories based on the folk tales and legends of China. In *The Rainbow People* he retells twenty stories adapted from the recollections of Chinese immigrants living in Oakland's Chinatown. The stories were recorded by U.S. government–sponsored programs during the Depression of the 1930s. Like all folk tales, Yep's stories are full of magic and other supernatural events. Yep is especially interested in stories that help young people live between two cultures. Yep's stories have been called bridge builders because they help readers understand the ways people in this world are alike and different.

Reading Standard 3.7
Analyze a work of literature, showing how it reflects the heritage, traditions, attitudes, and beliefs of its author (biographical approach).

The Buried Treasure

a Chinese folk tale, retold by Laurence Yep

There was once a rich man who heard that there was no lock that could not be picked. So he put his money into jars and buried them in secret places. In fact, the whole town nicknamed him "Old Jarhead."

Now, Jarhead had two sons. The older son, Yuè Cang, already managed the family's lands and properties. However, the younger son, Yuè Shêng, cared neither for books nor for business. Old Jarhead scolded and begged him to change, and each time the young man promised

10 to behave. However, he never remembered his promise.

Since Yuè Shêng was also a friendly fellow, he never turned a guest away from his door. Often he had to provide meals for three or even four guests a day. Everyone took advantage of him. As a result, his money poured through his hands like water.

One day when Old Jarhead fell sick, he **summoned** his sons to his bedside and told them the contents of his will. To the older son, he left everything. His younger son, Yuè Shêng, would receive nothing.

20 Hurt, Yuè Shêng sighed. "Well, it isn't as if you didn't warn me."

Alarmed, Old Jarhead tried to sit up but could not. "I'm not trying to punish you," he wheezed. "I have money set aside for you. But if I gave it to you now, you'd spend it all. You'll get it when you've learned the value of hard work."

From *Tree of Dreams: Ten Tales from the Garden of Night* by Laurence Yep. Copyright © 1995 by Laurence Yep. Published and reprinted by permission of *Troll Associates, LLC.*

Pause at line 15. How do Old Jarhead's two sons differ?

_____

_____

_____

_____

_____

_____

_____

_____

summoned (sum′ənd) *v.:* called or sent for.

In lines 23–26 is an important detail. When will the younger son get his money? Circle the father's words that tell you.

_____

_____

Despite his faults, Yuè Shêng was a good son. Bowing his head, he said, "Father, may the day of your death never come. May you live a thousand years."

30   However, Old Jarhead grew steadily worse and died shortly after that. Yuè Shêng wept until his eyes were purple, for he truly loved his father, though he had not listened to him. His older brother hardly shed a tear, for he had loved their father's wealth more than their father. When Yuè Shêng asked his brother about the burial, his brother replied, "I'm too busy. You handle it." So Yuè Shêng organized everything by himself.

Old Jarhead had been an important man in town. Yuè Shêng was determined that he should have a proper

40   funeral. He ordered an elaborate coffin and then asked a priest to name a good date on which to bury his father.

On the appointed day, Yuè Shêng hired a band of musicians and scattered lots of glittering ghost money. Ghosts were too stupid to tell the shiny paper money from real money. They would be so busy trying to pick it up that they would leave Old Jarhead's ghost alone. At the grave-side, Yuè Shêng set out a banquet for his father's spirit. At home, he put out yet another feast for the many mourners. He even let his father's tenant farmers have seats, though

50   his older brother protested.

Everyone in town said the elaborate funeral was fitting for someone as important as Old Jarhead. Although Yuè Shêng had arranged everything, his older brother took all the credit.

Yet when the bills came due, the older brother passed them on to Yuè Shêng. "I would never have ordered anything so extravagant," Yuè Cang said. "This is much too wasteful. I refuse to pay."

IDENTIFY

Draw a box around details that tell you about Chinese burial traditions.

IDENTIFY

By the time you get to line 54, the **conflict** in the story is clear. What is the problem in the story?

The funeral had indeed been very expensive, so Yuè
60 Shêng sold everything he owned to settle the debt. But
when Yuè Shêng lost his house, he lost his friends. None
of them would give him so much as a bowl of rice.

   Naturally, Yuè Shêng went to his brother to borrow
some money. He found Yuè Cang tearing down their
father's old house. That upset Yuè Shêng very much.

   "Why are you destroying all of our memories?" Yuè
Shêng demanded.

   "This old pile is riddled with[1] termites," his older
brother explained, "and I've found a much better place
70 to build. I'm very busy, brother. What do you want?"

   When Yuè Shêng asked for help, his brother sniffed.
"Humph, I'm not going to feed every moocher in town.
You're still much too wasteful." He gave Yuè Shêng only a
few copper coins. "These will keep you from starving if
you're careful. I have expenses of my own."

   After this, Yuè Shêng went down to his brother's fields.
Yuè Cang rented the fields to farmers who paid him with a
share of their crops.

   The **tenants** were surprised to see Yuè Shêng there.
80 "Please show me what to do," Yuè Shêng humbly
begged them. "If I don't work, I'll starve."

   One of the tenants, a fellow named Turnip Nose,
grunted. "So your brother's so small-hearted that he turned
his back on you. Well, your father was a nice gent. For his
sake, I'll give you part of my share. But you'll have to work
very hard."

   "I'm not afraid to use my hands," Yuè Shêng said.

   Each season, then, Turnip Nose told him what to do.
In the spring, Yuè Shêng pulled the plow himself to turn up

---

1. **riddled with:** full of.

Laurence Yep   **281**

IDENTIFY

Why does the younger
brother lose his home
and his friends (line 61)?

_____

_____

_____

_____

_____

_____

_____

_____

IDENTIFY

Pause at line 70. How does
the older son show disrespect
for his heritage?

_____

_____

_____

_____

VOCABULARY
DEVELOPMENT

tenants (ten'ənts) *n.*: people
who pay rent to use land or
a building.

Circle the definition provided
in the context of the previous sentence.

Pause at line 99. What do
you predict is going to
become of Yuè Shêng?

90 the soil. Next, he planted seed and weeded the rice plants and tended them. When the crops ripened, he harvested them, and Turnip Nose gave him a small part of what they had grown. If Yuè Shêng was careful, it would be just enough rice to live on.

As year followed year, Yuè Shêng became lean and tough as wood. One day when he was washing up, he saw his reflection in the bucket and thought, If Father could see me, he would laugh. I certainly know all about hard work now.

100 That night, Yuè Shêng dreamed that he was walking on their old estate. He passed by two pine trees growing from the same trunk. Behind them was an old well that had been filled in. Next to it were the ruins of an old brick wall. Right at the corner, he dug beneath the foundation. And there in the dirt was a jar of gold.

As soon as Yuè Shêng awoke the next morning, he jumped up. Trembling, he went back to the site of his father's house. The walls had all been torn down, but the twin pine trees still grew. Beyond them, he found the well

110 that his brother's men had filled in. Then he traced the remains of the wall until he came to the corner. With his hoe, Yuè Shêng began to dig.

When he reached the foundation, he heard a clink. Falling to his knees, he scrabbled in the dirt. Gradually, he uncovered a jar. With shaking fingers, he unsealed the lid. The jar was crammed with gleaming gold ingots.[2]

Yuè Shêng lifted some of the heavy ingots into his hands. The sun shone from their sides. "This is the gold Father intended for me when I learned what work meant,"

120 he said aloud. Yet as he stared at them, he felt guilty. "But

IDENTIFY

Pause at line 116. Folk tales often include dreams that guide the hero. What does this dream lead Yuè Shêng to?

2. **ingots** (in'gəts) *n.*: bars of cast metal; here, of gold.

father left the house to my older brother. By rights, the jar still belongs to him."

The honest man put back the gold ingots and covered the jar again. Then he went to his brother's house. However, the gatekeeper would not let him inside. "I'm sorry, young master, but your brother has ordered me not to let you in. He doesn't want to see you anymore. Please don't beg."

So Yuè Shêng asked for ink and paper to write a note.
130   In it, he told his brother where the treasure was. Folding it up, he asked the gatekeeper to take it to his brother.

At first, Yuè Cang was just going to tear the note up without reading it. However, his wife scolded him, saying, "Your brother could be very sick. Imagine what people would say if we let him die?"

Reluctantly, the older brother read the note. As soon as he finished, he jumped up and called for his servants. "What's wrong?" his wife asked.

The older brother rushed from the room, bellowing
140   to his servants. Some brought his sedan chair;[3] others snatched up shovels and hoes. Cursing and shouting, the older brother guided everyone to the ruins of the old house. Getting out of his sedan chair, he went to the spot described in the note and commanded his men to dig there.

When they had uncovered the jar, Yuè Cang told them to stand back. Then he knelt and lifted the lid. Immediately, he fell backward with a scream. When the curious servants peeked inside, they saw the jar was full of snakes. After the
150   older brother had recovered himself, he straightened his

IDENTIFY

What conflict has the gold caused for Yuè Shêng?

_____

_____

_____

_____

_____

_____

_____

_____

_____

_____

_____

_____

_____

IDENTIFY

Folk tales often include supernatural events. What fantastic event has happened in line 149?

_____

_____

_____

_____

---

3. **sedan chair:** covered portable chair used for carrying a person, with horizontal poles that rest on the shoulders of the carriers.

VOCABULARY DEVELOPMENT

bewildered (bē·wil′derd) *adj.*: confused hopelessly.

INFER

What magical change has happened in lines 165–166? Circle Yuè Cang's explanation for this strange event.

_____

_____

_____

INTERPRET

What moral lesson do you think this folk tale teaches?

_____

_____

_____

_____

_____

_____

_____

robes and dusted himself off. "This is not a funny prank at all," he said sternly.

Getting back into his sedan chair, Yuè Cang ordered his servants to take him and the jar to his brother's hut. Yuè Shêng was sitting outside, eating a simple meal of rice with a few salted vegetables.

160

When Yuè Shêng saw the jar in a servant's arms, he set down his bowl and stood up. "What are you doing here?"

His brother glared from his sedan chair. "I'm returning your jar to you."

"But Father gave the house to you. The jar is yours," Yuè Shêng protested.

"No. It's all yours," his brother said, then gestured to his servants. As they all marched forward, one threw the jar at Yuè Shêng's feet. When it shattered, shining gold ingots spilled around his ankles.

"Where are the snakes?" the older brother asked, **bewildered.**

170

"There was only gold in the jar when I looked," Yuè Shêng explained.

Then Yuè Cang understood. "It's a sign from our father that this gold is destined only for you," he said. "This is the share he always meant to give you."

Although Yuè Shêng offered him the gold again, his brother refused to take even a share. So Yuè Shêng used the money to buy a house and fields of his own. But he was always careful with his money, for he knew his father was not likely to send him another dream.

OWN THE STORY

PRACTICING THE STANDARDS

Author's Attitudes   Fill out the story-attitude chart on the next page. Then, discuss with a partner the writer's attitudes or beliefs that you think are reflected in "The Buried Treasure." Use details and quotations from the story to support your answer. Score each other's charts from 1 to 4, with 4 the highest score. The more details from the story you use to support your ideas, the higher your score.

KEEPING TRACK

Personal Word List   List the vocabulary words you learned from this story, in order of difficulty, in your Personal Word List.

Personal Reading Log   How much did you enjoy this folk tale, and why? Write your response to the story in your Personal Reading Log. Then, give yourself 4 points on the Reading Meter.

Checklist for Standards Mastery   If you answered the side questions as you read the story, your ability to analyze fiction should be improving. Use the Checklist for Standards Mastery to see how well you have done mastering the standards and where you can improve.

The Buried Treasure ▪ *Interactive Reading,* page 279

Interact with a Literary Text

Story-Attitude Chart   Writers sometimes express their attitudes through what their characters say and do. But writers don't always agree with all their characters' statements and choices. Often the writer's attitudes are only implied, or suggested. The reader infers the writer's attitudes by reading between the lines. Guess at Lawrence Yep's attitudes toward life by filling in the following chart.

In the Story . . .	Possible Writer's Attitude
Yuè Shêng is humble enough to take work as a laborer.	
Yuè Cang is careful with his money, but he does not show any generosity.	
Yuè Shêng spends money, but he does not worship it. He is rewarded at the end.	

Information

BEFORE YOU READ

King Midas was a king in an ancient country that is now Turkey. He was famous as a real king in his own time, but he has since become more famous for the myths that are told about him. In one myth, Midas wishes that everything he touches would turn to gold. He gets his wish—but what happens is not what he expected.

The following article presents some facts about the real King Midas and explains how today's scientists learned about him.

Reading Standard 2.7 Evaluate the unity, coherence, logic, internal consistency, and structural patterns of text.

from Muse *magazine*

THE FUNERAL BANQUET OF KING MIDAS

John Fleischman

Hercules, they say, could kill a lion with his bare hands. The great Achilles, the story goes, could only be wounded on the heel. And King Midas turned everything he touched to gold. Well, Hercules and Achilles may have been myths, but there really was a King Midas. Recently we even found out what they served at his funeral.

The real King Midas lived in what is now central Turkey 2,700 years ago, in a kingdom called Phrygia. We know there was a King Midas because his neighbors, the
10 mighty Assyrian kings to the east, wrote about him. They called him Mita. The Greeks, who lived west of Phrygia, also knew about him. The Greek historian Herodotus said Midas was the first "barbarian" (or non-Greek) to dedicate an offering to Apollo at his shrine at Delphi. After he died,

IDENTIFY

How do we know there was really a King Midas (lines 8–14)?

_____

_____

_____

WORD KNOWLEDGE

Circle the definition of *barbarian,* which is given in context.

How do people use the word *barbarian* today?

_____

Use this map to find Midas's kingdom, called Phrygia (frij′ē·ə). What countries are on either side of Phrygia?

_____

_____

_____

_____

_____

Circle the words that help you picture what sixty-eight meters is like (lines 25–27).

archaeologists (är′kē·äl′ə·jists) *n.*: scientists who study the culture of the past, especially by excavating ancient sites.

Circle words in this passage that give you a clue to what archaeologists do.

excavating (eks′kə·vāt′iŋ) *v.*: uncovering or exposing by digging.

avalanche (av′ə·lanch′) *n.*: mass of loosened snow, earth, rocks, and so on, suddenly and swiftly sliding down a mountain.

the Greek poets turned the man into a legend, giving him the curse of a golden touch and a shameful pair of donkey's ears. But we were reintroduced to the real King Midas when **archaeologists** dug up his tomb in 1957.

Rodney Young, an archaeologist at the University of 20 Pennsylvania Museum, was searching for Midas's tomb in the ruins of Gordion, the ancient capital of Phrygia. It was Young's seventh season **excavating** the city, and he was exploring the base of a massive burial mound. To explore the mound without destroying it, he brought in Turkish coal miners to dig a horizontal shaft. After tunneling 68 meters (about as far as 68 people holding hands would reach), the miners struck a smooth stone wall. When they broke through, a wave of rubble spilled out, blocking the tunnel. Young had them clear as much as they could 30 without bringing down the clay ceiling. Beyond the rubble was a rough wall of heavy logs. The men sliced through that and unleashed another stone **avalanche.** Once it was cleared away, they found an inner wall of beautifully crafted boxwood and cedar.

Young carefully sawed open a hatch, pushed his light into the **interior,** and found himself staring into the eye sockets of King Midas. The king was facing him, laid out on what Young thought was a bed (it turned out to be an open coffin carved from a single tree) in a tomb stuffed with

40 ancient textiles, wooden furniture, iron tripods, and bronze vessels—but not a speck of gold.

Archaeologist Ellen Kohler, who also worked on the dig, says the skeleton of King Midas rested on what looked

"like a million blankets," with a cover of thick felt over uncounted layers of fine-woven linens in purple, white, and pink. When the tomb was first opened, there was a strong, clean smell of freshly cut wood. "It smelled like the inside of a

50 cedar chest," she says. "The wood still looked freshly cut."

The archaeologists were astounded to find cloth and wood in such good condition because these materials usually rot quickly. Amazingly, the cloth and wood in Midas's tomb were saved by the decaying body of the king. Midas had been sealed under a burial mound of clay 49 meters high, making the tomb both dry and nearly airtight. As the bacteria that cause decay worked on his body, they also used up nearly all the oxygen in

60 the tomb. Lack of oxygen slowed down the decay process so much that the textiles and wooden furniture were preserved for centuries. Unfortunately,

More photos and info about Midas's tomb is at http://www. museum.upenn.edu/ Midas/intro.html

TEXT STRUCTURE

What are the topics of the two paragraphs beginning at line 7 and ending at line 34?

_____

_____

_____

_____

_____

_____

VOCABULARY DEVELOPMENT

interior (in·tir′ē·ər) *n.:* the inner part of anything. The opposite of *interior* is *exterior.*

Interior is usually used as an adjective, meaning "located within."

IDENTIFY

Describe the process that kept King Midas's burial clothes and wood in such good condition.

_____

_____

_____

_____

_____

_____

What humorous comments are found in the captions? What do you think of them? Would such comments be found in a serious scientific article written for archaeologists? Why or why not?

_____

_____

_____

_____

_____

_____

_____

_____

Find where the words *hatch*, *sarcophagus*, *caldron*, and *fibulae* are used in the captions. Using clues from the photographs and context clues, define each word.

_____

_____

_____

_____

_____

_____

_____

Knock! Knock! Anybody home? The sawed-open hatch that leads to the inner tomb.

Midas, the banquet's guest of honor. He's resting inside a wooden sarcophagus that was originally covered with cloth.

Inside this caldron are pots that held the meat stew. (And you thought the food in your school cafeteria was bad.)

Inside the Tomb

This drawing of the inside of the tomb was made before anything was moved, and all the objects were photographed in place.

Near the front of Midas's collapsed sarcophagus, some bronze fibulae pour out of a torn sack. (Fibulae are sort of like ancient safety pins.) People must have thought they'd come in handy in the underworld, since Midas's sack held about 100 of them.

Carved wooden panels from the front of the buffet tables. On the right is a fallen bronze bowl.

No, it's not an elephant tusk. It's the wooden leg of a table that has collapsed, spilling more bronze bowls onto the floor.

IDENTIFY

According to the paragraph beginning at line 66, how did scientists prove this was the tomb of Midas?

_____

_____

_____

_____

_____

_____

_____

TEXT STRUCTURE

What new question is introduced in the paragraph beginning at line 76?

_____

_____

_____

TEXT STRUCTURE

What topic unifies the two paragraphs beginning "McGovern climbed the museum stairs" and ending with "funeral banquet" on the next page?

_____

_____

_____

_____

once moist outside air entered the tomb, the textiles crumbled and turned a muddy brown within days.

But how could anyone be sure this was the tomb of Midas and not of some other Phrygian big shot? The answer has to do with that inner wall of boxwood and cedar. You could still see tree rings in the wood—wide ones
70 the tree added in good years and narrow ones the tree added in bad years. Peter Kunihom of Cornell University was able to match the pattern of wide and narrow rings to the patterns in trees whose age was known. In 1996, he said that the timbers were cut no later than 718 B.C., which was when the Assyrians said King "Mita" ruled in Phrygia.

But something had been overlooked in the excitement of the big discovery. At the bottom of all those bronze cauldrons and cups there was a dry, powdery sludge. The powder was poured into paper bags, which were rolled shut,
80 labeled, and shipped back to the University of Pennsylvania Museum of Archaeology in Philadelphia. There they sat on a shelf for 40 years.

Recently, Elizabeth Simpson of the Bard Graduate Study Center in New York, an expert on the Midas-tomb furniture, wondered what had happened to the sludge. She called Patrick McGovern, an archaeochemist at the Penn museum. Could he find the bags and run modern tests on their contents?

McGovern climbed the museum stairs and found the
90 bags on a bookshelf in Ellen Kohler's office. Examining the powdery remains, he realized that there were two different kinds of sludge, one from the tomb's big cauldrons and pots and another from the drinking vessels. He guessed that the cauldrons were used for meat, and the vessels for alcoholic beverages. Both sludges had thoroughly dried

over the centuries, but there was a good chance the food
molecules hadn't broken down and could still be identified.

100 McGovern did some of the analysis himself, but also
sent samples to several chemical laboratories that had more
advanced equipment. The chemists used technology that
wasn't available to Rodney Young in 1957. When the results
of the tests came back, McGovern had the menu for
Midas's funeral banquet.

They started with barbecue, either sheep or goat
roasted over an open fire and basted with olive oil, honey,
and spices. Part of the barbecued meat was for sacrifice,

110 probably to the Phrygian's most
powerful goddess, Matar. The rest
became the main ingredient of a
stew. The Phrygians added beans
(probably lentils), more olive oil

The 49-meter (about 160 feet) tall burial mound of Midas. It was almost 3000 years before anyone bothered to check if there was anything inside.

FLUENCY

The boxed paragraph is highly descriptive. Read it aloud to yourself at least twice. Record which parts you read faster and which you read more slowly.

TEXT STRUCTURE

What is the topic of the paragraph beginning at line 104? (The topic is announced in the last sentence of the preceding paragraph.)

_____
_____
_____
_____
_____
_____
_____
_____
_____
_____
_____
_____
_____
_____
_____

WORD KNOWLEDGE

In the paragraph beginning at line 104, underline the words *Matar, kykeon,* and *mead,* which are probably unfamiliar to you. Look for context clues, and circle them.

TEXT STRUCTURE

Sum up the main idea of the paragraph that begins on line 122. In other words, how is the question in line 122 answered?

and honey, wine, anise or fennel, and more spices. The second sludge turned out to be from an alcoholic drink called a *kykeon* by the Greeks; we'd call it a punch. It's a mixture of grape wine, barley beer, and a fermented honey drink known as mead. Part of this punch would have been poured out on the ground or an altar stone as an offering to Matar. All the cauldrons, bowls, and dishes that were packed away so carefully inside the tomb were used for 120 offerings to the goddess. The food and drink were part of the religious ceremony for the dead king.

So how did Midas end up with a golden touch? "I think Greek myth is really hard to fathom," says archaeologist Elizabeth Simpson. She believes that any king who was as wealthy as Midas would have been seen as a great man, especially by the poorer Greeks along the coast. Long after his death, his great burial mound at Gordion

Patrick McGovern with bags of sludge from Midas's tomb. In front of him is a white plaster bust of the king—a reconstruction based on the shape of his skull.

would have impressed them. "It took a long time and a lot of precise engineering to build that," says Dr. Simpson. "I say the Gordion earthwork is the counterpart of an Egyptian pyramid."

130

But great monuments don't guarantee great fame. Aside from King Tut, how many pharaohs can you name? How many of the great kings of Assyria? How many emperors of Persia? But if you were asked for the kings of little Phrygia, you would remember at least one "golden" name.

Review the article, and find its various features. What is the purpose of these features?

_____

_____

_____

_____

_____

_____

_____

_____

_____

• • • • • • Notes • • • • • •

_____

_____

_____

_____

_____

_____

_____

_____

_____

_____

_____

OWN THE TEXT

Outline   Complete the information outline on the following page with details from the article. Compare your outline with a classmate's, and note similarities and differences between them.

Structural Patterns   With a partner, evaluate the structure of this article. Was it easy to follow the writer's main ideas? Did the illustrations help? Use details from the text to support your evaluation.

_____

_____

_____

_____

_____

_____

_____

_____

KEEPING TRACK

Personal Word List   Record the vocabulary words in your Personal Word List. Can you think of how all these words are connected?

Personal Reading Log   What did you think of the way the selection combined humor and seriousness? Did it hook your interest in the topic of King Midas or archaeology in general? Write a response in your Personal Reading Log. Give yourself 3 points on the Reading Meter.

Checklist for Standards Mastery   Use the Checklist for Standards Mastery to see how far you have come in mastering the standards. Text structure is a challenging concept. Be sure you continue to watch for structure in what you read. Understanding how a text is structured will help your reading comprehension.

The Funeral Banquet of King Midas ▪ *Interactive Reading,* page 287

Interact with an Informational Text

Information Outline   Use this form to outline the supporting details for each of these main topics of "The Funeral Banquet of King Midas."

I. King Midas: Who, When, and Where

1. _____

2. _____

II. Excavating Midas's Tomb

1. _____

2. _____

3. _____

4. _____

III. How Did They Know It Was Midas?

1. _____

2. _____

IV. What Is the Sludge?

1. _____

2. _____

3. _____

V. The Findings

1. _____

2. _____

MYTH

BEFORE YOU READ

You have read a factual article on the real King Midas. Now you'll read the myth about the king who was unwise in his wishes. An important god appears in this myth. Bacchus (bak′əs) is the god of wine and merrymaking. He is often shown with grapevines twisted in his hair. Bacchus's old teacher is Silenus (sī·lē′nəs). Silenus is a woodland god who has goat feet, shaggy legs, and pointy ears. (The Greek name for Bacchus is Dionysus.)

THE GOLDEN TOUCH

Greek myth

COMPARE & CONTRAST

Pause at line 16. How are Midas and Marigold different?

_____

_____

_____

_____

_____

DECODING TIP

The flower name *anemone* (ə·nem′ə·nē′) comes from the Greek word meaning "wind" (line 18). Of the two *e*'s in *anemone,* the first is short and the second is long. Watch for anemones: They appear several times in this myth.

There was once a very rich king named Midas. The columns of his palace were inlaid with gold, and his treasure room was filled with jewels, yet he was not satisfied. He longed for greater wealth. He did not care for music or flowers, or indeed for anything else except his beautiful little daughter and his riches.

Midas wished to give his daughter, Marigold, the finest dresses ever made, the most beautiful beads and jeweled bands for her hair. This was one reason why he longed to

10 have gold and riches. But Marigold loved to wear a short white frock, and to go barefoot over the grass with only a band of ribbon on her head.

She liked to feel the cool wind blow through her curls; she loved roses and violets much better than jewels. Sometimes she begged King Midas to leave his treasure room, where he liked to sit, to walk in the woods with her.

"The birds are singing," she would say, "and the very first anemones are in bloom."

But Midas would pat her head and tell her to run out
20   and play—just as all busy fathers have told their little girls
ever since.

One day, as Midas sat counting his riches, a stranger
walked into the room and touched him on the shoulder.
Vines twined around the visitor's head, and a leopard skin
hung from his shoulders.

"Who are you?" cried Midas in alarm, "and how did
you pass the guards?"

"I am Bacchus," said the stranger. "I have come to
thank you. Not long ago you were kind to my old teacher,
30   Silenus. The gods do not forget such things."

Then Midas remembered that one evening an aged
man had stumbled into the palace. Midas had given him
shelter and food and fresh clothing. In the morning
the king had sent him on his way with a companion to
guide him.

Midas rose to his feet—as even a royal **mortal** should
stand in the presence of the gods—and bowed low to
Bacchus, inviting him to be seated. Bacchus looked at the
chair inlaid with gold. He saw the table **strewn** with jewels
40   and coins and glittering bowls. He shuddered and moved
farther away from Midas.

"I cannot stay in this room," said Bacchus. "There
is no sunshine here, nor any sound of the wind in the
vine leaves."

Midas looked at the god in amazement.

"You talk like my daughter, Marigold," said he. "True,
there is no sunshine here, but look! See the golden lights on
these bowls, and the red glow on the jewels!"

"Have you seen the colors of grapes when the sun
50   shines through them, purple and red and amber?" asked
Bacchus.

VOCABULARY
DEVELOPMENT

mortal (mor'tّl) *n.:* here, a
human being who must one
day die.

What does *immortal* mean?

_____

_____

_____

_____

_____

_____

strewn (strōōn) *v.* used as
adj.: scattered; spread about.

COMPARE &
CONTRAST

Pause at line 44. How are
Bacchus and Midas different?

_____

_____

_____

_____

_____

_____

_____

_____

_____

_____

_____

_____

_____

_____

_____

PREDICT

Pause at line 60. What is going to happen now?

_____

_____

_____

_____

_____

_____

_____

_____

VOCABULARY DEVELOPMENT

rigid (rij'id) *adj.*: stiff and hard.

"No," said Midas, "I like grapes only when they are brought to me on a golden platter. There is nothing in the world so lovely as gold. I wish that everything I touch might be changed into that beautiful metal. Then I should be happy."

"You shall have your wish," said Bacchus, hurrying away out of the gloomy room to his vineyards on the sunny hills.

60   "I shall have my wish!" whispered Midas delightedly. "Can he really mean it?"

Just then the palace servants struck the big gong and called the king to dinner.

Midas locked the door of his treasury and walked toward the room where his dinner awaited him. He glanced down at the great key in his hand. It was gold! His sleeve, too, gleamed a dull yellow and felt stiff to his touch. His girdle was changed into the same metal. His sandals, everything he wore, was shining gold.

70   He touched a marble column as he passed, and it turned yellow. The curtains which he brushed in passing grew **rigid** and gleaming.

Marigold came dancing in from the woods, her hands full of white anemones. She sat down in her tall chair beside the king's.

"Why, Father," she said, "when did you buy that funny, stiff robe? And your yellow sandals, where did you get them?"

Midas smiled delightedly as he sat down. "They are

80   solid gold, my dear! The gods have given me the Golden Touch. You may have anything in the world that you wish."

"Look at your chair, Father!" cried Marigold.

"No doubt it also is gold," smiled Midas, turning to see. "It seems more comfortable than ever. I shall have every chair in the palace made over."

He took his white napkin in his hand and shook it out. It was wonderful to see the golden color spread over the snowy linen, almost as if a yellow flame ran up the folds.

Smiling more than ever, he reached for his spoon. "We shall have all the golden dishes we like," he said.

Then he raised a spoonful of the savory soup to his mouth. He tasted it, and it was very good. But oh, horrible! When he tried to swallow it, the taste vanished and there was nothing in his mouth but a hard lump. He choked and sputtered and coughed.

He looked at his plate in surprise.

"Can there be a stone in my soup?" he wondered. Midas tried another spoonful, but the same thing happened. He broke a piece of white bread, and it turned to gold as he raised it to his lips. He touched an apple and a pear. They became hard and glittering.

"Oh!" shouted the king, "I do not want my food to become gold. Everything else, O great god Bacchus, but not my food!"

Bacchus did not hear. He was far away in his vineyards listening to Pan's music. Marigold climbed down from her tall chair, and ran to the king.

"O dear Father," she said, "what has happened?"

She put her arms around his neck and her cheek to his. At the same moment her skin grew dark and yellow. The pink and white of her cheek vanished. Only her hair remained its own color, for her curls had always been like spun gold.

IDENTIFY

What problem has developed with the golden touch (line 95)?

_____

_____

_____

_____

_____

WORD KNOWLEDGE

Pan (line 106) is the god of shepherds, wild animals, and woodlands. He has the horns and legs of a goat and is often shown playing a flute. The word *panic* comes from Pan's name. That feeling of sudden fear people sometimes have in forests was said to be caused by Pan.

IDENTIFY

What other tragedy happens as a result of the golden touch (lines 110–113)?

_____

_____

_____

_____

_____

_____

_____

THINK-ALOUD

Pause at line 120. What responses do you have to this key scene?

_____

_____

_____

_____

_____

_____

_____

_____

_____

· · · · · · Notes · · · · · ·

_____

_____

_____

_____

_____

_____

_____

_____

_____

Midas put his hand on her to caress her, then drew away in terror. For his little daughter was now cold and hard, a golden statue.

"O Bacchus, O great Bacchus!" cried Midas, leaping to his feet, "take away this dreadful gift. My daughter has become a golden image. Everything I touch grows hard and cold. Give me back my little girl, or let me die!"

Bacchus heard at last, and came down from the hilltop and entered the palace.

"Well, Midas," he asked, "do you still care so much for gold?"

"No, no!" said the king. "Take away the Golden Touch and give me my Marigold."

Bacchus smiled wisely at the king.

"Perhaps now you will like the sunshine as much as gold," said the god, "and the glowing lights in grapes better than the glitter of stones. Perhaps now you will leave your treasure room sometimes and walk in the woods with Marigold."

"I will, I will!" promised Midas. "Only let her live again!"

"Then go to the river and wash," said Bacchus.

Midas ran as fast as he could out of the room and down the marble steps, which turned to gold as he passed. In the garden, the rosebushes which he brushed lost their green color and became tawny yellow. The gravel path changed, and the grass where he walked showed his footprints in yellow tracks.

Down the river bank Midas stumbled, and splashed into the water. His garments became soft and white. His girdle and sandals were of leather once more. But the river

sands where he washed became golden, and remained
so forever.

He ran back to the palace and took the golden figure
of little Marigold in his arms. At first she felt hard and cold
to his touch, but in a moment Marigold's arms moved, her
150 color returned, and she grew soft and warm.

"O Father," she said, "I had a strange dream. I dreamed
that I could not speak, or move, or—"

"Never mind, my sweetheart," said the king, "that is
all over."

"And I dreamed that your robe was made of gold—"

"But see, it is soft white linen now," said Midas. "Let
us eat."

The servants brought more hot food, and Midas and
his daughter finished their dinner. Never had soup tasted so
160 good to him, nor fruit so juicy. His napkin seemed more
beautiful in its snowy whiteness than any golden fabric he
had ever seen.

When they rose from the table, Marigold showed him
the white anemones.

"There are whole banks of them in the woods," she
said. "And when the sun shines on them, and the wind
blows, they look just like little dancing nymphs with
yellow hair and white tunics. Won't you come with me
and see them?"

170 "Indeed, yes," said Midas.

He put his hand in Marigold's and walked with her
to the woods. There he found more happiness than he
had ever known in his treasure room, and learned to love
the white buds of flowers more than the largest pearls in
his coffers.

INTERPRET

Pause at line 146. Myths
often explain how some
aspects of nature came to be.
What does this detail explain
about the river?

_____

_____

_____

_____

WORD
KNOWLEDGE

Based on the context clues,
what do you guess *coffers*
are (line 175)?

_____

_____

_____

INTERPRET

Myths reflect the heritage,
traditions, attitudes, and
beliefs of the people who
first told them. What
message in this ancient
tale is still relevant today?

_____

_____

_____

_____

_____

_____

OWN THE STORY

Interpreting Attitudes   Discuss with a partner how "The Golden Touch" reflects the mythmakers' attitudes about money and greed. How is the message of the myth relevant today? Use details from the myth and real life to support your ideas.

_____

_____

_____

_____

_____

_____

_____

_____

_____

_____

_____

_____

_____

_____

KEEPING TRACK

Personal Word List   Add any words you learned in this selection to your Personal Word List. Then, use each word in a sentence.

Personal Reading Log   What did you enjoy most about this myth, and what did you enjoy least? Write your reaction to "The Golden Touch" as you enter the tale in your Personal Reading Log. Give yourself 3 points on the Reading Meter for completing it.

Checklist for Standards Mastery   You have finished reading this chapter. Use the Checklist for Standards Mastery to see how much you have learned.

The Golden Touch ▪ *Interactive Reading,* page 298

Go Beyond a Literary Text

Retell a Myth   You can show that a myth has a universal theme by retelling it in a contemporary setting. Either independently or with a partner, rewrite the myth of King Midas so that it takes place in the United States today. Pick a specific U.S. town, city, or area for your setting. To help you plan, fill out the following chart.

In the Myth	In My Myth. . .
Midas is a king who loves gold.	
A god rewards him for being nice to a traveler.	
Midas wishes everything he touches would turn to gold.	
His food and his daughter are turned to gold.	
The god answers Midas's pleas by removing the Golden Touch.	
His daughter comes back to life, and they live happily together.	
The myth demonstrates the belief that greed is harmful.	

Now, retell your myth. Add lots of details—even a twist or surprise if you are so inspired.

Chapter 8

Reading for Life

Chapter Preview In this chapter you will—

Strategy Launch:
"Close Reading"

READING FOCUS: DOCUMENTS

You get information from documents every day.

➤ **Workplace documents** do two things: communicate and instruct. E-mail, memos, and reports communicate information you need to do your job. Employee manuals instruct you about what is expected on the job. User guides tell you how to operate equipment.

➤ **Public documents** are posted by public agencies and not-for-profit groups. They give information about voting issues, health concerns, community decisions, and various other subjects.

➤ **Consumer documents** give you product information to help you select, purchase, and use the things you buy. Instruction manuals and technical directions tell you how to set up and use products. Consumer documents such as contracts and warranties define your legal rights and responsibilities.

A STRATEGY THAT WORKS: "CLOSE READING"

When you read documents, you should read carefully and slowly. In other words, you should apply a strategy called "Close Reading."

Here are some pointers for using "Close Reading":

➤ Identify your purpose for reading the informational materials. Are you looking for instruction on how to make something, or are you trying to find out whom to contact for more information?

➤ Skim the text, and notice its features. Take note of heads, lists, and special features.

➤ Read carefully, and absorb what the text has to say. Refer to diagrams and illustrations for guidance. If a glossary or footnotes have been provided, use them.

➤ If any information is confusing, re-read to clarify.

Reading Standard 2.1
Compare and contrast the features and elements of consumer materials to gain meaning from documents (e.g., warranties, contracts, product information, instruction manuals).

Reading Standard 2.5
Understand and explain the use of a complex mechanical device by following technical directions.

Reading Standard 2.6
Use information from a variety of consumer, workplace, and public documents to explain a situation or decision and to solve a problem.

Although years roll by, some things never seem to change. Customers in ancient Rome, for example, had to beware that sellers wouldn't take advantage of them. You may have heard the Latin phrase *caveat emptor,* meaning "let the buyer beware." A thousand years from now, buying and selling products we can't even imagine yet, people might still be having the same problems.

Get ready to read a funny story about what it might be like to be a customer in the future! This selection is organized in an unusual way—as a series of letters of complaint and a company's responses to them.

The Runaround

Richard Cohen

TEXT STRUCTURE

A letter of complaint is a special type of business letter sent from a consumer to a company. Circle the address of the person sending the letter.

TEXT STRUCTURE

Underline the name and address of the company receiving the letter.

· · · · · · Notes · · · · · ·

_____

_____

_____

_____

1560372 Winfrey Way
Chipsville, CA 90000

February 3, 2053

Consumer Service Center
DigiPet Global, Inc.
8 State Highway 13,005
New Austin, TX 78700

Dear DigiPet Global:

I recently received a DigiCat as a present and opened it as
10 soon as I could. (I was on vacation when it was delivered. I
found the box on my porch, dented on one side, when I
returned.) I took Fifi out of her box and assembled the
parts as the instructions showed. I inserted the batteries,
plugged in the power pack, and set the switch to "On,"

letting Fifi charge up for twelve hours, as your brochure recommends. Then I said to her, "Come, Fifi." To my surprise, she did not move! She remained in the sleep **mode** for nearly an hour. When Fifi did finally wake up, she ran all over the house, jumping on furniture and climbing the

20 living room drapes. I feel that I have been shipped a defective product. I hope you will agree to repair or replace this DigiCat **promptly,** as your advertising materials imply you will. Please let me know as soon as possible how to return the pet.

Sincerely,

Merton Morton

Merton Morton

Consumer Service Center
DigiPet™ Global, Inc.
30   8 State Highway 13,005
New Austin, TX 78700

April 10, 2053

Mr. Merton Morton
1560372 Winfrey Way
Chipsville, CA 90000

Dear Mr. Morton:

As Assistant Regional Communications Specialist for DigiPet™ Global, Inc., Consumer Service Center, I want to thank you for your recent interest in one of our DigiPets™.

40 Please do not return Fifi to this office. As your warranty materials indicate, the Consumer Service Center is not

VOCABULARY DEVELOPMENT

mode (mōd) *n.:* state of functioning or operation.

Name some modes that a human has.

_____

_____

_____

_____

_____

_____

TEXT STRUCTURE

A letter of complaint always has a specific purpose. Underline the words that tell what the writer wants to happen.

VOCABULARY DEVELOPMENT

promptly (prämpt′lē) *adv.:* on time; soon.

WORD KNOWLEDGE

The little ™ superscript next to the name DigiPet (line 29) indicates that the name is a trademark. Companies put the sign on their product names in order to retain ownership of the names.

Underline the two places
Mr. Morton is told to find
information.

How would you describe
the tone of the company's
letters?

A limited warranty (line 59)
is a guarantee of service and
quality, but the guarantee
has limits. What is one of the
"limits" of this warranty for
DigiPet™? Underline the
details that state the
limitation.

equipped to make repairs. Look in your DigiPet™ owners'
manual for a list of authorized DigiVet™ service providers
located near you.

I certainly understand your desire to have Fifi perform as
effectively as possible. The behavior you have described is
normal for a DigiCat™. In fact, it's normal for a cat. We at
DigiPet™ Global, Inc., pride ourselves on being able to
duplicate exactly the personality types of living felines and
50   other creatures. Sleeping, scratching, and jumping are parts
of the feline behavior grid that our engineers have been
working on for almost half a decade. Although DigiPets™
come out of the box full-grown for your convenience, they
do need a few weeks for their responses to "settle down."
Many of our customers find that their DigiCats™ are at
their most lovable during this "kitten" phase. Give yourself—and Fifi—time to get adjusted to your new situation.

Finally, Mr. Morton, thank you for describing the box's
condition. Under the terms of our limited warranty,
60   DigiPet™ Global, Inc., is not responsible for damage that
occurs during shipment. Also, please note that having a
DigiPet™ remain on your porch, exposed to the weather,
for more than 48 hours constitutes neglect as defined by
our limited warranty. For your convenience in consulting
the limited warranty, I am enclosing a new copy.

Sincerely,

Jen Bishop

Jen Bishop
Assistant Regional Communications Specialist

70   encl.

DigiPet™ Global, Inc.
DigiCat™ Division Limited Warranty

In the event of defective manufacture, workmanship, or materials, DigiPet™ Global, Inc., will repair this product free of charge for one year from the original date of purchase. Proof of purchase is necessary. Repairs must be done at an authorized DigiVet™ Service Center. (See page 748 of the owner's manual.)

80 According to our limits-and-exclusions clause, only those defects that occur during normal use are covered. This warranty does not cover damage that occurs during shipment. Also not covered are defects caused by products that are *not* made by DigiPet™ Global, Inc., such as batteries. DigiPet™ Global, Inc., does not cover defects caused by accident, misuse, abuse, mishandling, neglect, **alteration,** modification, or introduction of foreign materials (including, but not limited to, dust, sand, water vapor, fruit juice, sports drinks, and other fluids). DigiPet™ Global, Inc., does not 90 cover any damage caused by an act or acts of God.

This warranty **excludes** incidental or consequential damages resulting from the use of this product.

CLOSE READING

Read this warranty carefully. Describe a defect you think this warranty would cover.

_____
_____
_____
_____
_____
_____
_____
_____
_____
_____

VOCABULARY DEVELOPMENT

alteration (ôl'tər·ā'shən) *n.:* change; adjustment.

excludes (eks·klōōdz') *v.:* refuses to consider or include. *Excludes* can also mean "leaves out."

CLOSE READING

Limited warranties are important and should be read carefully. Number each condition of this warranty. You should find nine.

1560372 Winfrey Way

Chipsville, CA 90000

June 2, 2053

Ms. Jen Bishop

Assistant Regional Communications Specialist

Consumer Service Center

DigiPet Global, Inc.

100   8 State Highway 13,005

New Austin, TX 78700

Dear Ms. Bishop:

Things are getting worse. Fifi is coughing up hairballs. How can a digital pet have hairballs? I thought one of the advantages of a DigiPet was that it didn't have these kinds of problems. My neighbor has a DigiCat, and hers never has hairballs. I even know people who own real cats that don't have hairballs. It seems to me that the existence of hairballs is proof that there is something wrong with this product

110   and that your warranty should apply.

Sincerely,

Merton Morton

Merton Morton

Consumer Service Center
DigiPet™ Global, Inc.
8 State Highway 13,005
New Austin, TX 78700

July 22, 2053

Mr. Merton Morton
120 1560372 Winfrey Way
Chipsville, CA 90000

Dear Mr. Morton:

Your letter to Jen Bishop was passed along to me as West
Coast Director for Consumer Relations. Please note that
per p. 682 of our Owner's Manual, hairballs are one of the
Cute Feline Traits™ that can be expected in a certain
percentage of DigiCats™. Hairballs may occur as a result of
excess static electricity caused by the owner hugging the
DigiCat™ without brushing the DigiFur™ afterward or by
130 brushing the DigiFur™ from head to tail rather than from
top to toe. As a DigiCat™ owner myself, let me point out
that if regular brushing does not completely resolve the
hairball question, you might want to open Fifi's Tummy
TrapDoor™ and perform a simple DigiVet™ operation in
your home, apartment, or motorized residence. Simply
locate Circuit A117 on the circuit diagram on p. 331 of
the Owner's Manual. Then, making sure not to touch any
other part of the DigiCat's interior, cut a small notch in
Circuit A117 with a penknife or small scissors. This will
140 disable the hairball function. Please be advised, however,
that by performing this task yourself rather than having a
licensed DigiVet™ make the repair, you will be invalidating
the Warranty.

WORD KNOWLEDGE

As used in line 125, *per* means "according to." *Per* can also mean "for each," as in "one apple per child."

CLOSE READING

What does the letter writer tell the customer to check in the owner's manual (lines 125–127)?

_____

_____

_____

_____

_____

_____

_____

CLOSE READING

Note the warning in lines 140–143. Is the consumer-relations director correct? Check the warranty on page 311 to find out.

_____

_____

_____

_____

_____

We at DigiPet™ would like to extend to you our wishes for a perfect day with your pet and our thanks for your continued customer loyalty.

Sincerely,

Charles "Chuck" Charleston

Charles "Chuck" Charleston

150 West Coast Director
Consumer Relations Department

1560372 Winfrey Way
Chipsville, CA 90000

August 1, 2053

Mr. Charles Charleston
West Coast Director
Consumer Relations Department
DigiPet Global, Inc.
8 State Highway 13,005
160 New Austin, TX 78700

Dear Mr. Charleston:

I disabled Circuit A117, but the hairballs didn't stop, and now Fifi is scratching my window screens to shreds. I took her to your repair center, but they told me it was something they couldn't fix, for some reason about its being "hard-wired into her circuits." I didn't completely understand the explanation. But obviously, if it's hard-wired into her circuits, it's a defect in manufacture. I insist that you allow the warranty to cover this, since you were the one

170 who told me to perform the operation.

Sincerely,

Merton Morton

Merton Morton

Consumer Service Center
DigiPet™ Global, Inc.
8 State Highway 13,005
New Austin, TX 78700

October 5, 2053

Mr. Merton Morton
180 1560372 Winfrey Way
Chipsville, CA 90000

Dear Mr. Morton:

Thank you for keeping in touch with DigiPet™ Global. As was clearly stated in our letter of July 22, the problems you describe are not due to defective manufacture. Therefore, we cannot take the specific step you requested. However, because we look forward to keeping you as a satisfied customer, please accept our gift of a cents-off coupon for your next pack of batteries.

_____

_____

_____

_____

_____

_____

_____

. . . . . . · **Notes** · . . . . . .

_____

_____

_____

_____

_____

_____

_____

_____

_____

_____

_____

190 Here's hoping that the upcoming winter holiday season will be a DigiWonderful One™ for you and yours.

Sincerely,

Laszlo Konwicki

Laszlo Konwicki

Intern, Consumer Relations Department

1560372 Winfrey Way

Chipsville, CA 90000

December 2, 2053

Department Head

200 Consumer Relations Department

DigiPet Global, Inc.

8 State Highway 13,005

New Austin, TX 78700

Dear Sir or Madam:

Before I file a complaint with the consumer relations Board, I would like to resolve this dispute in a friendly way, if possible. I'm sure you would, too. So here's one more chance: Just let me trade in Fifi, and I'll drop the whole thing. I really do want a pet, and I still feel that DigiCat

210 offers many advantages.

Fifi hasn't done anything bad for three days now. Maybe she's outgrown her problems. She really is kind of cute. I'm keeping my fingers crossed.

Sincerely,

Merton Morton

Merton Morton

Consumer Service Center
DigiPet™ Global, Inc.
8 State Highway 13,005
New Austin, TX 78700

220

January 16, 2054

Mr. Merton Morton
1560372 Winfrey Way
Chipsville, CA 90000

Dear Mr. Morton:

I am glad that you are more satisfied than ever with Fifi. Even if the problems you describe were covered by our limited warranty, your one-year warranty period on Fifi **expired** yesterday. Therefore, we can no longer replace or repair the item free of charge. If you are still not 100 percent pleased with Fifi as a household addition, we recommend that you donate her to our popular DigiCats for DigiKids™ program, which allows youngsters from all walks of life to participate in the joy of digital pet ownership. It's tax deductible!

230

VOCABULARY DEVELOPMENT

expired (ek·spird′) *v.:* became inactive or invalid.

Name some things that expire.

CLOSE READING

What do you notice about
the identities of the letter
writers?

_____

_____

_____

_____

_____

_____

_____

_____

_____

_____

_____

_____

_____

_____

_____

_____

_____

_____

_____

_____

_____

_____

_____

Because we wish to continue serving you, we are proud to offer you a gift certificate for 10 percent off the price of this year's model DigiCat™, which has been improved in many respects compared with the previous model.

240   Sincerely,

Trudi Tranh

Trudi Tranh
Administrative Officer
Consumer Relations Department

1560372 Winfrey Way
Chipsville, CA 90000

February 15, 2054

Consumer Relations Department
DigiPet Global, Inc.
250   8 State Highway 13,005
New Austin, TX 78700

Dear Whomever:

Enclosed is my check for the purchase of this year's model, with the 10-percent-discount certificate. I think what Fifi might need is a DigiFriend to keep her company.

Sincerely,

MERTON MORTON

Merton Morton

PRACTICING THE STANDARDS

Close Reading   DigiPet's warranty presented information about legal rights. Make a list of all its terms. Compare your findings with those of one or more partners to be sure you've identified them all.

_____

_____

_____

_____

_____

_____

_____

_____

_____

_____

KEEPING TRACK

Personal Word List   Add the words you learned in this selection to your Personal Word List. You might want to look for some of those words in warranties you have at home.

Personal Reading Log   Note this selection in your Personal Reading Log. How helpful was it to you as a consumer who might someday need to deal with companies? Give yourself 4 points on the Reading Meter.

Checklist for Standards Mastery   Use the Checklist for Standards Mastery to see how far you have come in mastering the standards. Note areas where you can improve and places where you have already begun to do so.

The Runaround ▪ *Interactive Reading,* page 308

Interact with Informational Texts

Warranty and Business Letter   Write a warranty for a made-up product. Cite at least five conditions the warranty will not cover. Clearly state the period of time covered by the warranty.

Then, write a business letter from a customer complaining about the product and asking for a refund. Follow the business-letter structure.

Have a classmate determine if the customer is entitled to a refund under the terms of the warranty.

Warranty

_____

_____

_____

_____

_____ ◄ **Writer's address**

Date ⟶ _____

Company's address ⟶ _____

_____

_____

_____

Greeting ➤ _____

Body of letter ➤ _____

_____

_____

_____

_____

_____

_____ ◄ **Closing**

_____ ◄ **Signature**

_____ ◄ **Name of sender**

Skateboard Park Documents

Interact with Informational Texts

Decision Tree   A decision tree shows the results that may arise from making one decision over another. Filling in this decision tree will help you complete the Practice on page 535 of *Holt Literature and Language Arts.*

In each box on the decision tree below, write at least one reason for making that particular choice.

To Build a Skateboard Park—or Not

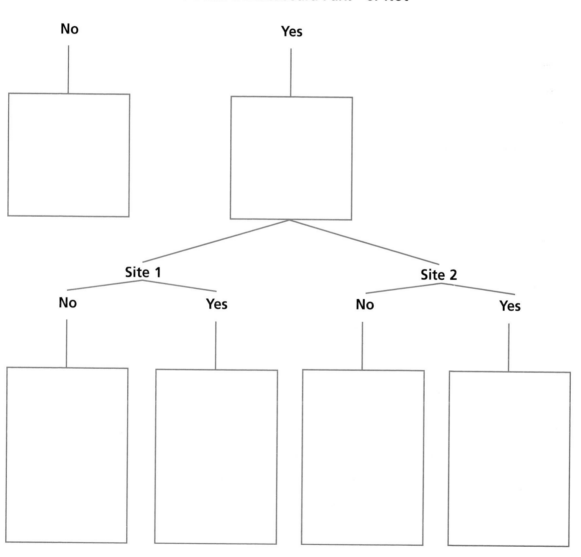

Leash-Free Dog Run Documents

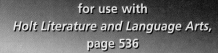
Interact with Informational Texts

Business Letter Template   Imagine that you are T. Wagger, Director of Parks and Recreation. You want to respond to the chairperson of the Site Committee of SouthPaws. To do this, use this business-letter template. State your preferred site on the line provided. Then, write your reasons on the lines labeled "Space," "Conflicts," and "Type of Area."

> 2222 Central Avenue
> Central City, CA 60000

December 14, 2002

A. K. Nine
Chairperson, Site Committee
SouthPaws
1111 South P. Street
South City, CA 60000

Dear A. K. Nine:

Thank you for your letter of December 12. It is important for us to work with the community in deciding where to put the dog park. Therefore, I would like to inform you that we favor the site at _____. Our reasons, in order of importance, are as follows:

1. Space: _____

_____

2. Conflicts: _____

_____

3. Type of Area: _____

_____

Thank you for continuing to work with us on this issue. I look forward to seeing you at the upcoming meeting.

Sincerely,

T. Wagger
Director, Parks and Recreation

WarpSpeedNet Documents

Interact with Informational Texts

Quick-Reference Guide   Consumer documents tell you what you need to know about something you're going to buy. These documents come with many products, from the battery-operated car you just bought for your sister to that new computer you saw while you were shopping.

The information that consumer documents provide can help you decide if a product meets your needs before you buy it, and it will help you understand how to use the product once you get it home.

Fill out the quick-reference guide below. Remember that *elements* define what the document is. *Features* tell more about the document. To get your elements and features, review the advertisement on page 541, the service agreement on page 542, the instruction manual on pages 543–544, and the limited warranty on page 545.

Quick Reference for Consumer Documents

	Basic Elements of Documents	Special Features of Documents
Advertisement		
Service Agreement		
Instruction Booklet		
Warranty		

SweetPlayer Documents

for use with
Holt Literature and Language Arts,
page 546

Interact with Informational Texts

Consumer Feedback Form   Read questions 1–4 in the questionnaire below. Then, based on those questions, fill in the correct name of each document the company is asking about (warranty, download directions, license agreement, advertisement). Then answer all the questions.

1. _____

   Were we honest about what SweetPlayer can do?

   [ ] Yes   [ ] No

   Was our sales pitch entertaining?

   [ ] Yes   [ ] No

2. _____

   Did we clearly show you how to get SweetPlayer onto your computer?

   [ ] Yes   [ ] No

   Did we state all the steps you needed to perform to start using SweetPlayer?

   [ ] Yes   [ ] No

3. _____

   Did we clearly state what you can and cannot legally use SweetPlayer for?

   [ ] Yes   [ ] No

   Did we clearly show you how to accept or not accept our terms?

   [ ] Yes   [ ] No

4. _____

   Did we clearly state what we would do in case of defective media?

   [ ] Yes   [ ] No

   Did we state what you need to do to inform us of defects?

   [ ] Yes   [ ] No

5. Which of our documents do you think needs the most improvement?
   Please explain what its weaknesses are and how you would improve it.

   _____

   _____

Computers

Interact with an Informational Text

Directions Check   Any time you set up complex equipment, be sure to read the directions slowly and carefully. "Computers" in *Holt Literature and Language Arts* contains a set of directions for setting up a computer. First, read through the step-by-step directions for setting up a computer. Then, re-read the directions to clarify any questions you may have. Also take note of things you are told *not* to do.

Fill in the chart below to be sure you understand the procedure for computer set-up.

1. What does the illustration next to step 1 provide?

   _____

   _____

2. According to step 1, which cord is to be plugged into the surge protector?

   _____

3. Step 3 contains a warning. What are you told *not* to do?

   _____

4. At what point do you connect the phone line and phone to the computer's modem?

   _____

5. In step 5, you are given specific instructions on when to do certain things. Number the following steps in their correct order:

   _____ Plug the power cord into a surge protector.

   _____ Turn on the monitor.

   _____ Plug the surge protector in the wall outlet.

   _____ Turn on the computer.

   _____ Attach the power cord to the computer.

Information

ARTICLE

BEFORE YOU READ

Suppose you're planning a trip to Costa Rica this summer. What do you need to do before you get there? Buy airline tickets, arrange for a place to stay, pack your stuff, go to the airport . . .

Wait a second. Did you remember to take your passport? For that matter, did you remember to get a passport in the first place? If not, you are going to encounter a big problem at the airport in Costa Rica. The following article tells you how to avoid that problem.

from Cobblestone, December 1994

Passports: Don't Leave Home Without One

Carolyn Liberatore Lavine

IDENTIFY

What does the illustration show you? Is it drawn to actual size? Use a ruler to find out.

_____

_____

_____

_____

_____

_____

_____

_____

_____

_____

If you decide that you would like to study art in Europe, pursue a career as a foreign diplomat, or simply travel abroad, you will need a passport. A passport is an official document used by both foreign countries and your birth country as proof of your identity and citizenship. It is a good idea to apply for a passport the minute you even suspect that you might be traveling

10   abroad. You will want to take off at a moment's notice when your appointment comes

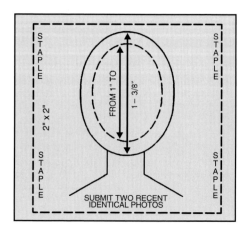

STAPLE   STAPLE

2" × 2"

FROM 1" TO 1 – 3/8"

STAPLE   STAPLE

SUBMIT TWO RECENT IDENTICAL PHOTOS

through as **ambassador** to Greece! Here is how to get a passport:

1. Get a passport application form. This form is available at some post offices and most county office buildings from the clerk of court. You also can get a form by writing to the U.S. Department of State, Bureau of Consular Affairs, Passport Services, 1425 K Street N.W., Washington, D.C. 20524.

2. Carefully fill out the one-page form. Type or print clearly and answer *all* the questions. Ask a parent to double-check them. If you do not have a Social Security number, fill in that box with zeros.

3. Obtain an official copy of your birth certificate. Visit or write to the county office building in the county in which you were born. You must have a *certified copy* of your birth certificate (one with a raised seal on it) to get a passport. A photocopy of the original will not be accepted.

4. Have two identical photographs taken of yourself alone. Check the yellow pages under "Photographers— Passport" for a photographer who knows all the rules about passport photos. Expect to pay ten to fifteen dollars for two photos. Remember to smile!

5. Take the completed application, official birth certificate, and photos to the county office that sent you the form. If you are under eighteen, a parent or guardian must accompany you. Your parent or guardian must show his or her driver's license or photo ID to the county clerk. If the person's last name is different from yours, he or she must provide a certified copy of his or her marriage license or divorce papers and proof of his or her citizenship. (A passport can be used for this.)

20

30

40

VOCABULARY DEVELOPMENT

ambassador (am·bas′ə·dər) *n.:* person who represents a nation while living in another nation.

IDENTIFY

Most of the information in this document is presented in a numbered list. Why might that be?

_____

_____

_____

_____

_____

_____

DECODING TIP

In "K Street N.W.," the *N.W.* stands for "Northwest" (line 20).

VOCABULARY DEVELOPMENT

obtain (əb·tān′) *v.:* get.

official (ə·fish′əl) *adj.:* having to do with a recognized authority, such as a government office.

WORD KNOWLEDGE

ID (line 40) is a shortened form of *identification*.

affirm (ə·fʉrm') *v.:* say that
something is true; agree.

What context clue helps you
figure out the meaning of
affirm? Circle it.

embassy (em'bə·sē) *n.:*
offices of an ambassador
and the ambassador's staff.

consulate (kän'səl·it) *n.:* office
of the consul, the person
appointed by a government
to aid and serve its citizens.

How is the information in
the passage beginning on
line 54 different from the
information presented
in the list?

_____

_____

_____

_____

_____

If you were to go get a
passport, what information
would you re-read?

_____

_____

_____

_____

_____

**6. Swear or <u>affirm</u> to the clerk that everything on your
application is true**—including that the photograph
attached is really you. Most passport photos are notoriously
unflattering.

7. Sign your name on the application form and pay the

50 **passport fee.** If you are under eighteen, the fee is thirty
dollars. Have a check or money order made payable to
"Passport Office." Be prepared to pay a ten-dollar
"execution fee" in cash to the county.

You can expect your passport in the mail four to six weeks
later. . . . A passport for children under eighteen years of
age is valid for five years. After that, a passport can be
renewed for fifty-five dollars plus the ten-dollar execution
fee. It is valid for ten years.

      If you do travel abroad, you will want to find out

60 about visas, too. A visa is an official document that is issued
by the country to which you are traveling. It sets some
limitations on the amount of time you can spend in the
country. Students who go abroad to study usually must
have a visa. Call the **embassy** or **consulate** of the country
you plan to visit to find out more.

OWN THE TEXT

Using Information from Public Documents   Test your knowledge by working with a partner. Have one of you play an employee at the passport office while the other asks questions about procedures. Switch roles after five minutes.

_____

_____

_____

_____

_____

KEEPING TRACK

Personal Word List   The vocabulary words in this selection will help you sound more official! Add them to your Personal Word List.

Personal Reading Log   How well did the article do its task of showing you how to fill out a passport application? Note any especially strong or weak points in your Personal Reading Log. Give yourself 1 point on the Reading Meter.

Checklist for Standards Mastery   Use the Checklist for Standards Mastery to gauge your progress in mastering the standards. Note your areas of biggest improvement and the areas you still need work on.

Passports: Don't Leave Home Without One ▪ *Interactive Reading,* page 326

Go Beyond an Informational Text

Passport Application   Fill out all the information on this sample passport application.

After you practice filling out this form, you might want to get a real passport for yourself. Re-read the article to find out where to get the application and a photograph. You might also try to find out how to get a passport application online.

UNITED STATES DEPARTMENT OF STATE
APPLICATION FOR ☐ PASSPORT ☐ REGISTRATION
(Type or print all capital letters in blue or black ink in white areas only)

1. NAME (First and Middle)

LAST

2. MAIL PASSPORT TO: STREET / RFD # OR P.O. BOX   **APT. #**

Sample

☐ 5 Yr. ☐ 10 Yr. Issue Date _____

CITY   **STATE**

R   D   O   DP

ZIP CODE   **COUNTRY / IN CARE OF (if applicable)**

End. # _____   Exp. _____

3. SEX ☐ M ☐ F   **4. PLACE OF BIRTH (City & State or City & Country)**   **5. DATE OF BIRTH** Month Day Year   **6. SOCIAL SECURITY NUMBER** (SEE FEDERAL TAX LAW NOTICE ON PAGE 2)

7. HEIGHT Feet Inches   **8. HAIR COLOR**   **9. EYE COLOR**   **10. HOME TELEPHONE** ( )   **11. BUSINESS TELEPHONE** ( )   **12. OCCUPATION**

13. PERMANENT ADDRESS (DO NOT LIST P.O. BOX)   STREET/RFD #   CITY   STATE   ZIP CODE

FOLD

14. FATHER'S FULL NAME Last First   BIRTHPLACE   BIRTHDATE   U.S. CITIZEN ☐ Yes ☐ No   **15. MOTHER'S FULL MAIDEN NAME** Last First   BIRTHPLACE   BIRTHDATE   U.S. CITIZEN ☐ Yes ☐ No

16. HAVE YOU EVER BEEN MARRIED? ☐ Yes ☐ No   SPOUSE'S OR FORMER SPOUSE'S FULL NAME AT BIRTH Last First   BIRTHPLACE   BIRTHDATE   U.S. CITIZEN ☐ Yes ☐ No

DATE OF MOST RECENT MARRIAGE Month Day Year   WIDOWED/DIVORCED? ☐ Yes Give Date ☐ No   Month Day Year   **17. OTHER NAMES YOU HAVE USED** (1) (2)

18. HAVE YOU EVER BEEN ISSUED A U.S. PASSPORT? ☐ Yes ☐ No   IF YES, COMPLETE NEXT LINE AND SUBMIT PASSPORT IF AVAILABLE.   **DISPOSITION** ☐ Submitted ☐ Stolen ☐ Lost ☐ Other

NAME IN WHICH ISSUED   MOST RECENT PASSPORT NUMBER   APPROXIMATE ISSUE DATE Month Day Year

It is necessary to submit a statement with an application for a new passport when a previous valid or potentially valid passport cannot be presented. The statement must set forth in detail why the previous passport cannot be presented. Use Form DSP-64.

STAPLE   STAPLE   2" X 2"   FROM 1" TO 1 – 3/8"

SUBMIT TWO RECENT IDENTICAL PHOTOS

19. EMERGENCY CONTACT. If you wish, you may supply the name, address and telephone number of a person not traveling with you to be contacted in case of emergency.

NAME

STREET

CITY   STATE   ZIP CODE

TELEPHONE ( )   RELATIONSHIP

20. TRAVEL PLANS (not mandatory) Month Day Year   Date of Trip   Length of Trip   COUNTRIES TO BE VISITED

21. STOP. DO NOT SIGN APPLICATION UNTIL REQUESTED TO DO SO BY PERSON ADMINISTERING OATH. I have not, since acquiring United States citizenship, performed any of the acts listed under "Acts or Conditions" on the reverse of this application form (unless explanatory statement is attached). I solemnly swear (or affirm) that the statements made on this application are true and the photograph attached is a true likeness of me.

FOLD

X _____ Parent's/Legal Guardian's Signature if identifying minor child   X _____ Applicant's Signature - age 13 or older

---

BEFORE YOU READ

"Recyclable! Earth-Friendly! Environmentally Safe! Biodegradable!" Nowadays, consumers are urged to buy products that are safe for the environment. Are these claims always true? What do terms like *recyclable* really mean? Read this article, reprinted from *Zillions* magazine, and you'll become your home's expert on what's *really* "earth-friendly."

from Zillions, April/May 1992

Earth-Friendly Products?

Can the People Who Bring You All That Trash Be Nice to Nature?

Eric is seriously Earth-friendly, and not just around his house. He tries to stay Earth-friendly when he shops, too. "When I buy something that I can recycle," he says, "I'm glad."

These days, it's easy to find products that make Eric feel good. More and more products claim they're

10 "recyclable," "recycled," "**biodegradable,**" or otherwise neat for the environment. Brian is **skeptical.** He believes many of the claims are phony. Lauren feels the same way: "I don't always trust them."

Are these *Zillions* readers right to be suspicious? Should Eric trust the claims made by many products?

PREDICT

Identify and circle the question that precedes the first paragraph of the article. Based on what it says, do you think the article will be on the side of the businesses that produce trash or on the side of the environment?

_____

_____

_____

_____

VOCABULARY DEVELOPMENT

biodegradable (bī′ō·di·grā′də·bəl) *adj.:* able to be broken down by the action of living organisms (such as bacteria).

skeptical (skep′ti·kəl) *adj.:* doubtful; having reservations about something.

_____

_____

_____

_____

_____

_____

CLOSE READING

According to this article, why are juice boxes difficult to recycle? Underline your findings.

DECODING TIP

Divide *polystyrene* (line 41) into syllables to help you pronounce this chemical name.

The prefix *poly-* is from a Greek word meaning "many." What is a *polygon*? What does *Polynesia* mean?

_____

_____

_____

_____

_____

_____

Recyclable?

Advertisers can say almost anything they want when it comes to "Earth-friendliness." There are no official govern-ment rules, for instance, about what can or can't be called

20 "recyclable."

Consider the juice box. You could tote your apple juice in a thermos, but "juice boxes are convenient, easier to carry than a thermos, and don't spill like cans," says Lauren. They also add up to a lot of garbage, say environmentalists. The four billion juice boxes sold in 1990 equaled about 80,000 tons of trash. Because they are made of several materials—six layers of paper, plastic, and aluminum foil—they are costly to recycle into useful stuff. Yet some ads claimed the boxes were "as easy to recycle" as newspaper.

30 "*I* can't find where to recycle them," says juice-box fan Lauren. No wonder—there are only a handful of places to do it. Most are in school programs partly paid for by the juice-box companies. For most of us, it's impossible to recycle the boxes.

"Recyclable" claims on many plastic containers are baloney, and not the kind you eat. One yogurt tub states: "This is a recyclable container." Its lid *is* made from a plastic that's easily recycled, but the tub itself isn't. It's made from a different plastic that's much harder to recycle.

40 Most plastic food containers are never recycled.

Another plastic that is rarely recycled is polystyrene (often referred to as Styrofoam). Maybe your school cafeteria has polystyrene trays or plates like the ones at RHAM Middle School, in Hebron, Connecticut. The kids there are helping their school explore whether the cafeteria should switch to another kind of tray. "We're looking into

CLOSE READING

Pause at line 56. What does the writer suggest you do before making your purchase?

_____

_____

_____

_____

_____

_____

_____

_____

_____

_____

_____

_____

cardboard or permanent trays," says Jessica. "Every kind has good and bad points."

50　　The reality of any "recyclable" claim always depends on your local recycling programs. "Before you buy, check whether the product can be recycled in your area," suggests Anthony. A product can be covered with "recyclable" labels. But if there's no place for *you* to recycle it, it's not recyclable. This may be true even for items like plastic milk jugs, made of one of the few plastics easy to recycle. Lauren's community doesn't collect them. Anthony's does.

Recycled?

Maybe you think a "recycled" product is made of stuff that has been used, then **reclaimed** from the trash, like old

60　　newspapers. That's sometimes true. But often these items are made from material that's never been used at all. It can be trimmings left over at the factory or items that could not be sold.

VOCABULARY DEVELOPMENT

reclaimed (rē·klāmd′) *v.*: rescued; recovered for use.

The prefix *re-* means "again." Think of at least five other words that use the prefix *re-*.

_____

_____

_____

_____

WORD KNOWLEDGE

Draw a vertical line between the syllables of *landfills* (line 85). What two words make up this word? What can you guess the word means?

_____

_____

_____

_____

WORD KNOWLEDGE

The **idiom** found in line 88 makes no sense if it is translated literally. Underline the idiom. Based on its context, what do you guess the idiom means?

_____

_____

_____

_____

VOCABULARY DEVELOPMENT

decomposition
(dē·käm′pə·zish′ən) *n.*:
decay; the breaking down of a substance into simple substances.

Composition, decomposition, and related words, such as *compose,* come from the Latin *componere,* meaning "put together."

For example, suppose a company makes too many large rolls of paper and can't sell them all. It can grind up the leftover paper, mix it with new paper, and sell it as "recycled" paper. That's true for much of the recycled paper we buy. This sort of re-use has been going on for many years. Suddenly, however, these products have acquired a "recycled" label, so people like Eric will feel good about buying them.

70

Real wastepaper is often used in making cereal boxes and other kinds of cardboard. To tell if your favorite cereal brand uses recycled paper, just cut through a box. If it's gray or brown under the coating, it's probably made from wastepaper. White all the way through? It's fresh from the tree.

Biodegradable?

A truly biodegradable product is something like an apple core. Once it's thrown away, it breaks down (rather quickly) into substances that aren't harmful to the Earth. People purchased one company's trash bags and another company's disposable diapers because ads made them think these products were better for the environment. But most trash bags and diapers end up in landfills where they are covered with piles of garbage. They are never exposed to the air, sunlight, and moisture that could make them break down.

80

We found a new wrinkle in environmental ad talk on a box of trash bags, which claims to be "Fighting Pollution." The label boasts that these bags "will not release harmful products of **decomposition** that can contaminate underground water supplies." That's trying to get some mileage out of the fact these bags are *not* biodegradable!

90

Buys 'R' Us?

Finding out what's *really* better for the environment has even the experts confused. And since companies can claim almost anything, you'd have to be a wizard at environmental ad games to know what to believe. To make less garbage, just follow the three Rs:

100   **Reduce:** This is the most important of the three. If you don't need it, don't buy it. Or use it. Lauren bought a teeny hairclip, but the clerk gave her a humongous bag. "I gave it back."

Re-use: Choose products (and packages) that can be used more than once. Avoid anything used just once and thrown away, like a juice box.

Recycle: Think of this as a last resort. According to one expert: "We're recycling products we probably shouldn't be using in the first place." Make the effort to find out what

110   can be recycled in your area. (The information on the next page can help you understand plastic codes.) If you're not

WORD KNOWLEDGE

Humongous (line 102) is slang for "very large." It is probably a blend of *huge* and *monstrous.* If you didn't know its meaning, what contrast context clue would help you guess? Underline the contrast clue.

WORD KNOWLEDGE

"As a last resort," line 107, means "as the last available possibility." *Resort* here means "resource." What other meaning does *resort* have?

_____

_____

_____

_____

_____

_____

_____

_____

_____

_____

_____

_____

_____

_____

_____

The **idiom** "take something with a grain of salt" (lines 112–113) means "be skeptical; not too trusting or accepting."

• • • • • • **Notes** • • • • • •

_____

_____

_____

_____

_____

_____

_____

_____

_____

_____

_____

_____

_____

_____

_____

_____

_____

_____

_____

_____

sure, swallow a product's environmental claims with a grain of salt. Or swallow the product. One of the world's most Earth-friendly containers is an ice-cream cone.

Plastics Decoded

If you turn over most plastic containers, you'll see a number from 1 to 7. What does it mean? It's a code for the type of plastic used. Jessica knew that plastics with higher numbers aren't very recyclable:

Code 1: Used for soft-drink bottles; often recycled.

Code 2: Used for milk and detergent jugs; often recycled.

Code 3: Used for shampoos and similar products; rarely recycled—produces toxic gases when burned.

Code 4: Used for plastic wrap; rarely recycled.

Code 5: Used for food containers; rarely recycled.

Code 6: Used for Styrofoam, fast-food containers, trays, cups, plates; sometimes recycled from schools and restaurants.

Code 7: All other types of plastic; rarely recycled.

OWN THE TEXT

Using Information from Consumer Documents Now that you have read about recycling, how should this information affect you as a consumer? Write three sentences stating your response to the article.

_____

_____

_____

_____

_____

_____

KEEPING TRACK

Personal Word List Write the words you learned while reading this selection in your Personal Word List.

Personal Reading Log You're now wiser about recycling. Enter this title in your Personal Reading Log. Give yourself another 3 points on the Reading Meter.

Checklist for Standards Mastery The Checklist for Standards Mastery is a good tool for checking your progress toward achieving the California standards. Track your progress now.

Earth-Friendly Products? ■ *Interactive Reading,* page 331

Go Beyond an Informational Text

Is It Recyclable? Using the "Plastics Decoded" feature in the "Earth-Friendly Products" article, do your own study of the plastic containers you use. Do this independently or with a partner.

First, find ten or more different plastic containers for products. Make a list of the code numbers that you find on each container. If you can't find enough containers at home, go to the grocery store, and take notes about the containers there. Then, find out which code numbers indicate plastics that can be recycled in your community. To do this, you may need to call your community recycling center or sanitation department.

Finally, present your findings in a visual form of your choice, perhaps as a chart or graph such as the ones shown below. Show the number and percentage of each recycling code among the containers you surveyed. Also show which ones are recyclable in your community.

Sample bar graph

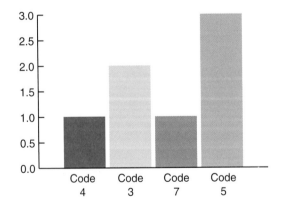

Sample pie graph

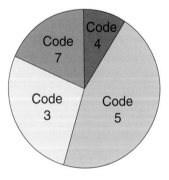

BEFORE YOU READ

The selection you are about to read will unlock the mysteries of that complex mechanical device—the lock! You'll learn about two types of locks, cylinder locks and electronic locks.

Reading Standard 2.5 Understand and explain the use of a complex mechanical device by following technical directions.

Locks

Neil Ardley

The need to secure valuables led to the development of one of the earliest inventions, the lock, which dates back about 4,000 years to ancient Egypt. Egyptian locks used wooden keys with **projections** that lifted pins inside the lock. Today's cylinder locks use metal keys that work in the same way. Each key has its own pattern of projections, which pushes up a set of pins in the lock to free a bolt. Losing a key can require replacing the whole lock, a problem avoided by combination locks. Their keys consist of
10 combinations of number or letters that the owner memorizes. Entering the correct combination on a set of dials or a keypad frees the bolt. The combination can be **altered** without changing the whole lock.

Cylinder Locks

A cylinder lock is often called a Yale lock after its inventor, Linus Yale. This lock uses a flat key with serrations along one edge. The key fits into a cylinder inside the lock. The

IDENTIFY

Underline the words that tell you how old locks are.

VOCABULARY DEVELOPMENT

projections (prō·jek′shənz) *n.:* things that jut or stick out.

altered (ôl′tərd) *v.:* modified or changed; made different.

COMPARE & CONTRAST

In what ways do cylinder locks and combination locks differ?

_____

_____

_____

_____

Circle the word *cam* in line
18. Use context clues to try
to figure out what a cam is
and what it does.

_____

_____

_____

_____

_____

_____

serrated (ser·āt′əd) *adj.:*
having sawlike notches
along the edge.

· · · · · · **Notes** · · · · · ·

_____

_____

_____

_____

_____

_____

_____

_____

_____

cylinder has a cam at one end that grips a bolt. Turning the
key rotates the cylinder so that the cam pulls back the bolt

20 and the door opens. However, the cylinder cannot rotate
unless the right key is inserted. The cylinder and body of
the lock have a set of holes that each contain a pair of pins
and a spring. The pins block the gap between the cylinder
and the body of the lock, preventing the cylinder from
rotating. When the key is inserted, its **serrated** edge pushes
up the pins by different amounts. This causes the gap in

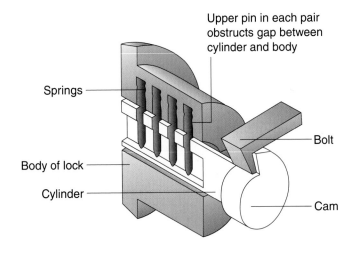

Upper pin in each pair
obstructs gap between
cylinder and body

Springs

Bolt

Body of lock

Cylinder

Cam

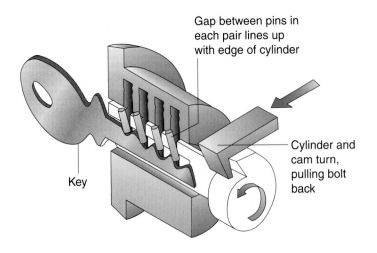

Gap between pins in
each pair lines up
with edge of cylinder

Cylinder and
cam turn,
pulling bolt
back

Key

each pair of pins to line up with the gap between the cylinder and the body of the lock. This frees the cylinder so that it can be turned by the key to pull back the bolt.

Electronic Locks

Many locks now use electronic rather than mechanical devices to free door bolts. Some office locks require a code number to be entered on a keypad at the door. The lock matches this number to a number in its memory and operates the bolt if the two numbers are the same. Hotel guests may use a card key that has a magnetic strip. The strip is programmed with a code number recognized only by the electronic lock of the guest's room. Some car locks use remote control units instead of keys. The driver presses a switch on the portable unit, which sends out an **ultrasonic** code signal that operates the car lock. A door lock can even send out a signal and open itself if an approaching person is carrying the correct unit.

Electronic lock and card key.

IDENTIFY

Pause at line 43. What three methods can be used to unlock an electronic lock? Underline them.

VOCABULARY DEVELOPMENT

ultrasonic (ul'trə·sän'ik) *adj.:* above the range audible to the human ear.

Ultra- is a prefix meaning "beyond" or "extreme." What is an *ultraconservative*? an *ultramodern* design?

_____

_____

_____

_____

_____

_____

CLOSE READING

Do you need to clarify any information you've just read? If so, go back and re-read.

· · · · · · **Notes** · · · · · ·

_____

_____

_____

_____

_____

OWN THE TEXT

Understanding Technical Directions   In your own words, tell how a cylinder lock works.

_____

_____

_____

_____

_____

KEEPING TRACK

Personal Word List   Some of the words in this selection are very common but are used in specialized ways. On your Personal Word List you might write down the more common meanings along with the more specialized ones.

Personal Reading Log   In your Personal Reading Log, sum up your responses to the selection. Do you still have questions about how a lock works? Add 1 point to your Reading Meter for completing these texts.

Checklist for Standards Mastery   Keep using the Checklist for Standards Mastery. How far have you come? What areas of the standards do you need to strengthen most?

Locks ■ *Interactive Reading,* page 339

Go Beyond an Informational Text

Diagramming a Mechanical Device   Think of a mechanical device that you are familiar with. Choose a device that is complex enough to have moving parts but simple enough for you to explain with one diagram and one paragraph of text. Then, create a diagram of the device, showing how it works. Also write instructions for using the device. Use reference books if necessary.

On the lines below, explain how the device works.

_____

_____

_____

_____

_____

_____

_____

_____

Personal Word List

Keep track of all the new words you have added to your vocabulary by filling out the following chart. Review these words from time to time to make sure they become part of your permanent vocabulary.

WORD	WORD
DEFINITION: _____ _____ _____	DEFINITION: _____ _____ _____

WORD	WORD
DEFINITION: _____ _____ _____	DEFINITION: _____ _____ _____

WORD	WORD
DEFINITION: _____ _____ _____	DEFINITION: _____ _____ _____

WORD	WORD
DEFINITION: _____ _____ _____	DEFINITION: _____ _____ _____

WORD	WORD
DEFINITION: _____ _____ _____	DEFINITION: _____ _____ _____

WORD

DEFINITION: _____

_____

_____

WORD

DEFINITION: _____

_____

_____

WORD

DEFINITION: _____

_____

_____

WORD

DEFINITION: _____

_____

_____

WORD

DEFINITION: _____

_____

_____

WORD

DEFINITION: _____

_____

_____

WORD

DEFINITION: _____

_____

_____

WORD

DEFINITION: _____

_____

_____

WORD

DEFINITION: _____

_____

_____

WORD

DEFINITION: _____

_____

_____

WORD

DEFINITION: _____

_____

_____

WORD

DEFINITION: _____

_____

_____

WORD

DEFINITION: _____
_____
_____

WORD

DEFINITION: _____
_____
_____

WORD

DEFINITION: _____
_____
_____

WORD

DEFINITION: _____
_____
_____

WORD

DEFINITION: _____
_____
_____

WORD

DEFINITION: _____
_____
_____

WORD

DEFINITION: _____
_____
_____

WORD

DEFINITION: _____
_____
_____

WORD

DEFINITION: _____
_____
_____

WORD

DEFINITION: _____
_____
_____

WORD

DEFINITION: _____
_____
_____

WORD

DEFINITION: _____
_____
_____

WORD

DEFINITION: _____

_____

_____

WORD

DEFINITION: _____

_____

_____

WORD

DEFINITION: _____

_____

_____

WORD

DEFINITION: _____

_____

_____

WORD

DEFINITION: _____

_____

_____

WORD

DEFINITION: _____

_____

_____

WORD

DEFINITION: _____

_____

_____

WORD

DEFINITION: _____

_____

_____

WORD

DEFINITION: _____

_____

_____

WORD

DEFINITION: _____

_____

_____

WORD

DEFINITION: _____

_____

_____

WORD

DEFINITION: _____

_____

_____

WORD

DEFINITION: _____

_____

_____

WORD

DEFINITION: _____

_____

_____

WORD

DEFINITION: _____

_____

_____

WORD

DEFINITION: _____

_____

_____

WORD

DEFINITION: _____

_____

_____

WORD

DEFINITION: _____

_____

_____

WORD

DEFINITION: _____

_____

_____

WORD

DEFINITION: _____

_____

_____

WORD

DEFINITION: _____

_____

_____

WORD

DEFINITION: _____

_____

_____

WORD

DEFINITION: _____

_____

_____

WORD

DEFINITION: _____

_____

_____

WORD

DEFINITION: _____

_____

_____

WORD

DEFINITION: _____

_____

_____

WORD

DEFINITION: _____

_____

_____

WORD

DEFINITION: _____

_____

_____

WORD

DEFINITION: _____

_____

_____

WORD

DEFINITION: _____

_____

_____

WORD

DEFINITION: _____

_____

_____

WORD

DEFINITION: _____

_____

_____

WORD

DEFINITION: _____

_____

_____

WORD

DEFINITION: _____

_____

_____

WORD

DEFINITION: _____

_____

_____

WORD

DEFINITION: _____

_____

_____

WORD

DEFINITION: _____
_____
_____

WORD

DEFINITION: _____
_____
_____

WORD

DEFINITION: _____
_____
_____

WORD

DEFINITION: _____
_____
_____

WORD

DEFINITION: _____
_____
_____

WORD

DEFINITION: _____
_____
_____

WORD

DEFINITION: _____
_____
_____

WORD

DEFINITION: _____
_____
_____

WORD

DEFINITION: _____
_____
_____

WORD

DEFINITION: _____
_____
_____

WORD

DEFINITION: _____
_____
_____

WORD

DEFINITION: _____
_____
_____

WORD

DEFINITION: _____

_____

_____

WORD

DEFINITION: _____

_____

_____

WORD

DEFINITION: _____

_____

_____

WORD

DEFINITION: _____

_____

_____

WORD

DEFINITION: _____

_____

_____

WORD

DEFINITION: _____

_____

_____

WORD

DEFINITION: _____

_____

_____

WORD

DEFINITION: _____

_____

_____

WORD

DEFINITION: _____

_____

_____

WORD

DEFINITION: _____

_____

_____

WORD

DEFINITION: _____

_____

_____

WORD

DEFINITION: _____

_____

_____

WORD

DEFINITION: _____

_____

_____

WORD

DEFINITION: _____

_____

_____

WORD

DEFINITION: _____

_____

_____

WORD

DEFINITION: _____

_____

_____

WORD

DEFINITION: _____

_____

_____

WORD

DEFINITION: _____

_____

_____

WORD

DEFINITION: _____

_____

_____

WORD

DEFINITION: _____

_____

_____

WORD

DEFINITION: _____

_____

_____

WORD

DEFINITION: _____

_____

_____

WORD

DEFINITION: _____

_____

_____

WORD

DEFINITION: _____

_____

_____

WORD

DEFINITION: _____

_____

_____

WORD

DEFINITION: _____

_____

_____

WORD

DEFINITION: _____

_____

_____

WORD

DEFINITION: _____

_____

_____

WORD

DEFINITION: _____

_____

_____

WORD

DEFINITION: _____

_____

_____

WORD

DEFINITION: _____

_____

_____

WORD

DEFINITION: _____

_____

_____

WORD

DEFINITION: _____

_____

_____

WORD

DEFINITION: _____

_____

_____

WORD

DEFINITION: _____

_____

_____

WORD

DEFINITION: _____

_____

_____

WORD

DEFINITION: _____

_____

_____

WORD

DEFINITION: _____

_____

_____

WORD

DEFINITION: _____

_____

_____

WORD

DEFINITION: _____

_____

_____

WORD

DEFINITION: _____

_____

_____

WORD

DEFINITION: _____

_____

_____

WORD

DEFINITION: _____

_____

_____

WORD

DEFINITION: _____

_____

_____

WORD

DEFINITION: _____

_____

_____

WORD

DEFINITION: _____

_____

_____

WORD

DEFINITION: _____

_____

_____

WORD

DEFINITION: _____

_____

_____

WORD

DEFINITION: _____

_____

_____

WORD

DEFINITION: _____

_____

_____

WORD

DEFINITION: _____

_____

_____

WORD

DEFINITION: _____

_____

_____

WORD

DEFINITION: _____

_____

_____

WORD

DEFINITION: _____

_____

_____

WORD

DEFINITION: _____

_____

_____

WORD

DEFINITION: _____

_____

_____

WORD

DEFINITION: _____

_____

_____

WORD

DEFINITION: _____

_____

_____

WORD

DEFINITION: _____

_____

_____

WORD

DEFINITION: _____

_____

_____

WORD

DEFINITION: _____

_____

_____

WORD

DEFINITION: _____

_____

_____

WORD

DEFINITION: _____

_____

_____

WORD

DEFINITION: _____

_____

_____

WORD

DEFINITION: _____

_____

_____

WORD

DEFINITION: _____

_____

_____

WORD

DEFINITION: _____

_____

_____

WORD

DEFINITION: _____

_____

_____

WORD

DEFINITION: _____

_____

_____

WORD

DEFINITION: _____

_____

_____

WORD

DEFINITION: _____

_____

_____

WORD

DEFINITION: _____

_____

_____

WORD

DEFINITION: _____

_____

_____

WORD

DEFINITION: _____

_____

_____

WORD

DEFINITION: _____

_____

_____

WORD

DEFINITION: _____

_____

_____

WORD

DEFINITION: _____

_____

_____

WORD

DEFINITION: _____

_____

_____

WORD

DEFINITION: _____

_____

_____

WORD

DEFINITION: _____

_____

_____

WORD

DEFINITION: _____

_____

_____

WORD

DEFINITION: _____

_____

_____

WORD

DEFINITION: _____

_____

_____

WORD

DEFINITION: _____

_____

_____

Personal Reading Log

The literature you read becomes part of your life, helping you to understand the human condition and unlock the mysteries of life. Take time to fill out a Personal Reading Log entry when you have finished reading a selection. Each time you complete a selection in *Interactive Reading,* you will have moved closer to meeting California's goal for students completing middle school—the goal of having the ability to read one million words on your own.

Reading Meter

If you read all the interactive selections in this book, you will have read close to 45,000 words, and you will have achieved 100 points. Fill in the Reading Meter to show how far you've come.

Number of Words in Selection	Points
About 500 words	1 point
About 1,000 words	2 points
About 1,500 words	3 points
About 2,000 words	4 points
About 2,500 words	5 points
Over 5,000 words	10 points
Bonus for reading every selection	10 points

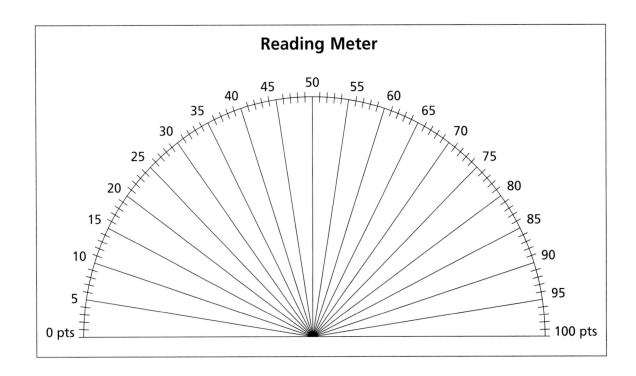

Reading Meter

DATE _____   Selection/Author: _____

Summary: _____

_____

_____

_____

_____

Comments and Evaluation: _____

_____

_____

_____

_____

| READING |
| METER |

DATE _____   Selection/Author: _____

Summary: _____

_____

_____

_____

_____

Comments and Evaluation: _____

_____

_____

_____

_____

| READING |
| METER |

DATE _____ Selection/Author: _____

Summary: _____

_____

_____

_____

_____

_____

Comments and Evaluation: _____

_____

_____

_____

_____

	READING METER

DATE _____ Selection/Author: _____

Summary: _____

_____

_____

_____

_____

_____

Comments and Evaluation: _____

_____

_____

_____

_____

	READING METER

DATE _____ Selection/Author: _____

Summary: _____

_____

_____

_____

_____

Comments and Evaluation: _____

_____

_____

_____

_____

| READING |
| METER |

DATE _____ Selection/Author: _____

Summary: _____

_____

_____

_____

_____

Comments and Evaluation: _____

_____

_____

_____

_____

| READING |
| METER |

DATE _____   Selection/Author: _____

Summary: _____

_____

_____

_____

_____

_____

Comments and Evaluation: _____

_____

_____

_____

READING METER

_____

DATE _____   Selection/Author: _____

Summary: _____

_____

_____

_____

_____

_____

Comments and Evaluation: _____

_____

_____

_____

READING METER

_____

DATE _____ Selection/Author: _____

Summary: _____

_____

_____

_____

_____

Comments and Evaluation: _____

_____

_____

_____

_____

READING METER

DATE _____ Selection/Author: _____

Summary: _____

_____

_____

_____

_____

Comments and Evaluation: _____

_____

_____

_____

_____

READING METER

DATE _____ Selection/Author: _____

Summary: _____

_____

_____

_____

_____

_____

Comments and Evaluation: _____

_____

_____

_____

	READING METER

_____

DATE _____ Selection/Author: _____

Summary: _____

_____

_____

_____

_____

_____

Comments and Evaluation: _____

_____

_____

_____

	READING METER

DATE _____ Selection/Author: _____

Summary: _____

_____

_____

_____

_____

Comments and Evaluation: _____

_____

_____

_____

| READING |
| METER |

DATE _____ Selection/Author: _____

Summary: _____

_____

_____

_____

_____

Comments and Evaluation: _____

_____

_____

_____

| READING |
| METER |

DATE _____ Selection/Author: _____

Summary: _____

_____

_____

_____

_____

_____

Comments and Evaluation: _____

_____

_____

_____

_____

	READING METER

DATE _____ Selection/Author: _____

Summary: _____

_____

_____

_____

_____

_____

Comments and Evaluation: _____

_____

_____

_____

_____

	READING METER

DATE_____ **Selection/Author:** _____

Summary: _____

_____

_____

_____

_____

_____

Comments and Evaluation: _____

_____

_____

_____

_____

| | READING |
| | METER |

DATE_____ **Selection/Author:** _____

Summary: _____

_____

_____

_____

_____

_____

Comments and Evaluation: _____

_____

_____

_____

_____

| | READING |
| | METER |

DATE _____   Selection/Author: _____

Summary: _____

_____

_____

_____

_____

_____

Comments and Evaluation: _____

_____

_____

_____

_____

| READING |
| METER |

DATE _____   Selection/Author: _____

Summary: _____

_____

_____

_____

_____

Comments and Evaluation: _____

_____

_____

_____

_____

| READING |
| METER |

DATE _____ Selection/Author: _____

Summary: _____

_____

_____

_____

_____

_____

Comments and Evaluation: _____

_____

_____

_____

_____

| READING |
| METER |

DATE _____ Selection/Author: _____

Summary: _____

_____

_____

_____

_____

_____

Comments and Evaluation: _____

_____

_____

_____

_____

| READING |
| METER |

DATE _____ Selection/Author: _____

Summary: _____

_____

_____

_____

_____

_____

Comments and Evaluation: _____

_____

_____

_____

_____

	READING METER

DATE _____ Selection/Author: _____

Summary: _____

_____

_____

_____

_____

_____

Comments and Evaluation: _____

_____

_____

_____

_____

	READING METER

DATE_____ **Selection/Author:** _____

Summary: _____

_____

_____

_____

_____

_____

Comments and Evaluation: _____

_____

_____

_____

_____

_____

| READING |
| METER |

DATE_____ **Selection/Author:** _____

Summary: _____

_____

_____

_____

_____

_____

Comments and Evaluation: _____

_____

_____

_____

_____

_____

| READING |
| METER |

DATE _____ Selection/Author: _____

Summary: _____

_____

_____

_____

_____

_____

Comments and Evaluation: _____

_____

_____

_____

_____

	READING METER

DATE _____ Selection/Author: _____

Summary: _____

_____

_____

_____

_____

_____

Comments and Evaluation: _____

_____

_____

_____

_____

	READING METER

DATE_____ Selection/Author: _____

Summary: _____

_____

_____

_____

_____

_____

Comments and Evaluation: _____

_____

_____

_____

_____

| | **READING** |
| | **METER** |

DATE_____ Selection/Author: _____

Summary: _____

_____

_____

_____

_____

_____

Comments and Evaluation: _____

_____

_____

_____

_____

| | **READING** |
| | **METER** |

Checklist for Standards Mastery

Each time you read, you learn something new. Track your growth as a reader and your progress toward success by checking off skills you have acquired. You may want to use this checklist before you read a selection, to set a purpose for reading.

✓	California Reading Standard (Grade 6 Review)	Selection/Author
☐	**2.1 Reading Comprehension:** Identify the structural features of popular media.	
☐	**2.8 Reading Comprehension:** Note instances of fallacious reasoning in text.	

	California Grade 8 Reading Standard	Selection/Author
☐	**1.0 Word Analysis, Fluency, and Systematic Vocabulary Development:** Students use their knowledge of word origins and word relationships, as well as historical and literary context clues, to determine the meaning of specialized vocabulary and to understand the precise meaning of grade-level-appropriate words.	
☐	**1.1** Analyze idioms, analogies, metaphors, and similes to infer the literal and figurative meanings of phrases.	
☐	**1.2** Understand the most important points in the history of English language, and use common word origins to determine the historical influences on English word meanings.	
☐	**1.3** Use word meanings within the appropriate context, and show ability to verify those meanings by definition, restatement, example, comparison, or contrast.	

✓	California Grade 8 Reading Standard	Selection/Author
☐	**2.0 Reading Comprehension:** Students read and understand grade-level-appropriate material. They describe and connect the essential ideas, arguments, and perspectives of the text by using their knowledge of text structure, organization, and purpose.	
☐	**2.1** Compare and contrast the features and elements of consumer materials to gain meaning from documents (for example, warranties, contracts, product information, instruction manuals).	
☐	**2.2** Analyze text that uses proposition and support patterns.	
☐	**2.3** Find similarities and differences between texts in the treatment, scope, or organization of ideas.	
☐	**2.4** Compare the original text to a summary to determine whether the summary accurately captures the main ideas, includes critical details, and conveys the underlying meaning.	
☐	**2.5** Understand and explain the use of a complex mechanical device by following technical directions.	
☐	**2.6** Use information from a variety of consumer, workplace, and public documents to explain a situation or decision and to solve a problem.	
☐	**2.7** Evaluate the unity, coherence, logic, internal consistency, and structural patterns of text.	

✓	California Grade 8 Reading Standard	Selection/Author
☐	**3.0 Literary Response and Analysis:** Students read and respond to historically or culturally significant works of literature that reflect and enhance their studies of history and social science. They clarify the ideas and connect them to other literary works.	
☐	**3.1** Determine and articulate the relationship between the purposes and characteristics of different forms of poetry (for example, ballad, lyric, couplet, epic, elegy, ode, sonnet).	
☐	**3.2** Evaluate the structural elements of the plot (for example, subplots, parallel episodes, climax), the plot's development, and the way in which conflicts are (or are not) addressed and resolved.	
☐	**3.3** Compare and contrast motivations and reactions of literary characters from different historical eras confronting similar situations or conflicts.	
☐	**3.4** Analyze the relevance of the setting (for example, place, time, customs) to the mood, tone, and meaning of the text.	
☐	**3.5** Identify and analyze recurring themes (for example, good versus evil) across traditional and contemporary works.	
☐	**3.6** Identify significant literary devices (for example, metaphor, symbolism, dialect, irony) that define a writer's style, and use those elements to interpret the work.	
☐	**3.7** Analyze a work of literature, showing how it reflects the heritage, traditions, attitudes, and beliefs of its author.	

Index of Authors and Titles

Vocabulary Development

Pronunciation guides, in parentheses, are provided for the vocabulary words in this book. The following key will help you use those pronunciation guides.

As a practice in using a pronunciation guide, sound out the words used as examples in the list that follows. See if you can hear the way the same vowel might be sounded in different words. For example, say "at" and "ate" aloud. Can you hear the difference in the way "a" sounds?

The symbol ə is called a **schwa.** A schwa is used by many dictionaries to indicate a sort of weak sound like the "a" in "ago." Some people say the schwa sounds like "eh." A vowel sounded like a schwa is never accented.

The vocabulary words in this book are also provided with a part of speech. The parts of speech are *n.* (noun), *v.* (verb), *pro.* (pronoun), *adj.* (adjective), *adv.* (adverb), *prep.* (preposition), *conj.* (conjunction), and *interj.* (interjection). To learn about the parts of speech, consult the *Holt Handbook.*

To learn more about the vocabulary words, consult your dictionary. You will find that many of the words defined here have several other meanings.

---

at, āte, cär; ten, ēve; is, īce; gō, hôrn, look, tool; oil, out; up, fʉr; ə *for unstressed vowels, as* a *in* ago, u *in* focus; ' *as in* Latin (lat'ʼn); chin; she; zh *as in* azure (azh'ər); thin, *the;* ŋ *as in* ring (riŋ)

Picture Credits

Page 16, Gary Soto; 17, PhotoDisc, Inc.; 29, British Museum, London, UK/The Bridgeman Art Library International Ltd.; 30, Vallee des Nobles-Tombe de Inherkha, Thebes/Giraudaon, Paris/SuperStock; 33, Archivo Iconografico, S.A./CORBIS; 41, Ashmolean Museum, Oxford, UK/The Bridgeman Art Library International Ltd.; 62, Paul Fetters/Matrix; 71, Conklin/Monkmeyer; 75, imageBlitz/Dynamic Graphics; 76, Dynamic Graphics; 82, Sheldon Collins/CORBIS; 100, Corbis; 104, Syndicated Features Limited/The Image Works; 118, Bettman/CORBIS; 120, 121, Keystone/Hulton Archive Picture Collection; 123, Ralph White/CORBIS; 127, PP/FA, Inc.; 145, Fitzwilliam Museum, University of Cambridge/The Bridgeman Art Library International Ltd.; 169, 170, 171, 172, 173, Anne Frank Fonds-Basel/Anne Frank House-Amsterdam/Archive Photos; 174, Gabriel Hackett/Archive Photos; 175, 176, Anne Frank Fonds-Basel/Anne Frank House-Amsterdam/Archive Photos; 177, Wolfgang Kaehler/CORBIS; 178, CORBIS; 182, PP/FA, Inc.; 204, Bettman/CORBIS; 234, PP/FA, Inc.; 241, Smithsonian American Art Museum, Washington, DC/Art Resource; 250, PhotoDisc, Inc.; 251, Paul A. Souders/CORBIS; 278, Rick Browne; 288, Rodica Prato/Muse; 289, *Muse;* 290, 291, University of Pennsylvania Museum; 293, (top) *Muse,* (bottom) University of Pennsylvania Museum; 294, University of Pennsylvania Museum; 326, PP/FA, Inc.; 328, Corbis; 330, PP/FA, Inc.; 333, Gary Buss/FPG International LLC; 335, EyeWire, Inc.; 336, Corbis; 340, PP/FA, Inc.; 341, PhotoDisc, Inc.